ENTREPRENEUR MAGAZINE
Organizing and Promoting Seminars

The *Entrepreneur* Magazine Small Business Series

<u>Published:</u>

Bringing a Product to Market
Guide to Integrated Marketing
Human Resources for Small Businesses
Making Money with Your Personal Computer
Small Business Legal Guide
Starting a Home-Based Business
Starting an Import/Export Business
Successful Advertising for Small Businesses
The Entrepreneur Magazine Small Business Advisor
The Entrepreneur Magazine Small Business Answer Book
Guide to Professional Services
Guide to Raising Money
Organizing and Promoting Seminars
The Encyclopedia of Entrepreneurs

ENTREPRENEUR MAGAZINE
Organizing and Promoting Seminars

Entrepreneur Media, Inc.

John Wiley & Sons, Inc.

New York • Chichester • Weinheim • Brisbane • Singapore • Toronto

This text is printed on acid-free paper.

This publication is designed to provide accurate and authoritative
information in regard to the subject matter covered. It is sold
with the understanding that the publisher is not engaged in
rendering legal, accounting, or other professional services. If
legal advice or other expert assistance is required, the services
of a competent professional person should be sought.

Library of Congress Cataloging-in-Publication Data:

Entrepreneur magazine: organizing and promoting seminars / by
    Entrepreneur Media, Inc. (The Entrepreneur magazine small business series)
       p.   cm.
    Includes index.
    ISBN 0-471-16289-2 (alk. paper)
    1. Entrepreneurship—Study and teaching.   2. Seminars—Planning.
    3. Congresses and conventions—Planning.   I. Entrepreneur Media,
    Inc.   II. Entrepreneur (Santa Monica, Calif.)
    HB615.E596   1998
    658.4'21'0715—dc21   97-31191

Printed in the United States of America

10 9 8 7 6 5 4 3 2 1

CONTENTS

INTRODUCTION

In 1989, Denise Dudley, PhD, and Jerry Brown sat on some borrowed orange plastic chairs in their new, small office in Mission, Kansas, and, using a borrowed flip chart, they set some goals for the future of their company. The pair had pooled their savings and their know-how—Brown is a marketing specialist; Dudley, a clinical psychologist—and were ready to take the plunge into the world of seminar promotion.

Today, their company, SkillPath Seminars, has 230 employees and grosses about $60 million per year. It has been ranked as one of the fastest growing companies in the country by *Inc.* magazine for the past five years, and on April 15, 1996—their seventh anniversary—Dudley and Brown celebrated serving their two-millionth customer.

Every year, hundreds of thousands of people pay to attend meetings and seminars where professional speakers encourage, enlighten, and enliven them. Some are sent by their companies to learn new skills; others are simply seeking personal growth—how to communicate better with family members, or manage the stress in their lives, or assert themselves. Seminar costs range from about $49 to more than $1,000.

A great deal of money is made by those who speak, by those who represent speakers, and by those who manage seminars that feature speakers.

COMING OF AGE

As an industry, seminar promotion is relatively new. Industry pioneers like Zig Ziglar, who has been speaking for more than 30 years, helped set the stage for the tremendous success of motivational speakers and seminars throughout the 1980s. Today, a few motivational speakers—Ziglar, Stephen Covey, Anthony Robbins, and Susan Powter—can fill a good-size auditorium on name recognition alone, but they are in the minority. Approximately 30,000 people earn at least part of their income by speaking before company meetings, sales organizations, trade associations, church gatherings, community groups, and the general public—and they're paid handsomely for their talents. Seminar promoters, collectively, make more than $100 million per year (Table I–1).

Table I–1   Seminar Promotion
Average Net Profit before Taxes: $177,372
Minimum Start-Up Investment: $15,480
Average Start-Up Investment: $55,583
Average Return on Investment: 319%
Stability: Moderate
Risk Factor: Moderate
Industry Growth Prospects: Good
Absentee Ownership Potential: No
Home-Based Business Potential: Yes

The Market

The seminar market is huge. Various associations sponsor keynote speakers at their annual conventions. Corporations often foot the bill to send hundreds of employees to seminars on developing effective work habits, excelling in a competitive world, motivating others, and similar topics. A survey by the National Speakers Association (NSA) in 1994 showed that the most popular topic among corporate executives and meeting planners who responded that year was "dealing with change." (The next NSA survey is scheduled for 1997.) Also popular were customer-minded orientation/customer service, global marketplace opportunities, and future strategies for success.

Targeting Customer Needs

What people want today, say experts, are speakers and seminars that provide them with the nuts and bolts, the "how to's" of excelling—or at least coping—in a busy and competitive world. In this age of downsizing, they want frank talk about what opportunities today's business world is really offering them, and what they can do to rise above the masses and still manage the stress of their ascent. In addition to topics that are strictly related to business, such as "How to Make Winning Cold Calls," speakers address subjects that are relevant to both businesspeople and the general public, for example, time management, organization, and self-motivation. The entire "self-help" area also appears to remain popular. According to Marketdata Enterprises, a research firm based on New York's Long Island, sales of self-help tapes, videos, books, and seminars top $1.5 billion per year.

Profit Potential

Large companies such as SkillPath Seminars and CareerTrack Seminars bring in tens of millions of dollars per year. Big-name speakers and celebrities on the speakers' circuit also earn millions of dollars per year. The 1994 NSA survey showed that professional speakers' regular fee is $2,000 per engagement in today's marketplace, and "a large percentage of professional speakers seem to have moved into the $2,000-to-$5,000 and $5,000-to-$10,000 categories when compared with the 1990 study." The survey noted that "there appeared to be a greater number of fees in the over-$10,000 and over-$25,000 categories, compared with results from the 1990 survey."

Newcomers to the business should not expect to generate large sums in the early stages, but they can make a good living. Promoters, especially, can realize profits early if they conduct proper market research and then plan and network their seminars effectively. Some promoters who stage only three or four seminars each year can realize net profit before taxes of $50,000 to $100,000. To achieve this level of success, you must be able to sign up speakers your audience is eager to hear, offer topics of keen interest, promote the event effectively and economically, and draw several hundred or even a couple thousand people, depending on the ticket price. Given these circumstances, you can earn an annual profit of more than $100,000.

A promoter who has successfully marketed a seminar should be able to realize, at a minimum, a 20 to 30 percent net profit. We spoke with a promoter who had put on two small-scale seminars: a two-day program and a one-day program. His expenses totaled $6,428 and his revenues were $11,530, leaving him a profit of $5,102. His net profit equaled 79 percent of his investment.

Getting Started

Most of the promoters we talked to were once professional speakers themselves, and many continue to make speaking appearances. They also have extensive sales or marketing experience—a background that is certainly helpful, if not essential, to a seminar promoter. To select effective speakers to feature in a program, promoters must know what it takes to be an effective speaker. A successful speaker at a seminar must be *dynamite* in front of an audience. "I worked with a professional clown for a year in order to learn clowning, juggling, magic, and that sort of thing," says Michael Podolinsky, an author, international speaker, and president of Key Seminars Speakers Bureau, in Eden Prairie, Minnesota. "I'm working with a professional voice coach who teaches Shakespearean actors and actresses. I'm learning about staging. I've taken professional modeling twice, and acting in front of the camera twice." Podolinsky now commands several thousand dollars per engagement and schedules up to 100 engagements each year.

Seminar promoters can often operate from their homes, as long as they have enough space and the appropriate office equipment. Promoters almost never need to meet seminar attendees in person, and they can interview potential speakers at an appropriate professional space (such as a rented meeting room, where they can audition the person's delivery and material). There is seldom a reason to spend money on office space. See Chapters 2 and 3 for more details.

As your business grows, you will probably need to hire at least one secretary and perhaps one or two other assistants to help you with daily activities. Depending on how you market your seminars, you may also need to hire salespeople. Information on hiring these individuals, and on the best way to select speakers for particular engagements, appears in Chapter 4.

1

DEFINING YOUR MARKET

You can offer seminars on virtually any topic imaginable, but, for your seminar to succeed, you must market it properly. One audience continually attracted to seminars is the business community. In fact, whether you are a speaker, run a speaker's bureau, or own a seminar promotion company, your largest clients are going to be corporations and their personnel.

SkillPath Seminars relies heavily on corporate clients, often tailoring their otherwise "highly controlled" speeches to meet the specific needs of the attendees. "People see a brochure and say 'Can you do this here?'" says SkillPath co-founder Dudley. "And we will tailor [the seminar] as much as anybody wants. We can either just present the very seminar that we present publicly, or we can actually redesign it around the company's own specific issues."

Many companies send groups of their people to prescheduled public seminars when they come to town. The annual Success series of seminars, which brings in more than 15,000 attendees per city, is reported to sell as much as 40 percent of its tickets to corporations.

In the bigger picture, however, all planners of meetings are potential clients: trade and professional associations, men's and women's organizations, senior citizens' centers, nonprofit companies, and others. Estimates peg the U.S. meetings industry as a $75-billion-per-year income generator. In 1993 (the most recent year for which figures are available):

- 801,300 corporate meetings,
- 206,500 association meetings, and
- 11,800 conventions.

were held in the United States, according to the "Meetings Market Report" in *Meetings and Conventions* magazine. More than 84 million people attended these meetings, creating *84 million potential customers for speakers and seminar promoters.*

Repeat Business

People who have attended a worthwhile seminar or have heard a phenomenal speaker are most likely to attend a seminar in the future—on their own, or through their company or association. A company that feels it has received tangible benefits (e.g., increased productivity or improved employee morale) from spending money on a speaker is most likely to either hire a speaker again in the future or send its employees to public seminars. "It's actually quite common that someone goes to a seminar and they say, 'This was so good! We have to have everyone at work hear this,'" says Dudley. "And so they go back and they talk to the decision maker—or maybe they are the decision maker, which is great—and they beg to have that seminar brought to their organization."

THE CORPORATE MARKET

An inherent benefit to targeting the corporate market is the fact that the U.S. Treasury Department regulations permit an income tax deduction for expenses undertaken to maintain or improve professional skills. Anyone can take advantage of the tax break (if the seminar topic qualifies), but corporations are often willing to pay the entire bill for attendance, including travel expenses. Whatever the economic climate, there is a continual need for management development, and companies of all sizes look to outside resources to train and motivate their workforce. Seminars such as SkillPath's "Managing Multiple Projects, Objectives, & Deadlines" or "Business Writing Basics" take on skills training that many companies, for lack of personnel or expertise, cannot offer in-house. Even companies large enough to employ human resource professionals often need to import an outsider who can work with their employees on topics such as how to build teams, focus on goals, or gear up for future competition.

Over the past decade, recessionary woes have affected the seminar and speakers' industry in many ways. Between 1990 and 1996, 15 huge

U.S.-based corporations either announced or carried out massive employee layoffs that eliminated nearly 400,000 jobs—in one case, 35 percent of a company's workforce. Such devastating downsizing brought about several changes for professional speakers and promoters. First, they had to look at the needs of their audiences differently. Executives needed people who could come in and train employees in how to work more effectively with fewer resources; employees needed trustworthy people who could give them that information, but who could also understand the pressures they were under in this era of job instability.

Second, speakers had to revise the tone of their speeches. The "hip-hip-hooray" cheerleading tone of the 1980s had to yield to a more subdued motivational, back-to-basics tone for the 1990s. "If employees are worried about getting axed, the purely inspirational speech just rubs salt in the wound," writes professional speaker Nancy K. Austin.[1] "Today's audiences are sick to death of happy talk, even from big-name motivators; they'd rather hear from somebody who will level with them."

Third, seminar promoters had to look at the people they were hiring to give speeches, and speakers' bureaus needed to have on board people who had actual experience in dealing with the skeleton-crew, globally restructured workplace of the 1990s. "Yes, we would love to have PhDs teaching our seminars, but some of our best seminar leaders don't even have college degrees, because that isn't really what it's about," says Dudley. "It's really about knowing something so well, you can teach it to someone else and you can be believable."

Austin agrees. "Regular people who have made something happen from inside their own companies are among the newest keynoters," she writes.[2]

Corporate downsizing and recessionary woes also placed more focus on the bottom-line results related to seminar attendance. Companies expect to see measurable changes in the way their employees work, relate, and innovate after they have been "inspired" by a speaker. If the speaker addressed the sales force, management wants to see more sales. If a seminar topic is a company's goals for the future, those goals better be met (management will expect that the sessions provided the tools and/or the framework for reaching those goals). Luckily, says Dudley, although the industry is still in a "consciousness-raising" period, companies are also beginning to lose their skepticism about the results that seminars can produce. "Many more companies are starting to figure out, 'You know, you send somebody to a one-day seminar and you spend an average of $99, and they come back motivated—they really do retain it!'" she says. "Plus they get workbooks and great ideas."

Laura Lodato, owner of a Priority Management franchise in Tampa, Florida, says her seminar programs are designed to produce just the results these companies are seeking. "Our [program] has three phases to it, instead of a single day or a single morning or afternoon workshop," she says. "There is a personal consultation, where we come out and work with each person individually after they come to the first workshop; a follow-up seminar; plus ongoing support and the opportunity for them to come back as many times as they want to re-attend the workshops. Our goal is to help them see habits change, so that it's a more long-lasting effect."

Where to Market

Before you promote your program, you need to decide which audience you will target. A target market is a specific group of people (or businesses) who are most likely to attend your seminar if given the opportunity. This selective approach, also known as niche marketing, saves you from wasting time and money advertising to groups that have no interest in your offering. Every topic on the market can be targeted to a specific group, although some topics may have a broader appeal than others. For example, seminars on self-improvement may appeal to people from all socioeconomic levels and types of employment. Business audiences may be easier to target because they specialize in one field. You can select companies by size, Standard Industrial Classification (SIC) code, area of specialty, number of employees, and other characteristics. Once you have selected the type of business, define your target market in greater detail by determining who, within the selected industry, would most benefit from the seminar: owners, executives, managers, and so on.

Let's say you're promoting a seminar on effective advertising for the floral industry. Your first step is to determine who would be the most likely candidates to attend the seminar. You know that within the floral industry there are growers, wholesalers, suppliers, and retail florists. Because the information you are presenting works best for a retail operation, you determine that retail florists are your primary target and wholesalers comprise a secondary audience. Your next decision: To which florists should you direct your promotions? You can select a nationwide audience and mail your flyers and brochures to all 35,000 florists in America, or you can identify the audience according to geographic market regions. Let's say you target the Pacific region. Next, you must select particular florists in this region. Your criteria might be the size of the shop, annual sales volume, or a special emphasis, such as flowers for weddings or funerals. If your seminar benefits all retail florists, then they are your market. Finally, which levels of the retail florist industry would benefit most? Is your seminar geared to owners, managers, employees, or all of the above?

Knowing all of the characteristics of your intended audience will help you determine many aspects of the seminar besides the subject matter. If you know that your audience is spread throughout the country, you have the option of either presenting one seminar in a central location to which attendees will travel (or connect electronically via a video hookup), or presenting the same seminar several times in different regions. Also, knowing the income range of your audience may help you to set the price for the seminar. If your audience consists of CEOs of Fortune 500 companies, they can afford to travel to a luxurious hotel and pay high seminar fees. On the other hand, a seminar aimed at secretaries probably would not attract a large audience if you had high fees or required attendees to travel to the event.

Eve Cappello, PhD, has been hired numerous times by hospitals and other large service providers to work with employees on communication skills in an increasingly diverse society. "I've worked with several Veterans Administration medical centers on how their doctors can more effectively relate to patients," says the speaker and author, whose books include *Act, Don't React* and *Why Aren't More Women Running the Show?* "[There are] a lot of gender, ethnic and cultural communications gaps, today, and I've worked with that a lot—specifically, at Pacific Bell Telephone, dealing with how men talk to women." More recently, two large financial organizations have approached her to discuss "women, money and power" with their sales team. "What they want is for me to actually come in and train their brokers to be able to speak to women—to speak to their female clients more effectively," she says. Among her clients: Mattel Toys, Paramount Pictures, and the U.S. Department of the Navy.

Corporations use speakers for annual meetings, national training seminars, quarterly executive meetings, and employee retreats, to name just a few occasions. And corporate attendance at public seminars remains popular. AT&T executives, for example, "sent their San Francisco people to Success 1994 on the same day the company announced that 15,000 jobs in its long-distance services unit would be eliminated in the next two years," according to *TIME* magazine.[3]

NONCORPORATE ORGANIZATIONS

Like corporations, organizations such as associations and clubs need professionals to train and motivate their members. Their goal is to offer their members a worthwhile benefit that adds value to their membership, for which they typically pay dues. If you are a speaker, these groups may hire you for conferences or special training meetings. Topics can be anything from family dynamics and learning to deal with the loss of a loved one, to investing for your future and still taking the vacation you've always dreamed of. If you target a narrower market with your seminars—for example, sales-oriented organizations—your topics will still be quite varied: making contacts that last; projecting a positive image; or making time for your family when you travel 200 days per year.

Associations

A single convention can bring in thousands of dollars to an association *if* members attend. To get them there, the agenda needs to deliver the message that "essential" information is going to be presented—information that won't be found anywhere else for the same value. Thus, from keynote speakers who kick off or wrap up conventions, to dynamic luncheon speakers and top-notch session trainers, associations provide a huge market for the seminar and speaker industry. Reportedly, more than 200,000 association meetings are held each year by approximately 16,000 national associations and their local chapters. Some speakers are hired to handle multiple engagements within a single conference. Others work to book themselves for multiple conferences in a single city. There is plenty of money to be made here.

As a seminar promoter, you can capitalize on this market by offering generous discounts to association members. The association benefits by providing its dues-paying members with a money-saving way to keep up to date on various personal and professional topics; the seminar promoter benefits by increasing the likelihood of greater attendance at seminars, as well as receiving "free" publicity by having the discount announced as a membership benefit. You can also look into "tacking on" your seminar to the beginning or end of an association convention or meeting. (Provide a discount to members while keeping the seminar open to the public and holding it at the hotel where the association convention or meeting is taking place.) You do not need the permission of an association to do this, but it is in your best interest to work with association representatives because you can benefit from the free publicity of having your seminar mentioned in the calendar of events or the convention/meeting program. Most hotels will provide you with a list of the conventions they will be hosting over the next several months.

Senior Centers/Social Clubs

Don't underestimate the importance of targeting small local organizations such as senior centers and local men's or women's groups. Their budgets may be more limited, but the experience you can gain as a speaker and the amount of market research you can glean as a promoter are priceless. Cappello was approached by the senior citizens center in Pasadena, California, when she moved to that city: Would she submit some topics that she thought might appeal to the population the center serves? The result was her new "Performance Is Everything" class, which focuses on teaching people about performing behavior, winning behavior, and so forth. She says: "We have a ball with this class! There is no other class like this; it's an original." Her current attendees are mostly housewives and retired professionals (as well as a couple of people who work for a local television station). What they desire to learn from her four-session class has a much broader appeal. "They're looking to become more assertive, to have more confidence, to build their self-esteem," says Cappello, who is already planning an advanced version of the program and new ways to market it. "This is going to go into a larger seminar kind of thing, and I'm also going to be promoting it at Pasadena City College."

If you plan to market your seminars to a professional organization, you should attend a few regular meetings beforehand, to become familiar with the background and interests of the members. Indeed, like a politician who knows nothing about a city where he is holding a rally, you as a speaker or promoter will fail if you don't know at least the basics about your audience. Look at your strengths and narrow down your target number of groups in the beginning. Then, approach these organizations and get to know as much as you can about each of them.

THE MASS MARKET

As shown by the thousands of individuals who buy every magazine, join every weight-loss program, or order every self-help book, there is a huge market of individuals who are intent on personal and professional growth and who enjoy the live "performance" of seminars. "Some [attendees] are practically addicts, trying one motivational session or program after another—individuals desperate for more control over their own lives. Each one wants more money, more power, more love, more happiness, more esteem or self-esteem," according to a *TIME* article on the Success 1994 tour.[4]

A one-day seminar costing $45 to $95 and covering nearly any subject can be promoted to the mass market. This is a risky area, however, because ticket costs must come out of the individual's pocket rather than from a generous corporate fund. The mass market generally responds well to seminars on investing money wisely and on ways to make money. Other popular topics include improving personal relationships, dealing effectively with stress, and achieving health in mind and body. "When you're really marketing or 'selling' seminars to the general public, a lot of [people] come in for confidence building, building self-esteem, or simply learning specific skills to do whatever it is that they want to do," says Cappello.

Therefore, just like corporations that desire a speaker to "jump start" their training process, individuals who sign up for seminars are hoping to receive a set of tools that they can take away with them to help them integrate your valuable lessons into their daily lives.

Professionals

Are you considering offering seminars that target specific professionals such as doctors, lawyers, accountants, teachers, and so on? An added bonus to this approach is that you can tap into a profession's continuing education requirements and generate an inherent "need" for your seminars. For example, Dudley notes that SkillPath's seminars generally count toward continuing professional educational requirements for nurses and hospital administrators (to name just two groups). Certified Public Accountants (CPAs), paralegals, teachers, and others also have continuing educational requirements that they must meet each year. In these cases, you would need to provide very specific and current information to specialized industries, and you would need highly qualified speakers.

The National Task Force on the Continuing Education Unit (NT-FCEU), which was formed several years ago to define exactly how much "classroom" time should count toward a professional's continuing educational requirements, allows seminar attendees to count every 50 minutes that they are in "class" as one-tenth of a CEU. The tax laws have recently changed to allow only a portion of this classroom time to be deductible, so be sure to review the continuing educational requirements for various professional groups when designing your seminar curriculum.

Salespeople

Anyone who sells for a living is a likely candidate for a seminar on successful selling and motivational techniques. Salespeople are in a high-pressure job, and they constantly need to boost their productivity. Their effectiveness can be measured by the number of sales they make and the number of clients they retain, and an informative seminar should have measurable results. Topics such as "Making Successful Cold Calls" and "Customer-Oriented Selling" can be quite popular in this sizable market. According to the U.S. Bureau of Labor Statistics, nearly 15 million people were employed in sales occupations in 1994, the most recent year for which data are available.

COMPETITION

Competition is growing, but this is an industry where the cream rises to the top—which means that your biggest competitor may be yourself. If you don't market yourself, you'll go nowhere. If you don't network, you're lost. As a speaker, you'll never benefit from the professional referrals given by your peers; and as a promoter, you'll never be able to attract the big-name speakers who will bring in high sales.

The biggest seminar promotion companies include SkillPath Seminars, CareerTrack Seminars, Dun & Bradstreet, Fred Pryor, and National Seminars. Less well known but highly successful companies like Peter Lowe International, in Tampa, Florida (promoter of the annual Success tours), also compete for the time and money of your target markets. And smaller companies specializing in topics like the Internet and computer software skills are cropping up every day.

If you choose to specialize in a professional area, your competition will also include national companies and organizations that are well known in their fields. For example, the Practising Law Institute specializes in seminars for the legal profession, and Springhouse Corporation (publisher of *Nursing 96* magazine) puts on successful continuing educational seminars for nurses.

For professional speakers, the biggest competition is other speakers. "You must keep on top of things—do personal research, update your material," says Cappello, who has been speaking professionally for more than 20 years.

Big-name sports figures and celebrities still command top dollar and stay busy, but not so much at the level of the corporate annual meeting or trade association convention. "There are fewer famous football coaches stepping up to the speaker's platform now," writes Austin. "Regular people who have made something happen inside their own companies are among the newest keynoters."[5] This probably has to do with the price of fame: The big names draw $20,000 and more for an appearance. Great coaches are still popular, however, and will probably compete with you on topics such as "Winning," "Overcoming Adversity," "Beating the Competition," and other motivational fare.

Before you get started, it is important to identify who your specific competitors will be, based on the geographic territory you plan to cover and the types of speeches you plan to specialize in or promote. "As in any growing market, the smart newcomers do as [Stephen]

Covey and [Susan] Powter do: specialize. For each problem, its own guru. Onetime real estate developer Brian Tracy teaches the psychology of selling. John Gray (bestseller: *Men Are From Mars, Women Are From Venus*) tells you how to run your love life. Gray shares the relationship market with his ex-wife, Barbara De Angelis, who wrote the best-selling book *How To Make Love All the Time.* Afraid your kids will go astray? Linda Eyre and Richard Eyre (bestseller: *Teaching Your Children Values*) tell you how to run your family life. Deepak Chopra (bestseller: *Ageless Body, Timeless Mind*) offers the secrets for a long and healthy life."[6]

Notice the common thread among your strongest competitors: Many are noted authors on one or more related subjects, which raises them to the level (or at least the perceived level) of "expert." This is why cultivating your own product lines, whether as a speaker or a seminar company, is so important (see Chapter 3) as your company gets going.

MARKET RESEARCH

Market research provides businesses with data that allow them to solve or avoid marketing problems. Many entrepreneurs skip this step in their business formation process, but the amount of money that you can save and the number of headaches that you can avoid by conducting some preliminary research into your business and your specific product (in this case, your speeches/seminars) are significant.

A thorough market survey forms the foundation of any successful business. It would be impossible to develop strategies such as market segmentation (identifying specific sales pockets within a market) and product differentiation (creating an identity for your seminars that separates them from your competitors') without market research.

According to William A. Cohen, author of *The Entrepreneur & Small Business Problem Solver*, the market research process consists of the following steps:[7]

1. Define the problems that you must solve.
2. Determine which problems require research.
3. List the goals and objectives that market research will define.
4. Identify the type of data that you should gather to meet those goals.
5. Plan the method you will use to acquire the desired information.
6. Define the sample audience that will best provide you with the data required.

7. Conduct your research and gather the information.
8. Analyze the data.
9. Develop conclusions based on the information gathered, and determine a course of action.

For example, suppose that for 20 years, you have been teaching math, Spanish, and geography at a private high school, and you are excited about the prospect of expanding a career you love to encompass teaching the general public in the seminar format. You face several problems. What are you going to speak on? Who is going to want to listen? How many other people also offer seminars on this topic? What are their qualifications as opposed to yours? To whom will this topic appeal most (corporations, city centers, poor people, women's groups)? Can you make money speaking on this topic, considering the demographics of the audience you are likely to draw?

The first question primarily takes some soul-searching—and common sense—on your part. The markets are going to be quite narrow and defined, for example, if you decide to start your own "Math Whiz Seminars" company. However, if you have taught Spanish for 20 years, you likely know quite a bit about the culture as well as the language of Spanish-speaking people. Is there a topic that you are knowledgeable on and feel quite certain would be of appeal to Spanish-speaking Americans? What about geography? Could you make money hosting a "Where in the World Is . . . ?" seminar series for business travelers, retiree vacationers, or people who want to understand more about their faith by putting religious history into a geographical perspective?

Each of these—and other—problems will require research. You can use four primary research methods that have been developed over time: (1) the *historical method,* (2) the *observational method,* (3) the *experimental method,* and (4) the *survey method.* The historical method relies on past data to define current conditions. The observational method uses current market data to predict future conditions. The experimental method tests the effectiveness of specific marketing activities. The most prevalent research method is the survey.

How to Conduct a Market Survey

A thorough market survey will help you make a reasonable sales forecast for your first and, ideally, your subsequent seminars. According to Dan Steinhoff and John F. Burgess, in their book *Small Business Management Fundamentals,* these are the steps you must take to assess your market and make a forecast:[8]

1. Determine the market limits or trading area of your business.
2. Study the spending characteristics of the population within this area.
3. Estimate this population's purchasing power, based on its per-capita income, its median income level, the unemployment rate, and similar factors.
4. Determine the present sales volume not only of the seminar industry itself, but also of the specific type of seminars you will offer.
5. Estimate the portion of the total sales volume you can reasonably obtain.

The fifth step is extremely important. Offering a "Making It in America" seminar series in a given community *won't* necessarily generate additional attendees in that area who are dying to try out a seminar; it may simply redistribute the business already there.

PRIMARY RESEARCH

In conducting your market research, you will gather two types of data. The first will be *primary* information, which you will compile yourself or hire someone to gather. Most of your research, however, will probably consist of *secondary* information—reports and studies conducted by government agencies, trade associations, or other businesses within your industry—which will already be compiled and organized for you.

Primary research essentially results in two types of information: *exploratory* and *specific.* Exploratory information defines a problem by presenting targeted consumers with fairly open-ended and general questions that elicit lengthy answers. This information is important because it may bring out additional problems that you had not considered yourself. Specific research concentrates on solving a problem that you have already defined. It usually involves more in-depth and focused questioning than exploratory research.

Many companies hire marketing firms to acquire primary data for them, and as a speaker or seminar promoter, you can consult experts who can help you with your marketing efforts. "I do a 'how to position, package, promote, and market yourself as a speaker' package," says Cappello. "It has a whole list of questions that I start with and that people really have to answer for themselves—everything from what appeals to them about being a speaker to what I call the 'psychographics': Who are the target audience? Who are the kinds of people that you're going to be approaching, and where do these people live? How are you going to finance this career? Do you have the kind of charisma, the kind of feeling about yourself, that you need to be successful?

"I really get them to delve into knowing themselves very thoroughly and how they are going to research their competition."

Should you decide to conduct your own primary research, you must first decide how you will question your target group of individuals. Three commonly used methods are (1) direct mail, (2) telephone surveys, and (3) personal interviews. You must then think about the questions you are going to ask.

A survey prepared for the 20-year veteran teacher might include questions such as the following:

- Do you speak Spanish?
- Do you speak any other languages (besides English)?
- Have you lived outside the United States? For how long?
- What are your most pressing concerns today?
- Are these concerns that you are anxious to resolve? Are you confident you can resolve them?
- What is your current income level? (Under $20,000, $20,000–$32,000, $33,000–$45,000, etc.)
- Do you consider yourself a confident person? (Definitely, Sometimes, Not usually, No)
- Have you ever traveled outside of the United States? Where?
- Could you indicate on a map where Mecca is? Jerusalem? Nazareth?
- Would you be interested in a fun way of learning where historical cities like these actually are (and how they tie in to your faith)?
- If you could have lunch with any one person in the world, who would it be?
- How many vacations do you take each year?
- How many business trips do you take each year?
- Do you often plan your vacations based on recommendations from friends, without really knowing much about where a place is located or what the country is like?

If you choose to use a direct-mail questionnaire, keep your questions short and succinct. Offer many multiple-choice questions and fewer open-ended questions. Most people don't like to be bothered with questionnaires, and your chances of receiving a strong response will drop if yours is too long or looks too difficult.

The same is true of telephone surveys. Most people, bombarded with phone solicitations, have become wary of unfamiliar voices on the telephone. When you combine this resistance with your invasion of their free time at home, you can see why the people you call might view you as an intruder. Many people, however, will give you a little bit of their time if your questions are few and concise.

Often, the best way to obtain primary data is to conduct person-to-person interviews. Once you have someone's attention and he or she has agreed to participate in an interview, it is easy to sit down and ask longer questions that will require detailed responses. Unlike direct-mail and telephone surveys, which impinge on the respondent's time with little or no warning, you can conduct personal interviews at a pre-arranged time that is convenient for the interviewee, making you less intrusive. In the seminar industry, such person-to-person interviews are generally arranged by offering a "free" seminar.

The "Free" Seminar

Even the entrepreneurs we spoke with who did not conduct thorough market research in the beginning always use surveys *after* their seminars. "This kind of research is a bit different, because these people are already *at* a seminar," says Dudley, "but it is still very helpful."

Offering a free seminar and simply gauging attendance will show you what type of interest there is in your topic. More importantly, by hosting a free seminar on your ideal topic and asking your attendees to fill out your questionnaire at the end of the seminar, you can generate a great deal of awareness about who you are and how good your seminars are.

You will need to decide whether your seminar should be truly "free" (no cost) or simply so inexpensive that cost will not be a consideration among those who attend. Do not expect attendance to cover your costs of putting on the seminar; market research takes some money, and you should count the cost of this seminar as a business expense. The only reason to consider charging a small fee is that some people believe strongly that you get what you pay for; thus, if your seminar is free, it may be perceived as worthless. For example, if your topic is likely to attract wealthy investors, you might charge a fee. Ralph Kydd, president of The Corporate Group, a consulting company in Toronto, Ontario, Canada, offered a low-cost seminar on banking and tax havens at the King Edward Hotel in Toronto. Writing on the seminar (one of many given by Kydd that year) in *Maclean's*, author Stevie Cameron noted that the seminar was so packed the hotel had to bring in extra chairs, and couples were separated in order to get a seat.

"By the end, the audience seemed dazzled by visions of tax savings dancing before their eyes. Kydd invited them to attend a $299 all-day seminar, or sign up as a client. . . . As they filed out of the Knights-bridge Room, most of the people stopped at the registration desk," says Cameron. "Those folks were sold."[9]

Offer an incentive to those who do attend, to ensure they fill out your questionnaire—a generous discount off the cost of a future seminar, a gift certificate to a local restaurant or theater, a drawing for a weekend getaway, etc. Also, be sure not to hand out the questionnaire until after the speeches are finished, when your audience is most likely to be excited about you and your company. Finally, be sure to take notes on everything you see: the ages of your attendees; their dress; how much they interact with the speaker(s); what seems to catch their interest the most; whether they come alone, in pairs, or in groups. All of these observations will be invaluable as you form your marketing plan.

SECONDARY RESEARCH

The value of secondary research information is that most of it will already have been gathered and organized for you, and you should be able to access it fairly easily and inexpensively. To obtain secondary research, all you need to know is where to search for agencies or organizations that have already gathered the information.

Associations

Not only are associations a great potential market for you, they also usually offer a wealth of information on the industries they serve: market statistics; lists of members; books and reference materials; and discounts on purchases from certain suppliers. By approaching these groups early, you can gather a wealth of very specific information on people who are likely to be among your future customers.

Census Tracts

Almost every county government publishes population density and distribution figures in widely available census tracts. These documents will show you the number of people living in specific areas—precincts, water districts, or even 10-block neighborhoods. Some counties publish reports on population trends, which compare the population ten years

ago, or five years ago, with the current demographics. An area with a declining, static, or small population is generally not a good area to which
to travel to conduct a seminar (although a seminar on "America's
Fastest-Growing Counties and How You Can Prosper There" might go
over well). An expanding population that desires your seminar information is ideal. Generally, seminar promoters warn against tackling cities
with population bases below 50,000, although you might target major
cities and surrounding cities (within, say, a 20-mile radius) which, taken
together, offer a large population. Census tracts can be extremely useful
for determining such statistics.

Maps

Maps of major trading areas in counties and states are available from
chambers of commerce, industrial development boards, trade development commissions, and newspaper offices. These maps show the major
areas of commerce and reflect the population's spending habits.

Colleges and Universities

Local colleges and universities are invaluable sources of information for
speakers and seminar promoters. Cappello, who began her working career as a singer-pianist in nightclubs before getting her PhD in psychology, says that her university teaching experience largely gave her an idea
of what markets she could target. "[The university] had marketing surveys that showed who their audience was, where they were coming from,
and what their interests were," says Cappello. "And it was interesting,
because I found that once people were in one class of mine they wanted
to be in others."

More than 650 colleges and universities have branches of the
Small Business Administration's Small Business Development Center
(SBDC), which offer business management information addressing
topics such as marketing, legal and financial concerns, and accounting.
They can also lead you to state and federal business assistance programs. The SBDC will help you prepare business plans and financial
statements.

Even if there is no SBDC near you, you may be able to obtain help
from a local college during your market research and start-up phase.
Many college business departments are eager to have their students
work in the "real world," gathering information and doing research at
little or no cost.

Media Sources

Ask the sales departments of local newspapers and magazines for copies of the business profiles used in their sales efforts. These organizations gather information on their local markets and use it in their own efforts to sell space to their advertisers. The profiles can help determine the financial situation of your potential seminar attendees or corporate clients.

Advertising managers, including those in local broadcasting stations, are another source of information on spending patterns in the community. The research they routinely conduct can help you determine whether there is a valid market for your seminars.

Finally, Dun & Bradstreet (likely to become one of your competitors in some capacity) has more than 9 million businesses and 15 million names on file to help you obtain marketing information, assess a customer's credit, acquire and maintain customers, or perform your market research. For more information on market research services, refer to Appendix B.

Community Organizations

Major cities have chambers of commerce or business development departments that encourage new businesses in their communities. They can supply useful information, usually free of charge, such as:

- Demographic reports on local, regional, and state populations.
- Seminars on networking, managing, financing, or developing a marketing plan.
- Relocation and site selection assistance.
- Directories that can lead a businessperson to a company's key purchasing decision maker.

This information will not only help you develop your market survey so you can partially gauge your likelihood of success, but it will also help you to develop your seminar business and run it efficiently.

2

LOCATION, SITES, AND FACILITIES

You know now that your market is broad because you can offer your services and target your topics to any number of groups, companies, or individuals. When you're ready to set up your office, an address anywhere in the country can be successful, because you can travel to your clients to give speeches or to put on a public seminar. Travel isn't cheap, however. If your clients are paying your travel tab (as is customary for hired speakers), you have no problem. If you are taking your seminars on the road, a number of logistical details must be worked out well ahead of time.

This chapter looks at the two locational decisions that affect your business: (1) locating and setting up your business office, and (2) selecting and preparing seminar sites around the country.

THE HOME-BASED OFFICE

Nearly everyone starting out in this business begins at home. Starting from home frees up money that would otherwise be spent on leasing an office. In fact, because the business is so favorably disposed to home-based operation, many established speakers, bureaus, and promoters never move into a commercial facility. There is very little need for clients to visit you; you can always arrange to meet with them at their facilities. Your actual presentations will take place in a hotel conference room or a similar facility. You will have few in-house employees until your business grows to a size where your revenues and personnel requirements make moving into a commercial location desirable.

A spare bedroom or den, converted into an office, provides the best home-based operation, as long as you have enough room for work space and equipment (desk, files, computer, fax, etc.) and for stored materials. If your office will be part of another room (such as a bedroom or kitchen), you will need to set aside additional secure space for shelving your brochures, handouts, letterhead, business cards, overhead slides, enrollment forms, props, and so on. A corner of the garage, a basement or attic room, or even a large closet with ample shelving can work, if you are well organized and the area is properly protected from moisture, temperature extremes, and casual access by others.

Keep overhead expenses as low as possible when starting out. Don't invest in fancy office fixtures and decor that your clients will never see; save your money for the costs of printing four-color brochures and upgraded visuals for your presentations. Do, however, invest in a professional image. At a minimum, rent a post office box to serve as your mailing address. (You can rent one monthly from either the local post office or a private mailbox rental facility. Renting from the latter allows you to affix a suite number to your post office box and appear as though you are operating from a commercial office location.) Even better, rent a "business identity" from a service that provides mail collection and phone answering. Laura Lodato, owner of a Priority Management® franchise in Tampa, Florida, uses such a service for less than $200 a month. Included in the monthly fee are the following:

- Business mail is received, sorted, and bundled at the commercial address. She can pick it up there each business day.
- Her calls are answered professionally (a voice introduces "Priority Management") and can be automatically forwarded to her home office.
- An after-hours voice mail service receives calls after business hours.
- Meeting rooms are available for those rare times when a client wishes to meet with her at her "office."
- Postage meters and copy machines can be used freely. "Tenants" are issued a pass card that calculates the number of copies they make and the amount of postage they use, and these charges are

added to their monthly rental fees. In essence, the business identity works like an executive suite (discussed below), except that Lodato does not pay for or receive any individual office space.

"The location is considered my physical address, so my business cards, my letterhead, everything that goes out from the local office of Priority Management®, all have the address of that business location," says Lodato. "It really works out well, because I have the flexibility of working from home, but I have constant phone coverage during the day. If I hired somebody to do that, even at minimum wage, it would cost much more than what I pay."

Home Office Tax Breaks

To take full advantage of the available tax breaks afforded home-based businesses, you must choose a room—not just a corner of a room—to use solely as an office. If your work area also contains a TV and stereo and serves as a den, your home office deduction probably won't hold up under an IRS audit. In January 1993, the Supreme Court ruled that to claim office space as a tax deduction, you must conduct the majority of your business there. Under the ruling, unless business owners spend most of their work time within the home, and use it for visits from clients, customers, or patients, the IRS will not allow a deduction.

To qualify for the deduction, the home office has to be:

- The principal place of business.
- A place where clients, customers, or patients visit on a regular basis.
- In connection with your trade if it is a separate place (e.g., the garage).
- Used exclusively and on a regular basis for business.

You may deduct from your income taxes a percentage of expenses equivalent to the percentage of space your home office occupies. If you live in an eight-room house and use one room solely as your office, you can deduct as business expenses one-eighth of your rent (or deed/mortgage payment) plus one-eighth of your utility, carpet cleaning, and similar bills. According to recent federal tax legislation, however, you cannot deduct any part of the base rate of the first telephone line into your residence, even if you use the telephone for business. Before you begin your business in a home office, review your local zoning codes. Zoning ordinances that prohibit or restrict business operations in residential areas may directly affect your home-based business. We will discuss taxes and zoning codes in Chapters 5 and 6.

Ask your insurance broker to judge whether your homeowner's insurance adequately covers the added liability risks of operating your business from your home. Insurance requirements are covered more thoroughly in Chapter 5.

OTHER OFFICE POSSIBILITIES

Should a home office be undesirable or unfeasible, you should look for a small office in which to begin your operations. As mentioned, your clients will have little or no need to visit your office, so you don't need to locate in the area from which they come. If, however, you plan to put on public seminars yourself, and to successfully target enough potential customers within, say, a two-hour radius of your office, then location becomes extremely important. Likewise, if your goal is to rapidly grow the size of your business and the number of employees you have working from your headquarters, you should carefully select the location of your business and the terms of your lease. Here are the key factors to consider.

1. *The rent-paying capacity of the business.* If you have done a sales-and-profit projection for your first year of operation, you will know approximately how much revenue you can expect to generate. For some high-volume businesses, rental expenses can be less than 1 percent of net sales. For small retail shops or businesses with uneven sales, the rent/net sales ratio can run as high as 10 percent. For the majority of businesses, rental expenses fall between 2 and 4 percent of net sales, although premium rental space in a new or highly developed commercial area can push the percentage much higher. To estimate your rental expenses (leased space plus any add-on costs), you can express the total amount you expect to pay—on a monthly or annual basis—as a percentage of projected net sales. Then you should take a close look at your business and decide whether the amount of money you will spend on renting a commercial facility is reasonable, given your current business needs. If your rental expenses will exceed 10 percent of your projected net sales, is this the wisest use of your funds? Perhaps you should consider extending your home-based operation for another year, or look for a less expensive commercial alternative. (More on commercial sites below.)

2. *Client/employee parking facilities.* Your site should provide convenient and adequate parking for employees, as well as easy access for individuals who come to visit you. It should be well-lit and secure.

Consider whether the parking area will soon need expansion, resurfacing, or striping—possibly at additional cost.

3. *Proximity to other businesses.* Because the majority of your customers will come from the business sector, it is desirable to locate in an area that has a large corporate presence. As a speaker, having a presence in the local community raises the likelihood of word-of-mouth referrals and facilitates valuable networking opportunities. As a seminar promoter, you can save substantially on travel costs by putting on seminars in your local area—at least at the outset—and targeting businesses in your area.

4. *Proximity to the airport and desirable hotels and meeting facilities.* Most largely corporate areas are conveniently located near major airports and hotels or other meeting facilities. It is important that you look into such availability ahead of time, however, so that you can be as close to a given meeting place as possible. Most experts advocate getting to a seminar site at least two hours ahead of time. If your seminar begins at 7:30 A.M., you won't want to have to leave home at 4:30 A.M. if you can avoid a long early drive.

5. *Terms of the lease.* Leasing considerations can sometimes be the deciding factor in your choice of site. Occasionally, an otherwise ideal site may have unacceptable leasing terms. The time to negotiate leasing terms is *before* you sign the lease. (See below.)

Business Parks and Office Buildings

You may want to consider locating your office within a business park or commercial office building. Business parks are usually composed of one or more office buildings located on the same lot and managed by the developer or a professional management company hired by the developer. Office space is commonly leased out on a triple-net basis, and tenants share in the maintenance costs of the building. Your rent will often include security and the cost of service to your own office.

Because you will not need much space when you begin your business, and because your clients do not need to visit you, an office in a business park or commercial building can be a good start-up option. A 500-square-foot office can run as low as $550 per month in some areas of the country. Shop around to negotiate the best deal.

Executive Suites

Another office option is an executive suite. Executive suites lease office space and provide secretarial services to a number of small—

often one-person—businesses like yours. According to the Executive Suite Network, the average executive suite occupies about 14,500 square feet and houses 50 offices. The average office is about 180 square feet. Monthly rent, running about $500 to $1,200 per month, varies by the market, the size of the office, and the location of the office within the building. Executive suites provide tenants with short-term leases, usually lasting from six months to one year. Suites usually include a telephone, use of common areas (lobby, conference room, kitchen, etc.), a receptionist, and incoming mail reception. Office utilities are also usually included in the tenant's monthly rent, and a professional office manager runs the group of suites. Faxing, photocopying, and word processing services are generally made available, and tenants pay only for the services they use. To find executive suite facilities in your area, look in the business-to-business telephone directory under "Executive Suites."

Office Layout

A single room as small as 150 square feet can start you off in this business, if you use the space wisely. First, plan out your storage area. You will need several shelves and/or cabinets to house all of your brochures, handouts, letterhead, business cards, overhead slides, enrollment forms, props, and miscellaneous materials. This area does not have to take up a great deal of space, but it must be situated in a portion of the office that permits easy access to needed items. (Ideally, your office will have at least one small closet in which you can store some of these items.) Next, set up your work area so that your desk and files are functional. Allow space for your telephone, fax machine, computer, printer, coffee maker, and copier (if you plan to have one), plus a small bookshelf for your resource materials.

If you feel sure that you will, for whatever reason, prefer to have clients visit your office from time to time—and you are not located in a facility with a common conference room—you will need at least 250 square feet to make your office functional. If you can afford more space, so much the better. Set up the front half of the office space as a reception/meeting area. Furnish it with a couch, two or three nice chairs, and a coffee table placed to form a small square. Another table holding brochures, a phone, and some coffee or water should stand off to one side. Between this reception area and your work/storage area, place some large, attractively potted plants in a row, to serve as a separation "wall." Decorate your reception/meeting area tastefully so that it looks quite professional despite its small size.

LEASING PROPERTY

Leases are strong contracts. If you sign a lease for $1,000 per month for a period of one year, you are agreeing to pay $12,000 regardless of what happens to your business. Therefore, some business tenants recommend starting out with the shortest lease term possible—ideally, a month-to-month lease—until the enterprise is established. It may not always be possible to rent premises on a month-to-month basis, but you should never feel pressured to accept whatever is offered to you. There will always be other sites available.

New ventures hold many surprises. Look for a lease that you can easily assign to another tenant, in the event you decide to move your business back home or need another, larger facility. A provision for assignment or subletting will allow you to close or move your business while permitting you to get another tenant to pay your rental obligation for the balance of the lease term. It will also allow you to sell your business to a new owner who can assume your lease under the same good terms you have.

Flat Leases

The flat lease, the oldest and simplest form of lease, sets a single price for a definite period of time. This lease is becoming hard to find but is naturally the best deal for the lessee. Do not be tempted to go along with a flat lease if the term is too short. A series of short-term leases could cost you more in the long run. Even if your business is successful in your present location, if your landlord increases the rent every time your short-term lease expires, a prime location can quickly become unprofitable.

The short-term lease is a built-in "escape clause" that enables you to leave the leased facility before your business goes bankrupt altogether, but it's better to find a good location that won't price you out in 2 or 3 years. Always do your homework. Sit down and calculate potential costs over the long and short terms. Insulate your business as much as possible from threats to your financial well-being.

Step Leases

Increases in the landlord's expenses are inevitable over time. Taxes *will* go up, insurance premiums *will* increase, and the cost of repairs *will* pace wage inflation. The step lease attempts to compensate the landlord and cover these increases by annually increasing the monthly rental rate throughout the term of the agreement. A typical escalation might be:

Step Lease

First Year, $450/month
Second Year, $480/month
Third Year, $510/month
Fourth Year, $540/month
Fifth Year, $570/month

In this example, the rent rises almost 30 percent over a five-year period. You will have to judge whether this is an advantageous type of lease agreement for you.

Net Leases

In contrast, a net lease requires you to pay only the exact amounts of increases when they occur. You pay a base rent and the dollar increase if and when taxes rise. There are net-net (or double net) versions of this lease that pick up added insurance premiums as well as tax increases, singularly or on a proportionate basis. Keep in mind that if you do something within your business that raises insurance premiums, you alone will pick up the tab.

Triple-net is the lease version most often encountered, especially in malls, strip centers, and business parks. Tenants share repair costs as well as taxes and insurance. Remember, however, that the repairs are not confined to your building. If you agree to pay taxes, insurance, and maintenance costs, the landlord might have little concern over whether these costs remain at a minimum.

Cost-of-Living Leases

This type of lease ignores specific expense items, ties everything together, and attaches itself to the Cost of Living Index. In short, it takes general inflation into account. At the end of the year, the government's cost of living figures are evaluated. If the inflation has been, for example, 6.8 percent, your rent will increase by the same percentage.

Lessees often complain that "cost of living indicators" depend on consumables' costs, while increases in taxes or insurance premiums tend to lag a year or so behind. Thus, when you pay that 6.8 percent to your landlord, you're paying for increases that the landlord won't feel for another year. Taxes and other rising costs vary nationwide; evaluate the cost of living circumstances in your area.

Negotiate before You Sign

A lease usually covers other important matters, such as remodeling to be done, who is to pay for it, liabilities and duties assumed by each party, and permission for the tenant to construct external signs, engage in additional lines of business, or make alterations if needed. Some landlords include other clauses in their lease contracts—clauses you may or may not want to pay for.

The lease prepared by the lessor is not engraved in stone; it is extended to you for your consideration. You may accept it without discussion, but you may be able to negotiate something better, particularly in terms of its length, simply by asking. If the landlord won't budge, you have lost nothing. You can always look elsewhere and come back to the first location if you don't find a better offer. Analyze your requirements thoroughly. When negotiating with the landlord, ask to have necessary additions or renovations made to the property *before* you rent. If the landlord won't bear the expense, see whether the landlord will defer, or waive, the rent for a beginning period.

SELECTING SEMINAR LOCATIONS

The information in this section pertains to seminar promoters and speakers who put on seminars in their own facilities. Professional speakers hired by companies to do in-house training will generally have facilities arranged for them by the company. Refer to this section if you ever need to make your own facility arrangements.

The two major steps in locating your seminars are: (1) select a particular city or community in which to hold the seminar, and (2) choose a site within that community to house the event.

Choosing a Community

When you must choose a community in which to hold a seminar, consider your answers to this quiz:

1. Is the population base large enough to support the seminar?
2. Does the community have a stable economic base that will provide a healthy environment for the event?

3. Are the area's demographic characteristics compatible with the market that is targeted?
4. Can facilities within the city accommodate the event within a reasonable amount of time? (In other words, can they fulfill your planning schedule?)

Population Required

Each year, the U.S. Bureau of the Census publishes Economic Censuses, which are comprehensive studies of the numbers of firms in various lines of business and the populations of the communities where they are located. For more information, contact the U.S. Bureau of the Census, Customer Services, Washington, DC 20233. The telephone number for the Bureau is (301) 457-4700, and the fax number is (301) 457-4714.

In general, seminar planners say that the larger the population base, the larger the turnout you can expect, but the larger the costs involved in holding your seminar there. "In little bitty cities, we're glad if we get 30 people—and that's OK. It's worth it as long as we can say that it was worth putting some mail into [the area]," says Denise Dudley, co-founder of SkillPath Seminars. "But some seminars just can't go to little cities, because there's not enough interest in them.

"Basically, the more specialized the topic, the larger the city you need to do it in. For example, we can go with a customer service seminar into just about any town; every teeny-weeny little town you've heard of has a 7-Eleven and a bank, and they're going to want to send people to a seminar on that topic. But we may not be able to take another type of seminar there."

Bill Hill, manager of seminar operations for CareerTrack, which holds seminars in 360 cities per year, says the company generally sticks to larger metropolitan areas. However, they include surrounding cities within a given area when planning. "We have such a huge database now that we know pretty much every market and how it's subdivided. For example, in Denver we know there's Aurora and Englewood and Littleton—all the little markets that surround that city," says Hill. Those breakdowns help in targeting the advertising efforts and selecting a centralized location within the larger city limits.

Economic Base

A community's economic base will determine your opportunities to some extent. The wealth produced in or near the community greatly affects local employment, income, and population growth, each of which plays a role in the success or failure of your seminar.

The occupational makeup of a community depends on the types of jobs its resources and location will support; its population density depends on the number of such jobs available. The nature and number of jobs largely determine income levels in the community.

To evaluate a community's economic base, research the following:

1. Percentage of people employed full-time, and the trend in employment.
2. Average family income.
3. Annual per-capita sales for seminars in the area.

You can obtain this information by studying the census data and business statistics mentioned earlier. You can also learn a great deal about your prospective community just by observing. If high school and college graduates have to leave town to find suitable employment; if other residents cannot find local jobs; if retail sales and industrial production are declining; and if local business owners, educational administrators, and other residents hold discouraging attitudes about the community, it's probably not a good choice for your seminar unless your topic is motivational and addresses the community's specific concerns. Favorable signs are:

1. Branch plants of large industrial firms locating in the community.
2. A progressive chamber of commerce and other civic organizations.
3. Good schools and public services.
4. Well-maintained business and residential properties.
5. Good transportation facilities to other parts of the country.
6. Construction activity accompanied by a minimal number of vacant buildings and unoccupied houses for sale.

Demographic Characteristics

To judge whether a particular community will be advantageous for your seminar(s), you must know the demographic profile of your potential customers. Evaluate the demographic characteristics of a community by looking at the following:

1. Purchasing power (amount of disposable income).
2. Educational attainment achieved.

3. Places and kinds of work.
4. Means of transportation.
5. Age ranges.
6. Family status.
7. Leisure activities.

Detailed demographic information should be available from established businesses within your industry or from a trade association. In addition, the Bureau of Labor Statistics publishes the Consumer Expenditure Survey (CES). The CES annually samples 5,000 households to learn how families and individuals spend their money. Unlike other surveys that might ask only how much people spend on one specific type of item, the CES questions participants about nearly every expense category, from alcoholic beverages and takeout food to pensions and life insurance. Bureau of Labor Statistics analysts then sort the information and group consumers by income, household size, race, age, and other factors. You can order a copy of the latest CES by calling (202) 606-5886 or writing to the Bureau of Labor Statistics, Division of Information Services, 2 Massachusetts Avenue N.E., Room 2860, Washington, DC 20212. You can also order this information over the World Wide Web at http://stats.bls.gov.

Facility Availability

Some topics are so hot that you will want to jump on them immediately in order to stay on top of your competition. At the same time, if your usual seminar route includes Chicago, Atlanta, and Las Vegas, you may have trouble getting a room in your favorite facility—or, possibly, *any* facility—in the time frame that you'd like. Dudley says that SkillPath tries to give a minimum of two months' advance notice to their planners when implementing a new seminar topic, so they can design and print brochures, mail them, and book a meeting place. "But we can't always plan sooner than that, so sometimes you miss out on a city," she says. Hill agrees, noting that some cities can almost always take reservations six months in advance; others need more than a year's advance notice for bookings. (More on this below.) Be sure to ask about the average lead times needed for hotel meeting rooms when you are considering any new city.

Watch for Changes in Your Communities

Once you've added a location to your seminar site roster, you must remain aware of the community's demographic characteristics. As cities and the people within them change, seminar promoters must either change their topics or redefine the markets they wish to serve. The alternatives are reduced revenue or eliminating certain cities from your route.

Conversely, you should constantly be on the lookout for "new" cities. "A few years ago, we 'discovered' Dubuque, Iowa," says Dudley. The city was a surprise success because, although it has a population base of more than 50,000, there aren't really any surrounding areas from which to draw attendees. "We're always looking for new cities. And for reasons that we really, honestly don't understand, sometimes [going to a new city] works and sometimes it doesn't."

She adds that it is important to really do your homework before trying out a new location. "We're so busy doing so many other things, and there are so many cities that *do* work, so you take risks carefully and slowly."

SELECTING SEMINAR SITES

Once you have decided on the cities in which you will hold your seminars, you must choose a specific site within each city. Most seminars are held in hotel meeting facilities. Not only are hotel personnel quite experienced at handling reservations for meeting functions, there are also plenty of resources to help you locate appropriate hotel rooms in any city in the country. The *Official Airlines Guide* (OAG) and *The Hotel Index* are two popular resources; each lists hotels in every imaginable city. Travel agents are also a great resource, especially while you are still in your start-up phase. Some chambers of commerce are more helpful than others (some, says Dudley, can take *forever* to help you), but they can be a great resource if you build a relationship with them. "They're great," says Hill, "because they're working for the hotels. They'll find out when your event is going to be and they'll call and try to negotiate prices for you."

You should also contact your local program manager (more on this in Chapter 4) and ask for referrals to appropriate hotels. A local resident is your best resource for finding out whether a hotel has recently begun major construction, undergone impressive renovations, started to deteriorate, and so on. "When you first go to a town, unless you can go and scope it out, or you know someone there already, you're kind of taking pot luck," says Dudley.

Here are the important questions to ask when you are considering a hotel or other facility for your seminar.

> *Has the hotel/facility planned for any construction during the date(s) of the seminar(s)?* "Hotels are renovating all the time, and you would

want to know if there's any renovation going on while you're there," says Hill. "I've had jackhammers, guys on the roof—we've actually moved people from one hotel to another hotel across the street during a break."

What events are going to be taking place in the room(s) next door to mine? "This is important, because you'll have these rowdy groups, or a jokester speaker next door, and you can hear them through the walls. It's very disruptive," says Lodato. Imagine a university organization singing fight songs while you are discussing productive ways to cope with job loss.

Does the hotel/facility use its own audio/video equipment, or do you need to rent it especially for an event? "Some hotels have to bring in A/V equipment, so check on this," says Dudley. Renting the equipment is not a problem in itself, but you must double- and triple-check with hotel personnel ahead of time, to confirm that the equipment is at the hotel, in working order, before your event.

Have the directions I've been given to your hotel from the airport/ freeways/Main Street changed? Is there ample parking available? Nothing is more frustrating to seminar attendees than to circle a business district endlessly looking for the correct hotel, or to be unable to find a place to park once they find the correct hotel.

The most important thing, says Dudley, is to survey your attendees for their input on any facility you choose. "We've had our share of disasters. We've looked up something in the book, we thought it sounded good, but our customers say to us, 'Hey, this isn't really the greatest part of town' or 'This place is hard to find,' and they put that on our evaluations at the end of the seminar," she says. "Enrollees are very, very cooperative. They're helpful. They want you to do well!"

Booking Meeting Rooms

As mentioned previously, some topics are so hot that you want to jump on them immediately, in order to beat your competition. In such cases, it may or may not be possible to book a room at your usual hotel or facility. "Every hotel is different," says Hill. "If a hotel books a lot of business, it is going to have what they call book-out policies. [This is usually the case] in the major metropolitan areas: Chicago, Atlanta, Denver. [At these hotels, the] main incentive is to book sleeping rooms; meeting rooms are kind of incidental. If they generate revenue off meeting rooms, that's great, but they hold them for the big groups that [book] all the [guest] rooms. If you don't block a lot of rooms, the hotels aren't going to release space to you. In smaller cities, you can pretty much book six to nine months in advance and they'll take the bookings."

Cost is a major factor when selecting cities and hotels/facilities. "In your major metropolitan areas, you'll run into more expense," says Hill. "In Los Angeles, we may not be as profitable because of the expense in the area. In more rural areas, we do better."

Dudley agrees. "In big cities, it costs a lot to put on a seminar. It's just unbelievable. Hotel room costs, a sound system, or just the travel to get there—you have to have a lot more people to cover the costs." Skill-Path's goal is to get from 100 to 200 people to attend a seminar in a major city—a goal that they achieve regularly because the company focuses its efforts in areas where they know they can draw from the larger population base and meet their target market profile.

Actual costs vary substantially from hotel to hotel. Meeting rooms can run from $35 to $1,500 or more per day, depending on the type of room desired, the number of people expected, and the elegance of the facility. The time of year can also affect rates. Areas that attract large numbers of tourists in the summer may lower their rates in the winter, and vice versa. Remember, however, that many other entrepreneurs and organizations will be vying for the same deals, so it's best to make your move as early as possible.

A Touch of Elegance

Lodato, who primarily targets executives in Tampa, Florida, and the surrounding region, decided that the best way to ensure a proper setting for her clients was to become a member of The Tampa Club, an elite facility with spacious and elegant meeting rooms available only to members. After paying an initiation fee and monthly dues on top of room rental charges, she still believes that the overall cost is reasonable for the environment she is able to present in. "It's pretty impressive for the executives that come to our workshops," she says. "It's much different from a room at [a local hotel] or whatever."

Though up-front costs will be higher, club membership can be a good alternative to hotels in major cities, where book-out policies are common. As long as you remain a member in good standing, pay your bills on time, and build a rapport with club personnel, you will likely be able to book a meeting room for at least your smaller seminars (drawing 30 to 50 people) at almost any time. Ask local clubs, in the areas you are targeting, about their membership rates, any meeting rooms they offer, and the lead times they require.

3

EQUIPMENT AND
INVENTORY

This chapter outlines both the equipment you need to run your business and the inventory items (audio and video tapes, books, and so on) you will eventually use to market yourself and increase your profits. We will also review the equipment used in seminar presentations; most of it will be provided for your use at the seminar sites. It's important to track and monitor your inventory so that you never come up short for your seminars.

SEMINAR EQUIPMENT

Let's take a look at the equipment commonly used in seminars. A key aid is a microphone, which can be either handheld or clipped onto the speaker's clothing. Many speakers choose to use a lectern, if only to keep their notes and backup material close by (in case something goes wrong with any equipment they plan to use). Some speakers like to use some sort of pointer to highlight visual information—anything from a simple wooden pointer to a "laser" pointer, which works like a flashlight, beaming a small pinpoint of light or an arrow onto a visual image.

Beyond these basics, the equipment to be used will depend largely on the size of the expected audience. If the group is small—say, 10 to 20 people—it may be most effective to stick to flip charts, chalkboards or dry-erase marker boards, an overhead projector and transparencies, and some audience participation exercises. "We've found that 92 percent of meeting leaders choose an easel and pad as one of their top three meeting supply tools, along with markers and overhead projectors," says Kelly Spaulding, senior product manager for Quill Corporation, a leading independent direct marketer of office supplies. On the other hand, if your audience is large, you may want to consider supplementing your overhead projector and transparencies with audio/visual equipment and either a large, up-front projection screen or several television monitors placed throughout the room where the seminar is being held.

What you select also depends quite a bit on how much you will charge your attendees. "We don't do [multimedia] very much because of cost—because of our price point," says Bill Hill, manager of seminar operations for CareerTrack, whose national seminars begin at $39. If your budget is tight, you can save money and offer impressive visuals by using a slide projector, but this will require an investment in the slides.

Hotels in large and medium-size cities have convention services departments that supply everything from registration tables to lecterns. If they don't have the equipment on hand, they can make arrangements to provide it. If you are using a meeting hall or a location that lacks the resources you need, contact a local party rental or audio/visual company. Keep in mind that facilities charge extra for additional microphones, lighting, projectors, screens, laser pointers, and so on. With a hotel, you might be able to negotiate a discount if you have a large seminar or use the hotel's catering department. Some basic equipment may even be included in the room rental agreement, but be sure you know exactly what equipment the hotel will provide and what, if anything, you will have to pay for.

Multimedia

Today, there are computer programs that allow presenters to give on-screen lessons to people in remote sites via their desktop computers. Equipped with pointers and messaging capabilities, those involved can speak to one another without disrupting the overall presentation and can ask questions of the leader right on the screen. There are also impressive machines that project three different slides onto a wall in sync with prerecorded audio tracks, and tie in perfectly with your well-planned and well-rehearsed presentation. Such presentation equipment appeals to a society that can do just about everything via television or computer: shopping, banking, networking, studying, and so on. According to 1995 figures from Nielsen Media Research, U.S. households continue to watch nearly 20 hours of television per week, on average. And numerous studies have shown that people retain up to five times as much information when it is presented both aurally and visually as they do when it is presented only aurally.

What does this mean to seminar promoters? "[Multimedia] is where the industry is going," says Hill. "And there is quite a bit of additional expense in that. For example, we have an Internet program, and we wanted to go online with that and shoot, basically, what was on the computer screen onto the wall. To do that, to get a phone line, to get a 3M projector and a couple of other things to make that happen, cost us about $1,200 a day." And that was just for the presenter to project the image; it did not allow for attendees to participate interactively.

Does this mean that you will have to spend big money up front to be competitive? Not necessarily. The key to any successful seminar still lies in the skill of the presenter. After all, high-tech visuals are practically a necessity if you are listening to a dry, monotonous presenter, but they can be both unnecessary and disruptive if they are competing with a dynamite speaker. If you can't put together a top-notch visual program, don't use anything visual at all. Nothing will undermine a speaker faster than to be backed up by slides or video-tapes of poor quality.

Keep abreast of what is being used in the industry, and know where the price points for these items are falling. For example, prices for film recorders that take computer images and convert them into high-quality slides have dropped as low as $3,000 for low-end, desktop models (mid-range models remain closer to $10,000). If you decide to specialize in seminars for the medical industry, this expense may be worthwhile; otherwise, you might have to spend much more to have slides of MRIs and Xrays done by an outside vendor.

Simply put, you must keep on top of the industry's trends, and plan and budget accordingly. As the 1995 *Guide to Professional Speakers*—a joint publication of the National Speakers Association and the American Society of Association Executives—points out, speakers began using videotapes of their presentations as marketing tools in the early 1980s. These videotapes allowed meeting planners to conveniently preview a variety of speakers before selecting one for a particular event. The *Guide* predicts that "speakers will [soon] be previewed on CD-ROM because of the convenience and time-saving element of planners being able to select the portion of the program they wish to preview—live speaking segments, testimonials, biographical materials, and so on."

BASIC OFFICE EQUIPMENT

As mentioned in Chapter 2, your primary office can be small, but it needs to be well equipped and organized. To get started, you'll need a large desk, a comfortable chair, one or two visitors' chairs, a standard file cabinet, and some type of shelving. You probably will also need at least one bookshelf for your resource materials, hotel catalogs, magazines, and pricing guides.

You can probably set up your office for less than $1,200 if you buy used furniture and shop around for it. In the classified sections of most metropolitan newspapers, you will find a host of used furniture and equipment bargains. Also check the "Business Opportunities" category. Businesses that are being liquidated or sold may have furniture or equipment for sale at substantial savings. Don't overlook suppliers of new equipment, either, when looking for bargains. They frequently have trade-ins or repossessions for sale for as little as 50 percent of the new purchase price. Judicious shopping will turn up some excellent bargains.

Other items that you'll need to get your business started include:

- Computer.
- Software.
- Modem.
- Copier.
- Fax machine.
- Cellular phone.
- Answering machine.
- Phone.
- Postage meter.

Computerization

Investing in a computer is a must in this business because the speed and efficiency that computerization brings to your operation are invaluable. You can use a computer for the following tasks:

- Computerized bookkeeping, including reports on profitability, break-even points, and most successful topics and/or cities (gauged by attendance, gross revenues, profit margins, and so on).
- Inventory control tasks, including activity, lead times, and client order/reorder schedules.
- Direct-mail databases, which can help you prospect for new clients and keep existing ones satisfied.

- Master calendar planning for scheduling seminar locations, sites, and dates across the country, and the speakers and/or program managers handling those events.
- Word processing and presentation graphics. (Many printers give lower prices to customers who can provide them with a diskette that contains the information to be printed.)

Despite popular myth, a computer system is no longer superexpensive. The minimum cost is usually about $4,200 for your first workstation, the hardware and software needed to run the system, and a laser printer. Each additional workstation will cost approximately $1,500. Although newspapers advertise PCs for less than $1,000, most of these computers are extremely limited and cannot run many of the programs you will want to use.

To get the most out of your computer and its compatible software, purchase a PC based on 486/DX technology, with 8 megabytes of RAM, a 525-megabyte hard drive, and a high-density 3 × 5-inch floppy drive. Couple that with an SVGA monitor, an SVGA graphics board, a 28,800-bps modem, a laser printer, and a mouse controller. This system will run all the latest, most powerful software, and will give you enough room for more software and hardware in the future. For a complete breakdown of computer-related costs, see Table 3–1.

Service contracts, if you decide to purchase them, usually run 10 to 20 percent of the hardware cost per year. If you hire a reputable consultant to help with the selection, installation, testing, and training process, add another 5 to 20 percent to the total system price.

Training is one of the most time-consuming aspects of computerizing, but some instruction is often necessary. The duration of your training will depend on your previous exposure to computer systems. There are user-friendly systems on the market that are easy to learn. Apple Computer's Macintosh uses a standard graphics interface for all of its programs, so you don't have to spend countless hours memorizing the proper commands and learning the quirks of each program.

To make the PC more user-friendly, Microsoft Corporation introduced "Windows" in the late 1980s. All programs written for Windows use the Windows interface, so they all look and feel the same, reducing training time considerably when compared to DOS-based programs.

Whether you choose a Macintosh or a PC, you will need to purchase stand-alone software (programs dedicated to doing a single task). For DOS, Windows, and Macintosh systems, examples of powerful stand-alone software are: Microsoft Word (word processing); Microsoft Excel (spreadsheet functions); Microsoft FoxPro and Microsoft

Table 3–1   Computer Equipment Table

HARDWARE	
486/33 Computer	$1,000
SVGA Monitor	460
SVGA Graphics Board	120
Modem-14,400 bps/Software	100
Laser Printer	810
Mouse	70
Surge Protector	15
Printer Stand	45
Total Hardware	**$2,620**
SOFTWARE	
Windows	$90
Word Processing	120
Spreadsheet	120
Database Management	495
Total Software	**$825**
MISCELLANEOUS	
Miscellaneous Supplies	$200
Magazine Subscriptions	45
Total Miscellaneous	**$245**
Total Costs	**$3,690**

Access (for database files and records); and Intuit's Quicken and QuickBooks, or Microsoft's Money, for accounting and bookkeeping. In addition to these programs, you may need telecommunication software for sending and receiving electronic information.

According to Ron Mansfield in *New Business Opportunities* magazine,[1] you should consider the following guidelines:

1. *Buy enough power.* Many first-time computer shoppers buy systems without enough power or expansion capacity. If you plan to purchase a business computer, you're better off buying one that is a little bigger and faster than you currently need.

2. *Take time to learn.* Many people purchase computers without learning how to use them. Most of today's new software comes with self-paced, on-screen tutorials and printed documentation. Spend time exploring these aids.

3. *Establish standards and procedures.* Failing to establish computer standards, policies, and procedures creates problems. You need policies regarding the use of virus-detection software, backups, and software piracy. Keep these policies updated.

4. *Make backups.* Don't get stuck spending days or even months trying to restore information that was lost or destroyed. If you don't make regular backups, you're destined to learn the hard way.

5. *Plan for expansion.* Find out what's involved in moving from single-user to multi-user versions of your software and hardware. Make sure your computers and printers can be easily networked.

6. *Quit "frittering."* Today's computers offer fun ways to turn out impressive documents, tempting you and your employees to add artwork, color, and even motion to your documents. Nip that tendency in the bud if it starts to get out of control.

7. *Train employees on your computer system.* Computer ignorance is a time-waster. Encourage each new employee to learn how to use the computers and software efficiently.

8. *Protect against viruses.* Never use disks that have been in someone else's computer. Virus-detection software is a necessity, and you must update it regularly. New viruses pop up all the time and may not be detected by older software.

9. *Keep it simple.* Overcomputerizing is a mistake. It's much easier to set up a huge database than it is to maintain one. Don't waste time collecting unnecessary information that makes your system hopelessly complex.

10. *Stay honest.* Software piracy can be expensive. Software makers are cracking down, taking even fairly small companies to court if they think software has been copied illegally.

Software Considerations

New businesses often run into a common problem: They purchase a computer and want basic office software, but don't know what to buy. Businesses may also rely on one major application, like the word processing or spreadsheet programs mentioned above, and then decide they want a complete range of computer capabilities.

One option is to buy an integrated software package such as ClarisWorks or Microsoft Works. A second option is the new "office suites" or software products from Microsoft and Lotus. In Microsoft's Office, you'll get Microsoft Excel, Microsoft Word, Microsoft PowerPoint, and Microsoft Mail. In Lotus SmartSuite, you'll get Lotus 1-2-3, Lotus AmiPro, Freelance Graphics, Lotus Approach, and Lotus Organizer.

Both integrated packages and software suites offer a full complement of office automation software: word processing, spreadsheet, database, graphics, and communications. The difference is that integrated software contains all these applications in one program, which means that each component has fewer features than its individual counterparts. Software suites, on the other hand, are bundles of full-featured software programs. For many small-business owners, an integrated software package is sufficient, and it comes with a lower price tag—$200 to $400, compared to $600 to $800 for an office suite. However, the latest versions of office suite packages offer more consistent user interfaces and better networking capabilities than those available in the past, making them a wise investment for entrepreneurs desiring the power of full-featured applications.

In addition, you may want to consider information management software programs such as ACT! by Symantec Corporation and contact management software such as ECCOPro by NetManage. The ACT! program allows you to keep detailed information on every contact you make, including date-by-date detailed notes of every phone call, letter, fax, or meeting between you and a contact. You can look up contacts or information in your database by first name, last name, company name, city, state, zip code, or other attributes. You can schedule meetings, phone calls, and so on, and alarms will alert you to your upcoming events, and print reports of all past, current, and future activity. Personalized letters, mailing labels, and envelopes can be printed from the database using an automatic mail-merge function.

ECCOPro, a multi-award-winning information management program, provides contact management features as well as calendar and scheduling functions. You can view your schedule by day, week, month, or year. It also features work management functions such as full outlining, Gantt charts, and time and expense tracking, plus an Internet address book of more than 2,000 sites. Users of DayRunner, Day Timers, Franklin, Priority Management, or Avery personal organization systems can also print their calendars, to-do lists, and so on in the proper format for their personal notebooks.

Laura Lodato, owner of a Tampa-based Priority Management franchise, says that what is most important is finding a software package that allows seminar scheduling, enrollment tracking, mail list maintenance, and "purchase tracking" so that you know when you need to reorder any materials you provide to your seminar attendees. (Priority Management franchisees receive software through the parent company.)

Upgrading Your PC

When people consider adding power to their computers, the first thing they think of is upgrading the central processing unit (CPU). There are three ways to add a more powerful processor to your computer:

1. Replace the motherboard.
2. Go through the manufacturer's proprietary upgrades.
3. Get the new industry-standard Pentium chip.

You may also need to analyze other options.

Adding random access memory (RAM) can improve your system's performance more than any other upgrade tactic. However, this booster helps only up to a point; after that, adding more RAM will not boost performance any further. Windows stores applications and data it is using in RAM; if there is not enough RAM, the applications and data will be stored in "virtual RAM," and this slows down your computer. By adding enough RAM to store your entire application and data—optimally, 16 megabytes (MB)—you can greatly speed your performance. However, having more RAM than your system needs will not produce any additional benefits.

If you decide you need to buy a faster hard disk, look at access times and transfer rates. The access time is the time it takes for the hard disk head physically to find the data on the disk; the transfer rate is the length of time it takes to transfer the data from the disk to the processor. If your computer runs at 20MHz or faster, look for a hard disk with an access speed of less than 20 milliseconds (ms) and a transfer rate of at least 700 KB per second—preferably 800 KB per second or faster. Also, be sure your new hard disk has the same kind of hard disk controller you already have.

Graphical applications, such as those that run in the Windows or Macintosh environments, can be quite taxing on any computer system. Graphics display and manipulation require a great deal of processor power, which in turn can greatly slow the operation of your system. Graphics accelerators, which you can buy for about $75 to $250, are add-in cards you install into the NuBus slots in your Mac or the expansion slots in your PC. These add-ins take on the burden of graphics processing, leaving the computer's CPU to do other processing. Companies such as Radius, RasterOps, and Mirror Technologies offer graphics accelerators for the Mac; ATI Technologies is a company that offers graphics accelerators for the PC.

Online Information Services

The birth of online communications services has been one of the most significant technological breakthroughs in personal computing. Their ability to link millions (and potentially billions) of computers allows individuals and businesses to communicate in ways never before possible, thereby gaining access to unlimited stores of information.

If you're a newcomer to the information superhighway, you may ask, "What are online services and how are they useful to entrepreneurs?" Online services are electronic networks that connect an infinite number of local computer terminals to each other. This allows the rapid transmittal of large amounts of information at the wink of an eye and a touch of the keyboard.

By logging onto an online service via a local access telephone number and a modem hooked up to a personal computer, a person can access many different types of information: local, national, and global news; reference materials usually available only in a well-stocked collegiate library; professional and financial data; and entertainment.

You may already be familiar with bulletin board services (BBSs). The board is simply a message board in electronic format, where people can write and post messages, and reply to messages from other BBS members. Bulletin board services also contain library file databases, from which members can download any kind of PC file, be it a text file, a graphic image, or an executable application.

Online services are simply large BBSs. Among the more popular commercial online services are Prodigy, CompuServe, and America Online (AOL). Each of these services has its own assortment of news information, message boards, file databases, and conference or "chat" capabilities, which allow you to hold live (or "real-time") conversations with people located anywhere in the world.

Many commercial online services offer "gateways" to the Internet, a giant international network made up of smaller networks, each with bulletin boards, file databases, and other information resources. Gateways serve to transfer data between separate networks or applications not normally connected to each other. America Online, for example, is a separate network from the Internet, but it offers gateways through which you can send and receive e-mail (electronic mail) from the Internet, as well as access certain parts of the Internet.

For more information about the Internet—what it is, and how to access and use it—look for *The Whole Internet User's Guide and Catalog* in bookstores, or order it directly from the publisher: O'Reilly & Associates, 103-A Morris St., Sebastopol, CA 95472; (800) 998-9938. You can use online services for research for your own business or for a client, and you can network with other entrepreneurs in your field or in other industries. Online services are also good for making contact with consultants and other individuals who can offer valuable advice. If necessary, you can even conduct business online with clients in other parts of the world. This part of the information highway can be very beneficial for home-based entrepreneurs.

If only to have the *possibility* of reaching valuable information sources, no matter how often they use them, entrepreneurs who subscribe to one or more online services have a distinct advantage over those who do not.

Modems

To access online services, you'll need a modem as a necessary link. Consider whether you need an internal or external modem and whether it should have fax capability, and, most importantly, how fast a modem your activities require. Internal modems are generally less expensive than external modems. External modems have status lights to let you know whether the modem is in use and connecting with the service. Portable notebook computers can be plugged into external modems.

If you fax messages on a regular basis, faxing directly from your computer via a modem can be very convenient. The modem's speed, measured in bits per second (bps), indicates how fast your modem will transmit and receive data. Experts recommend that you buy a modem with a speed of 14,400 bps or more. The rate at which your modem processes data depends on the phone line you use and the software you have, as well as the type of information it processes. Graphic images with photographs, drawings, and even video and audio files will take more processing time than text.

Copiers

A copier is a fixture in any modern office. A few years ago, only companies with sizable equipment budgets could own copiers. The average personal copier cost $10,000 or more, and was housed in a huge console. Today's copiers are far more compact—and far more affordable. They're small enough to place on a desktop and are designed for easier maintenance.

Not every business needs a copier, but if you distribute handout materials that you have created, and can afford a high-quality copier, owning or leasing one may be to your best advantage—particularly if you don't have a rapid-service copying shop nearby. Some copiers offer features such as automatic document feeders, collating for multipage documents, color reproduction, paper cassette choices that range from the standard $8\frac{1}{2} \times 11$-inch sheet to ledgersize, and reduction and enlargement of the image.

Some important features to consider when purchasing a copier are: the number of copies per minute, reduction and enlargement capabilities, collating and sorting options, paper tray sizes and capacities, and two-sided copying. Include the expense of toner cartridges and regular servicing when you plan to purchase a copier.

You may need only a basic copier with multiple paper trays for different sizes of documents, or you may need one with most of the features listed above. A basic copier is suitable for the reproduction of one-page documents such as invoices and correspondence. The high-end machines will be most appropriate for lengthy documents and materials that require color reproduction.

Basic copiers with a minimum of features are often priced around $1,500; office copiers with a range of features cost several times that amount. You can also lease a copier on a monthly basis. Your monthly lease payment will vary, depending on the type of copier you select, the number of copies you make each month, and the duration of the lease. Very broadly speaking, lease charges will begin at about $200 per month and rise from there. Call your local Xerox, Canon, Sharp, or 3-M dealer for more information.

Personal copiers—compact (or mini) copiers for home and private use—handle anything from single sheets (which the user must manually feed in) to 10 copies per minute (cpm). Major players in the personal copier industry are Canon, Sharp, and Xerox, as well as Mita, Panasonic, and Sanyo. You can get a low-end, no-frills personal copier with replaceable toner cartridges for less than $400. However, plan to use this type of copier only for your personal office work. If you photocopy any materials you will hand out at your seminars, they must be of the best quality.

A bit higher on the scale are desktop copiers. Even the plainest desktop copiers have speeds of 10 cpm, which is considered the minimum for a business copier. Many go as high as 20 to 25 cpm. They can handle anywhere from 800 to 20,000 copies per month. For about $2,000 to $3,000, you can get a desktop copier with considerable speed (20 or more cpm) and useful extras like front-loading paper trays, the ability to enlarge originals up to 11 by 17 inches, and zoom reduction/enlargement capabilities.

Most businesses buy desktop copiers through dealers because service and support are thrown in with the deal. Buying from a dealer costs from 10 to 20 percent more than buying from a discounter, computer superstore, or mail order company. The advantages are: an on-site service center, and a contract guaranteeing a certain number of service visits throughout the year. You pay a little extra for the service contract, but most alternative vendors do not even offer the contract as an option. Most copier vendors offer their own warranties, which generally cover your machine for 90 days to 3 years.

Ninety-eight percent of all businesses with fewer than 100 employees own at least one copier or plan to buy one in the near future, according to BIS Strategic Decisions.

Fax Machines

Fax machines are a must in today's business ventures. Last-minute contracts, hotel confirmations, speaker arrangements, and other critical information can be transmitted to one or more locations instantly. If you are in business at all, you will be expected to have a fax machine.

Fax machines range from small desktop units to the larger models that many offices use. "Personal" fax machines usually offer built-in telephones and photocopiers with an automatic feed capability. Some models even include an answering machine. Priced as low as $200, personal fax machines are well worth the cost, especially for home-based entrepreneurs. Check your local Sharp, Xerox, or Canon dealer for more information on their models of personal fax machines.

Because all communication takes place through the phone wire, consider whether you should install a second phone line. You can hook up your fax machine to any phone jack, so you could, in theory, get away with using one phone line for both your phone and fax. However, with a shared line, you can't use the phone while sending or receiving a document. Clients and others trying to call you will get either a busy signal or the shriek of a fax machine in their ear. A business fax machine should ideally be hooked up to a second phone line.

One alternative: Invest in an automatic voice/data switch. Plugged into your phone line, this device can instantly tell the difference between a data transmission and a voice call, and adjusts the machine accordingly. Some fax machines include an automatic switch, as well as a telephone and answering machine.

You also have to decide what kind of paper you want. Thermal-paper fax machines are less expensive, as is the paper supply. The drawbacks are that thermal paper is flimsy, has an irritating tendency to curl, and fades after a while. Plain-paper machines, especially laser-driven, cost more, but the output quality is much better. Think about who will see your faxes, how often you'll end up copying them onto plain paper anyway, and the kind of data you will receive.

Some other points to consider:

- *Memory:* You need memory for saving transmissions if you run out of paper, for sending batch transmissions at a later time, and for saving and accessing confidential faxes. Low-end models usually carry enough memory to store up to 30 pages.

- *Transmission speed:* The speed determines how long it takes to transmit one page. Average transmission speeds range from 10 to 20 seconds per page, but a page with photographs or illustrations can take longer to send.
- *Document feeder:* This feature allows you to transmit multipage documents without having to feed the paper through the machine page by page.
- *Delayed transmission:* You can program the fax machine to send a document at another time, such as during off-peak hours when long-distance rates are lower.
- *Polling/Broadcasting:* The fax machine automatically calls a group of selected fax machines and either receives documents from them or sends a document stored in memory.
- *Automatic redial/Alternate number redial:* These features allow your machine to redial a number after receiving a busy signal, or dial a different assigned number.

Before you buy a fax, give this purchase some thought. Fax machines vary in features, price, speed, and image quality. Do a little investigating and a lot of comparison shopping. You'll not only make a better choice; you'll learn how to get the most from your fax machine.

Computer Telephony

Computer telephony, as the term implies, refers to the integration of the functions of the telephone with those of the computer. This technology is still developing, but a small business owner might find it useful to incorporate into the computer some of the functions originally associated with the telephone, the fax machine, and voice mail.

New add-in cards, coupled with the right software, can turn your microcomputer into a fax machine. You can also use many of these cards to turn your computer into an answering machine or a voice mail system with an unlimited number of mailboxes. These cards feature fax modems (in some cases, data/fax/voice modems) that transmit at 14.4 Kbps or 28.8 Kbps. Some of these cards also come bundled with sign-up kits to major online services, like CompuServe and America Online, and offer access to the World Wide Web through these services. You can buy these add-in cards, and their accompanying software, for about $200 to $250. Major computer manufacturers such as AT&T, IBM, and AST are offering computers preloaded with such cards and software, and additional communications tools such as telephone directories, voice-recognition systems that allow you to use voice commands to perform various operations on your computer, and contact management software. You can buy such computer systems for about $2,300 to $2,400.

Multifunction Devices

If you find yourself short on space and on funds when you plan to start your business, consider buying a multifunction device. This piece of office equipment combines the functions of a printer, copier, fax machine, scanner, and even a telephone and answering machine into one small, relatively inexpensive unit. You can buy such machines for about $750 to $3,000. They generally do not take much more space than a good business fax machine would occupy. Many of the multifunction devices on the market are designed to work only with IBM-compatible computers; if you have a Macintosh, you may have trouble finding a compatible multifunction device, although they are available.

Multifunction machines can save space and money, but they do not have the same capabilities as their single-function counterparts. In other words, you shouldn't expect to enjoy all the benefits of a high-end, full-featured printer, photocopier, or answering machine if you buy a multifunction device. Before you purchase one of these machines, consider what kind of work and how much of it you will be doing, and what quality you require. If you expect to do a great deal of high-volume, high-quality printing, for instance, you'll probably be better off with a laser printer. Many multifunction devices use ink-jet printing technology, which is fine for a number of tasks but not as sharp as laser printing. Similarly, if you plan to do a great deal of faxing, photocopying, or scanning, you might be better off buying devices devoted to those tasks.

Keep in mind that although a multifunction device can perform a number of tasks, it may not be able to perform them simultaneously. Carefully compare your needs against a multifunction machine's capabilities before you buy one of these devices.

Cellular Phone

Although they were considered a luxury in the past, cellular phones are becoming standard equipment for many entrepreneurs. If you are a speaker or seminar promoter, they can be a lifesaver—especially when you are traveling in new cities or must be out at a site for a day and still keep tabs on your office.

There are basically four types of cellular phones:

1. *Mobile cellular phones.* These units are permanently installed in a car and are powered by the car's battery.
2. *Transmobile cellular phones.* Designed for in-car use, transmobile cellular phones plug into the vehicle's cigarette lighter outlet, but are not permanently installed; instead, you can remove them and reinstall them in any number of vehicles.
3. *Transportable cellular phones.* You can also plug these units into a car's cigarette lighter outlet, but they have their own rechargeable batteries and you can use them outside the car. Transportable phones come with a carrying case, which houses a battery, and they are somewhat bulkier than other types of cellular phones.
4. *Portable cellular phones.* Designed to be carried in your hand or pocket, portable cellular phones contain small, lightweight batteries, and you can mount them in cars.

Many cellular phones can be mounted in more than one way. (You can buy a mobile phone, for instance, and convert it to a transportable phone.) The complete price for a cellular phone will often depend on the mounting option; prices for the phone alone will usually fall between $175 and $350. Don't forget about the other costs usually involved with purchasing a cellular phone: a fixed monthly service charge plus "airtime" charges and any "roaming" fees for calls outside your local cellular service area.

Car phones are available with a number of special features designed to make them safe and easy to use. Phones with speakers built into the handset allow you to keep both hands on the wheel and carry on a conversation without lifting the phone off the hook. Many models can be set to answer automatically after a specific number of rings, or they allow you to continue your conversation after you've turned off the ignition, thanks to call-in-progress protection, a feature that is standard on most phones.

Other useful features are standard on most cellular phones. Use the mute feature if you want to speak privately to a passenger in your car while maintaining contact with a caller on your cellular phone. If you dial a number and get a busy signal, use the automatic redial to keep trying to reach the number until you get through. Call timers are handy for helping you keep track of phone usage.

Perhaps the most important standard feature is memory, which allows you to scroll through stored phone numbers until you find the one you want to dial. Once you find it, the "SEND" key on your phone will dial the number. You can also assign a two-digit speed-dial code to important numbers. Phones with numeric memory store only phone numbers; those with alphanumeric memory store both numbers and names. Pause dialing lets you access important number sequences, such as your calling card number, from memory and append them to the phone number you are dialing. "Scratch pad" memory, another convenient feature, lets you input numbers into memory while you speak on the phone. Speed dialing and scratch pad memory are especially useful when you're on the road. They let you devote your attention to driving.

Cellular phones also offer a number of options to make in-car use even more convenient. Voice recognition systems let you "dial" a number by saying it, instead of punching buttons. Another option, automatic radio mute, turns off your car's audio equipment whenever you make or receive a call. If you're often outside your car, but still near it (for instance, if you visit construction sites), you can take advantage of an optional horn-alert feature, which signals incoming calls by sounding your car's horn.

Postage Meter

Because you will send out so much literature to customers and potential customers, consider buying a postage meter and scale. Stamping packages with the appropriate postage and mailing them directly from your place of business might be more convenient than taking them to a post office and having them stamped there. (Currently, the U.S. Postal Service will not mail any packages weighing more than 16 ounces that have stamps affixed and are deposited in postal collection mailboxes, due to heightened security measures. Metered mail, however, will still be processed.)

You can rent a postage meter for as little as $17 per month, after establishing an account with the U.S. Postal Service. If you buy a given amount of postage, you can stamp that much postage on the mail that goes through the meter. If you need to buy more postage, you may be able to do so over the telephone, if you have the right kind of postage meter. If you would like to be able to ship items via United Parcel Service (UPS) or Federal Express, these companies can provide you with the appropriate paperwork and procedures. Be sure to keep accurate records for yourself, so you can include your freight costs into your pricing.

TELEPHONE

Most small businesses will find a single-line phone system adequate. However, if your company outgrows the single line, you will want to invest extra money and install a multiline (push-button) phone system that allows you to switch back and forth between lines while on one phone. As your business grows, you may need a computerized, electronic switchboard and a receptionist to operate it.

Whether you choose a single line or multiline system, here are some features you may want to consider when deciding on a phone:

- *Automatic redial.* The phone redials the last number called, or it may dial and redial a number at regular intervals until it gets through. This is now an automatic feature on some telephones, but you can add it to a phone through an attachment.
- *Programmable memory.* You can store phone numbers and call them automatically by entering a code or pushing a single button. If you call long-distance numbers frequently, this feature is especially helpful.
- *Call forwarding.* This feature allows you to transfer incoming calls from your home receiver to another number. You can answer there, rather than having clients leave messages at your home.
- *Call waiting.* This feature signals you if someone is trying to reach you while you're on the phone. You can take the incoming call while holding the original call.
- *Speakerphone.* A speakerphone allows you to hear the other person's voice without using the receiver. You can easily write down information, research a file placed away from the phone, or just move around for comfort.
- *Cordless phone.* Cordless phones offer the obvious convenience of freedom of movement, but they vary widely in quality. Research the latest models in *Consumer Reports* before buying.

Your local phone company's business sales rep should have a range of products that answer your specific needs.

Answering Machines

You may want to purchase an answering machine to receive calls while you're away from the office, especially if you work from home and do not have voice mail. Answering machines come with a variety of features. All you'll need is a simple machine that will record messages and play them back. Make sure your message is professional and gives your name as well as the name of the company. Ask callers to leave their name, number, and a brief message. If a client or prospective client has a specific question in mind, you can then research it and have the answer ready when you call back. Many answering machines also function as speakerphones and have speed dialing and other features. For a suitable answering machine, you should expect to pay between $40 and $150.

Voice Mail

Any business owner—or customer, for that matter—knows the one essential ingredient in running a successful business: customer service. You can be hard-working and dedicated, have a flawless business plan and a bottomless source of financing, but if you don't keep customers satisfied and coming back, your business will never succeed. Customers' primary complaints regarding the service they've received often center on phone service; they've called only to hear a busy signal or an endlessly ringing phone, or they are placed on hold indefinitely.

A voice mail system answers and directs incoming calls, takes messages, and costs less than hiring more employees. Formerly available only to large corporations, voice mail is now within the reach of small and even home-based businesses. By contracting with a voice mail service for less than the cost of a cup of coffee a day, you can receive your customers professionally without any equipment to buy, operate, or repair. You can also install, in your computer, software that allows you to create voice mailboxes. For taking calls from prospective attendees, we recommend using a receptionist or a voice mail system. Answering machines work fine for business-to-business messages, but you never want a prospective attendee to hit your machine when it's full or to hear a long, annoying "beep" when you're getting near capacity. Instead, through voice mail, you can allow callers to feel as if they have called a large corporation and are simply leaving a message in the proper voice mailbox.

Long-Distance Carriers

Since deregulation, the competition in the telecommunications industry has grown fierce among the primary contenders: AT&T, MCI, and U.S. Sprint. Buying long-distance services from one of the Big Three means buying years of research and development, millions of miles of telephone lines, and the assurance of a well-established company that stands behind its product. Brand awareness is a big factor in purchasing long-distance services, and many business owners prefer to stick with what they know.

Your next option is to use regional carriers. Regional carriers have their own facilities and switching equipment, but usually cover only a limited region: a tri-state area or the Southwest, for example. They are sometimes called switch-based resellers because they augment their own lines with time purchased from the big carriers.

Regional carriers such as ITT, Metromedia Long Distance, Cable and Wireless Communications, and Allnet Communications Services are gaining popularity with small businesses that place the bulk of their calls to very specific areas. For example, if 80 percent of your customers are within a 100-mile radius, you could negotiate a good deal with a regional carrier covering that area. On the other hand, if your seminars will be held all over the map, it might not be worth the inconvenience of using several different regional carriers.

Some business owners find it advantageous to sign with the smaller long-distance companies, which, they say, often respond more quickly to customers' problems. But not all regional carriers are created equal; some of them may not offer all the amenities you want, like calling cards or dedicated data lines. Most cities are served by numerous regional carriers. Look in the telephone directory under "Telecommunications" or "Telephone" for representatives, and ask for a consultation.

Another option is going through switchless resellers, a small but growing group of competitors out to get a piece of the long-distance pie. Their edge? The same service—for less money. Switchless resellers are companies that buy long-distance time in bulk, then resell it to individuals or small businesses. Because they buy in bulk, resellers receive a substantial discount, part of which they pass on to their customers. One reseller in Illinois says that about 95 percent of his customers are small and medium-size businesses.

Before making the switch, however, research the reseller. Some fraudulent companies are promising big discounts, then reneging. When you call a reseller, ask to be referred to one or two of its customers, whom you can ask about service, billing, and any problems they may have had. When choosing a long-distance carrier, keep in mind that the major network providers—AT&T, MCI, and Sprint—offer direct line service, and a host of national and regional carriers lease lines from the major providers and offer long-distance service; or, they act as "fiber carriers" and sublease those lines to yet another carrier.

Your choice of carrier depends on a number of factors. Analyze the calling patterns of your business and consider these factors:

- Which distances will you call most frequently (regional, national, worldwide)?
- At what time of day will you make most of your long-distance calls?
- How much do you anticipate spending on long-distance calls each month?

- Do you foresee a seasonal trend in your calling patterns?
- Can the company customize its services to fit your business needs?
- Can it provide all the services you need: calling cards, conference calling, data services, 800 numbers?
- How responsive is the company; that is, how willing and/or able is the company to solve your problems quickly?
- What billing increments does the company use? Does it offer "first dollar" discounts, or is there a minimum threshold you must cross before a discount kicks in?
- Is billing customized? Can it reflect specific reporting information such as length of call, time of day, and area codes called?
- How many carriers does the company contract with? If it uses more than one, does it consolidate all your charges on one bill?
- Can you consult the company if you need specialized help, for example, on installing dedicated data lines or linking two office buildings?

Most carriers offer specialized services structured for both small and large businesses. If your business deals only with customers or clients within your state, a regional dedicated WATS (Wide Area Telecommunication Service) line could be the most cost-efficient option.

Be sure to read the fine print in telephone company brochures. Some carriers charge installation and/or start-up fees for their services. Others charge minimum monthly usage or flat monthly fees. Make sure you can meet any minimum usage requirements, or that the discount or service you receive warrants the flat monthly charge. If you require computer telecommunication services, find out whether this option is available. When choosing a long-distance carrier, you should be familiar with accounting codes, billing units, calling card availability, dedicated access/dedicated line, hotline connection, Local Access and Transportation Area (LATA), least-cost billing, magnetic tape, mileage-sensitive/distance-sensitive/time-of-day-sensitive, retail billing, speed dialing, volume discounts, WATS, and any other services that are available.

THE 800 TELEPHONE NUMBER

The 800 number exploded in the early 1970s as a national and regional marketing tool. For a seminar promoter, this number is a necessity. If you promote seminars nationally and do not provide a toll-free line, your customers will be scattered across the country and will have to invest in a long-distance call to get in touch with you. This is a strong deterrent; many potential customers won't spend the money to find out what you have to offer. An 800 number lets them call without spending a cent. Even on a regional level, the 800 number tells your prospective enrollees that this opportunity is so important, you will pick up the cost of the call.

800 numbers are so common these days that businesses that market and sell throughout a wide territory and don't have one are at a competitive disadvantage. An opposing argument is that an 800 number, if not handled properly, encourages a certain number of "shoppers"—unqualified leads—on whom your time and money are largely wasted. It is now often possible to have an 800 number that covers only a small geographical area, saving you from paying for the service to customers who will never actually cross the country to attend your seminars. The installation, monthly service charges, and usage rates can add up to a substantial sum, so weigh the costs against the value of the service.

When acquiring an 800 number, ask whether the carrier offers call reports that show where calls to your number have come from. You can use this information to direct your marketing efforts toward your most likely customers, as well as to pinpoint successful seminar sites. If you want to attract business from overseas, see whether you can offer 800 numbers in the countries you hope to target.

Toll-Free Answering Services

There are toll-free answering services that will take enrollments for your seminars or orders for your products over the phone. Usually, customers can dial an 800 number 24 hours a day. For a per-order fee of about 25 cents to one dollar, the service's operator will take the name and address, credit card number, and whatever other information is needed from each caller.

Hiring a service does cut into your profits, but if you wanted to install your own inbound WATS line, hire operators, and do the paperwork, it could cost you several thousand dollars each month. These companies will give you access to that level of service without taking money directly from your pocket. If you need to establish a high-profile professional image for your seminar business, you will most likely be better served by customer service operators whom you employ and train. They can answer numerous questions as well as take basic enrollment information, but their employment will be an added expense.

LEASE OR BUY EQUIPMENT?

If your equipment investment will be substantial, compare the potential tax savings available through leasing to those realized by buying. See your accountant for current rulings and to determine whether your potential leases are suitable for write-offs.

You can often stretch a limited amount of start-up capital through leasing. Leasing significantly lowers your initial cash outlay. If you have a legitimate tax-deductible lease, however, you do not acquire equity in your equipment and therefore do not build up your balance sheet. A financial statement showing a strong net worth is important to any business. In addition, the total cost of leasing over a period of years is higher than the cost of purchasing the same items. Consult your accountant about the wiser choice for you.

The tax laws generally make the purchase of equipment, whether new or used, more attractive than leasing. Some financing sources offer no-money-down options for equipment purchases or leases. No-money-down leases enable you to own the equipment when you reach the end of the lease.

Asset Remarketing

To save money on equipment costs, you can purchase used equipment through asset remarketers or equipment leasing companies. Some of these companies work through wholesalers and dealers; others deal directly with business owners. Leasing companies may run ads in the classified section of your local newspaper, and keep their equipment in warehouses that you can visit. When purchasing equipment from these companies, look for name brands, and always inspect the equipment before you consider purchasing it. Many business owners are thoroughly satisfied after buying repossessed equipment.

Contracts for Equipment Purchase

Two types of credit contracts are commonly used to finance equipment purchases: (1) a conditional sales contract, in which the purchaser does not receive title to the equipment until it is fully paid for; and (2) a chattel-mortgage contract, in which the equipment becomes the property of the purchaser on delivery, but the seller holds a mortgage claim against it until the purchaser has paid the amount specified in the contract. (See Table 3–2.)

Table 3–2   Equipment Table

Item	Low	High
Computer	3,690	9,500
Chair(s)	60	350
Desk(s)	65	230
File Cabinets	50	300
Calculator/Tape	80	160
Answering Machine	80	160
Bookcase	0	120
Rolodex	22	28
Pencil Cup	7	10
Copier	0	2,100
Fax Machine	400	850
Phone(s)	80	260
UPS/Parcel Post Scale	200	500
Total Expenses	**$4,734**	**$14,568**

DEPRECIATION

There are two kinds of depreciation: (1) cash-value and (2) tax-related. Cash-value depreciation is based on the difference between the initial cost of the equipment and its current fair market value. If a piece of equipment that cost $15,000 in January had a market value of $11,000 in December of the same year, the cash-value depreciation would be $4,000. In other words, the actual expense of owning the equipment would have been $4,000 a year, or $333 per month.

Tax-related depreciation is purely an accounting device that takes advantage of the maximum deduction permitted by law when figuring annual net taxable income. Tax-related depreciation is determined by a formula in the Internal Revenue Code. It has nothing to do with the actual condition of the equipment or its decline in value at the end of each year's use.

The 1986 Tax Act created a new form of accelerated depreciation. In general, for any equipment purchased throughout the year, one half-year of accelerated depreciation is allowed, whether the equipment was purchased in January or December. The remaining half-year of depreciation is recognized in the year the equipment is sold or abandoned.

There is a critical exception to this "half-year convention." If more than 40 percent of a company's equipment is purchased in the last three months of the year, all the asset purchases for the year are subject to the "midquarter convention," which weights depreciation substantially more for assets purchased in January through March and correspondingly less for equipment bought in October through December.

Many entrepreneurs wait until the end of the year, see how much money they have left, then buy their equipment. This approach, however, may throw them into the midquarter convention instead of the half-year convention for depreciation. If you recognize in September that you need to buy equipment, make your purchase before October, to qualify for the extra depreciation.

Cash-Value Depreciation

If you buy a piece of equipment, you should include depreciation of its cash value as an expense on your monthly operating statement. If you lease a piece of equipment, the monthly lease payment will be a part of your monthly operating expenses. (Cash-value depreciation is frequently figured into the cost of an equipment lease; you need not necessarily figure it separately.) Many equipment-leasing agreements have a clause providing for a depreciation reserve, an amount of money set aside to correspond with the declining value of the equipment. When the lease is up, the equipment will be sold either to the lessee or to a third party. If it sells for more than its depreciated value, the difference can be refunded to the lessee. If, however, the equipment is sold for less than its depreciated value, the lessee must pay the difference to the lessor. This is where the depreciation reserve comes into play. It is usually a part of the lease and should be considered a monthly expense of running the business.

Straight-line or uniform depreciation is the most frequently used method of depreciating new equipment. In straight-line depreciation, the equipment loses the same portion of its total value during every year of its life. Suppose you buy a $15,000 multiline telephone-call routing and forwarding system with a 10-year useful life, according to your accountant's schedule. You would calculate the straight-line depreciation rate by dividing its price by its useful life ($15,000 divided by 10 years, or $1,500 a year). If you are in the 28 percent tax bracket, $1,500 in depreciation will save you $420. Suppose you only need 20 percent down to buy the $15,000 machine. Suppose, too, that you financed your telephone purchase on the installment plan. The interest you pay on any amount you owe will be another deduction for you. That means your total cash savings of $4,536 [($420 multiplied by 10) + $336] will more than offset your down payment of $3,000.

Depreciation for Taxes

The depreciation method you use on your financial statements may differ from the one you use on your tax return. For your tax return, your accountant will usually use whichever tax-approved depreciation will reduce your taxes the most.

The Tax Reform Act of 1986 revised the depreciation rates that you may use for federal income tax purposes on all equipment, real estate, and so on, purchased after December 31, 1986. These new methods are often referred to as MACRS. The method used for assets acquired before that date is called ACRS.

Assets purchased before that time and used in your trade or business are depreciated using methods different from those discussed here. Those earlier methods generally give you a larger depreciation deduction than the current rates. You should also keep in mind that, in many states, an entirely different set of rules applies.

Section 179 of the Internal Revenue Code gives a tax break that allows small businesses to expense up to $17,500 in equipment each year. Entrepreneurs cannot take the Section 179 deduction if it creates a loss; they may, however, carry forward the unused portion of the deduction to future tax years. You can learn the rules regarding depreciation of assets used in your business by ordering Publication 17 (entitled *Your Federal Income Tax*) from the Internal Revenue Service and ordering Form 4562 with the accompanying instructions.

Depreciation Schedules

If you are depreciating real estate used in your business or held for investment, the time period over which you depreciate it depends on whether it is residential property (such as apartments) or commercial property (such as stores, offices, etc.). Residential real property is depreciated over 27.5 years using the straight-line method. Commercial real property is depreciated over 31.5 years using the straight-line method.

Several different depreciable lives are possible for depreciable personal property used in your trade or business. Those lives include 3-, 5-, 7-, 10-, 15-, and 20-year periods. Almost all equipment such as automobiles, trucks, typewriters, desks and machines will be depreciated using either a 5-year or a 7-year life. Consult IRS publications to determine which types of assets use other life classes.

Equipment that fits into the 5- or 7-year life classes can be depreciated using the 200 percent declining balance rate. This means that the equipment is depreciated using twice the straight-line rate. However, in the years in which the property is acquired and disposed of, only one-half of a full year's depreciation can be taken, regardless of the month of the year when the property was purchased.

Some of the items included in the 5-year depreciation class under MACRS are:

1. Automobiles and light trucks.
2. Typewriters, computers, calculators, copiers, computer-based telephone switching equipment.
3. Research and experimentation property.

The 7-year MACRS depreciable life property accounts for most forms of office furniture used in business (such as desks, chairs, and fixtures) and any other equipment that does not have a class life and is not otherwise classified. Certain properties, such as luxury automobiles used less than 50 percent of the time for business, are limited to straight-line depreciation. Automobiles used for business that cost more than $12,800 are limited to $2,560 depreciation in the first year, $4,100 in the second year, $2,450 in the third year, and $1,475 for all subsequent years.

Except for automobiles, under Internal Revenue Code Section 179, you can immediately deduct up to the first $17,500 of equipment purchased for your business each year and avoid depreciating it over a period of time. However, if you place in service personal property worth more than $200,000 in any one year, the $17,500 is reduced dollar for dollar for all property purchased in excess of the $200,000. In addition, the $17,500 deduction is limited to the taxable income of your trade or business before taking this deduction. If the equipment is sold, this deduction must be recaptured.

We emphasize that these points are current at the time of publication but may change from year to year. Make sure your financial adviser(s), particularly your tax adviser(s), will be made aware of any changes that may occur in tax-related depreciation guidelines. Your adviser should pass all relevant information on to you.

INVENTORY

Your inventory will consist mainly of items such as tickets and various signs used for each seminar. Product sales can make up a large part of your income and, if you are a speaker or you work with the same speakers repeatedly, you may want to keep relevant books and tapes in stock. If you plan to offer a given program several times, using the same speakers, titles, and subjects, consider printing a large quantity of brochures. For each seminar you put on, you'll need to stock a quantity of workbooks, evaluation forms, and similar aids.

MATERIALS FOR THE SEMINAR

Although each seminar is different, most will require the following supplies:

- Tickets.
- Signs.
- Workbooks.
- Evaluation forms.

Most of the necessary material can be purchased at an office supply store or composed either by a freelance graphic artist or through the use of a computer that accepts page layout and design or word processing software.

Tickets

After you have scheduled a speaker and a site for your seminar, the job of selling tickets for the program begins. Instead of individual tickets, use tickets that come in stapled books. D. Michael Frank, past president of the National Speakers Association and an experienced seminar producer, suggests using numbered tickets attached, via a perforated edge, to correspondingly numbered stubs. You can use the stubs to keep track of who bought which tickets on which date. (If you have a computerized record-keeping system, you can add this information to your mailing list.)

Frank also suggests printing "universal" tickets, which don't specify any particular dates. In this way, you can save money by printing tickets in bulk, and you can use the same ticket books for years. Don't print any prices on the admission tickets. Your rates may change with time, or you may choose to offer volume discounts. The tickets should carry a printed statement that the ticket is good for admission to any seminar offered by your company. The tickets should have a feature that makes them hard to copy. Numbering them is one way to prevent duplication. Another method is to print them on heavy or colored paper stock that would be hard to duplicate.

Signs

Although you won't need a huge supply, signs are among the necessities for each seminar. You will need signs for your registration table and your products tables. If you have your handouts and workbooks on a separate table, you will need a sign there as well. If your speakers are well known, you may want to set up a table at which they will sign autographs for attendees at the end of the presentation. (An autograph table may also boost product sales. After all, an attendee who is motivated to buy a book after seeing its author deliver a seminar will be further motivated by the chance to buy a signed copy.) Your signs should be fairly simple: "Registration," "Please Take One" (for workbooks, etc.), and "Autographs" should be sufficient. Be sure to collect your signs at the end of each seminar, so that you can use them again. Store them with enough care to keep them looking new; if they look worn, replace them. Although signs are fairly inexpensive, you should save as much money as you can. Don't print new signs for a seminar unless you need to.

Workbooks

You will most likely hand out a workbook at each seminar. If you have more than one speaker, each speaker will probably have a separate workbook. These items are usually fairly short, straightforward booklets summarizing the main points of the talk.

Speakers generally supply the material for the workbook to the producer of the seminar, who is expected to make copies of it for the attendees' use. The speakers generally leave the cover text and design up to the producer as well. You can then print your own title, such as "Acme Seminars Presents 'Sales Secrets' by Phil Jones." Your company's name, address, and telephone number should appear on the cover, so that attendees can contact you directly if they are interested in any future seminars.

With workbooks, as with everything else, aim to present a professional image, but don't spend more money than you have to. Have your workbooks professionally printed or copied. Print two pages on each side of each sheet of paper you use, then fold the sheets in half and staple them in the center, to create a small workbook. This format should give you a nice product at a reasonable price.

Evaluations

Another important item to include in the materials you hand out to your attendees is the evaluation form. You can insert this one-page document in your workbook or you can hand it out with a schedule at the registration desk.

Speaker evaluation forms are useful for several reasons. First, they let speakers know what their audiences think of them. Attendees have the chance to criticize the speaker's style of presentation and subject content. You can use these comments to help decide whether to invite a given speaker to any future seminars. Second, the audience has a chance to evaluate the seminar as a whole. This information is essential if you are to survive in the seminar promotion business. Use the evaluations to see how your attendees feel about the site, food service (if any), ticket-selling approach, and other decisions you made.

The form should be only one page long. Michael Frank says that you should use the form to get only the information you really need. Ask about the number of speakers on the program, the schedule, whether you should serve food (or different food), the price of the program, its length and starting time, the strength of the speaker, any speakers attendees would like to see in the future, any topics attendees would like to see covered, and any additional comments. Make all questions easy to answer. You might begin a question with the phrase, "On a scale from one to five, rate such-and-such quality of the seminar." Give attendees the option of not revealing their names and addresses. This option encourages candid responses; people more freely write any negative comments they may have if they can do so anonymously. (Names, addresses, and phone numbers for your database can be obtained from enrollment materials.)

You may want to create a new evaluation form for each seminar, or you can adapt a standard form to all of your programs. If you put on a program with more than one speaker, you must decide whether to have a workbook and evaluation form for each speaker, or one large workbook and one detailed evaluation form covering the whole program.

SELLING PRODUCTS

Seminar promoters who use dynamite speakers can boost their profits through product sales—either by producing them and giving a cut to the speakers and/or employees at their seminars, or by taking a cut of the sales of their speakers' products. Many speakers, especially better-known speakers like Zig Ziglar and Anthony Robbins, have a variety of such products.

Audiotapes/Videotapes/Books

When people attend your seminars, they will feel empowered, excited, and ready to take on the world. When they take something away with them, it promotes retention and allows them to revisit the information you've shared again and again.

Professional speakers report making anywhere from 30 to 60 percent of their income from product sales, once they have become polished. But they don't make this money when they first start out, and not every speaker sells products. If you plan to speak yourself, you should consult marketing and speaking professionals to find out what types of products will best complement your seminars and topics. As a promoter, your best bet is to sell products on consignment, at least at first. In that way, you can return any unsold items to the speaker.

You will need a contract or agreement with the speaker covering all the details regarding product sales: which products to sell, how many of each item to offer, how much to charge for each, how to divide the profits, and how to handle any unsold items. Our sources indicate that producers usually split the profits equally with the speaker, but the speaker's share can range from 20 to 60 percent of the product revenues. When dealing with profit splits, specify up front whether you are splitting net or gross profits from product sales.

Taping the Seminar

Videotapes are a part of the seminar industry in many ways. Speakers are often hired based on tapes of their performances; videos are used to supplement the message being given at a particular seminar (one speaker we interviewed said she often provides videotapes of her speaking on a topic to other speakers, who use the videos as part of their presentation); and videotapes provide a souvenir for attendees. These tapes are often recorded at a live seminar. A video production company conducts the actual taping, which requires a minimal investment of about $1,000 for a single-camera shoot. If you want to use more cameras, count on spending more money. You would also need to have the proper lighting arranged at the seminar.

If you are not the speaker, draw up an agreement that gives you permission to tape the speaker's presentation and the terms for how to distribute the tapes, how much to charge for them, and how to share the revenues, if any. Apart from the expense of filming the seminar, you have to add in the cost of duplicating, packaging, and storing the tapes.

Before you invest any of your precious resources in a videotape or audiotape venture, make sure that a market exists for the tape. Wait until your seminar promotion business is well established and profitable before taking on the task of videotaping a program and selling the resulting product. Prices for any printed materials or tapes that you produce and sell or distribute at your programs—your workbooks, tickets, and evaluation forms—will vary according to the quality of the materials you use and the quantity of the products you order. The fewer units you order, the more you have to pay for each one. Conversely, the more units you order, the less each one costs. It may actually cost less to order 2,000 workbooks than to order 1,500. When you have anything printed, estimate your attendance as accurately as possible. Then order as many materials as you need at the best price, without ordering too few or too many.

OFFICE SUPPLIES

Your business stationery and supplies are a reflection of your business, so choose them carefully. The creation of a business logo, which you will imprint not only on your letterhead, business cards, and envelopes, but also on your sign or on your company vehicle(s), is not something you should take lightly.

If you have sufficient artistic skill, you may want to create the logo yourself. If you do not have this skill, hire a freelance designer or graphic artist to create the logo for you. Although the cost will vary from region to region, most freelance graphic artists will handle your job for $500 to $1,000. Have them present the logo in camera-ready form according to letterhead and business-card specifications. If you will imprint envelopes, have them provide the art for that as well.

When you shop for your business stationery, check stationers and office supply stores as well as printers. Many of these places provide business start-up packages of letterhead, business cards, and envelopes for about $300 to $400. If you have camera-ready art, the price could be lower. For the best results and the lowest possible cost, have your stationery printed at a local quick-print shop. Get several estimates before placing your orders, and always insist on getting the quality you asked for (or were promised). Your business materials are a reflection of your company's image and should be of the highest possible quality.

Local stationers and office supply stores will have most or all of your miscellaneous operations materials. A few hundred dollars should buy you all the blank stationery and envelopes, record-keeping equipment (files, ledgers, and index cards), sales slips, invoices, bags, boxes, labels, tagging guns, and other paraphernalia you need. (You can order specially printed sales receipts, but keep your startup costs down by buying standard two-copy receipt books.)

Ask for referrals from other businesspeople or check the telephone directory under "Paper Products—Wholesale," "Office Supplies," and "Stationers—Retail." You may also find a "Pricing [or Marking] Devices" listing for labeling equipment.

INVENTORY CONTROL

Many small business owners fail to realize the importance of inventory control. An adequate stock control system will tell you what inventory has been used, what remains, what is on order, when it will arrive, and who is up for reordering. With such a system, you can plan purchases intelligently and quickly recognize the fast-moving items that you need to reorder and the slow-moving items that you should mark down or specially promote.

Merchants frequently devise their own inventory systems or adopt those recommended by accountants. Your inventory needs and planning will be quite different from those of a retail merchant, whose inventory sales directly impact the success of the business. Sales of products are a great bonus for seminar promoters, but they are a secondary source. Your primary income comes from attendees at your seminars, and from proper planning and management of your finances as a producer of seminars. Still, if you are going to offer items for sale at your seminars, you need to know the basics of inventory control and management.

Lead Time

Lead time—the length of time between reordering and delivery of a product—should be factored in well in advance of your seminars so that you don't run short of needed materials the day before a big program. For instance, if your lead time for videotapes is four weeks, and a particular video sells 10 units on average per weekly seminar, then you must reorder before the inventory on that video falls below 40 units. If you do not reorder until you actually need the videos, you will run low and lose sales.

Many small business owners protect themselves from shortfalls by incorporating a safety margin into basic inventory figures. The right safety margin for your business depends on the external factors that can contribute to delays. You must determine your safety margin based on past experience and anticipated delays.

Excess inventory, on the other hand, creates extra overhead, and that costs you money. Inventory that sits in your storeroom does not generate sales or profits; it generates losses that will shrink your bottom line. The natural reaction of any businessperson to excess inventory would be to reduce the price and sell it quickly. Although this solves the overstocking problem, it also reduces your return on investment. If you overstock and reduce your prices by 15 to 25 percent to jettison the excess inventory, you're losing money you had counted on when ordering.

The answer: Pay close attention to your inventory in order to establish a plan that allows you to avoid accumulating excess inventory while establishing a realistic safety margin.

Dealing with Suppliers

Reliable suppliers are assets to your business. They can bail you out when your customers make difficult demands on you, but they will do so only as long as your business is profitable to them. Suppliers, like you, are in business to make money. If you argue over the fine points of every bill with them, ask them to shave prices on everything they sell you, or fail to pay their bills promptly, don't be surprised when they stop calling—or accepting your orders.

At first, don't expect to receive the same kind of attention a long-standing customer gets. Over time, however, you can develop excellent working relationships that will be profitable for you and your suppliers. Be open, courteous, and firm with your suppliers, and they will respond in kind. Tell them what you need and when you need it. Have an exact understanding of the total cost, expect delivery on schedule, and pay them on a timely schedule (see Table 3–3). In other words, expect from your suppliers what your customers demand from you.

Table 3–3   Inventory Range

Item	Low	High
Tickets	$170	$400
Signs	450	1,200
Workbooks	2,600	6,400
Evaluation Forms	10	48
Letterhead/Envelopes	140	600
Business Cards	65	195
Brochures	1,600	2,600
Large Envelopes	30	420
Mailing Labels	36	360
PRODUCTS		
Video Tapes	$0	$20,300
Books	0	16,400
Order Forms	85	575
Miscellaneous	200	500
Total Expenses	**$5,386**	**$49,998**

INVENTORY ACCOUNTING

If you spend a few minutes considering the size of your inventory, how you account for that inventory, and the taxes you must pay on it, you'll never again question the validity of employing an accountant. Two methods are used for inventory valuation: LIFO and FIFO.

LIFO, an acronym meaning *last in, first out*, assumes that you will sell first to your customers the goods you received most recently. An easy way to grasp LIFO is by considering two lots of 10 widgets each. You purchased the first lot of 10 widgets a year ago at $1 each. A week ago, you purchased a second lot of 10 widgets at an inflated price of $2 each. By employing the LIFO method, you sell your customers the $2 widgets *first*, which allows you to keep the less expensive units (in terms of your inventory cost) in inventory. Then, when you have to calculate inventory value for tax purposes, LIFO allows you to value your remaining inventory (the $1 widgets) at substantially less than the $2 widgets.

FIFO, which stands for *first in, first out*, was the traditional method used by most businesses prior to the years of rapid inflation. Under FIFO, the goods you receive first are the goods you sell first, and you value inventory at its most recent price. FIFO is usually employed during periods of relatively low inflation, because high inflation and increasing replacement costs tend to skew inventory accounting figures.

To differentiate between the two methods, remember that LIFO establishes the value of your inventory based on the last quantity received, and FIFO establishes the value of your inventory based on the oldest item on hand. You can use either dollar control or unit control with these methods. Match your system to your needs, based on your accountant's recommendations.

4

PERSONNEL

FINDING SPEAKERS

Whether you speak at seminars yourself or have other speakers deliver the seminars you promote, this section can be helpful because it covers what seminar promoters and speakers bureaus look for in a speaker.

Promoters and speakers bureaus do not actually hire the speakers they work with. Professional speakers are independent contractors who, for a fee, speak at a specific function (or functions) on a contract basis. Some estimates place the number of professional speakers (those who are paid at least half of the time for any speeches they give) at around 30,000 nationwide.

Associations

The National Speakers Association (NSA), headquartered in Tempe, Arizona, is a good place to start looking for potential speakers. The NSA currently has more than 3,500 members who specialize in more than 60 different topic areas. Among other publications, the NSA compiles the *Meeting Planner's Guide To Professional Speakers*, a listing of its members alphabetically, by topic, and by location.

The organization's goal is to ensure a standard of excellence in professional speaking, and it offers a certification program whereby members can show that they have met certain standards. To become a Certified Speaking Professional (CSP), members must, among other things:

- Be active as a professional speaker for a minimum of 5 years, or 5 out of 6 years.
- Serve a minimum of 100 different clients in the 5-year period represented in the application. (Speakers who work for seminar companies or the same client repeatedly can count every 5 engagements as a single client, up to 50 clients.)
- Earn an average income of $50,000 per year as a speaker, speaking no less than 20 times per year on a paid basis and accumulating 250 paid engagements over the 5-year period.
- Submit 20 testimonial letters (minimum) from 20 different clients.

Completion of continuing professional education units each year is also required. Currently, there are more than 250 CSPs. Because the certification process is a long one, speakers actively pursuing the CSP can be classified as *certification candidates* after they complete two years' worth of specific qualifications toward the CSP. (See Appendix A for contact information.)

Another good resource is the International Platform Association (IPA) in Winnetka, Illinois. The oldest international association in the United States, the IPA traces its roots back 165 years. Members have included Theodore and Franklin Roosevelt, Richard Nixon, Herbert Hoover, John Kennedy, Nelson Rockefeller, Harry Truman, David Brinkley, Art Buchwald, Henry Kissinger, Barry Goldwater, Winston Churchill, Gerald Ford, Mario Cuomo, Ted Turner, Bob Hope, and numerous other political, TV, radio, newspaper, and entertainment icons. Membership is by recommendation only and is subject to the IPA's Board of Governors approval. (Refer to Appendix A for contact information.)

Speakers Bureaus

There are well over 150 speakers bureaus across the country. These organizations represent professional speakers in return for a commission, usually between 20 and 30 percent of earnings from the speaking engagements that they arrange. Some bureaus specialize in representing speakers on a single topic (e.g., family dynamics, business management, international affairs, empowerment); others represent only celebrities or politicians. Most speakers bureaus represent a wide variety of generally top-notch professionals who have proven track records. Michael Podolinsky, president of Key Seminars Speakers Bureau in Eden Prairie, Minnesota, says that bureaus become interested in speakers when they are so well known that they almost don't need a bureau. "Most bureaus don't want to deal with people until they are a known commodity, because their reputation goes on the line," he explains. Key Seminars represents such big names as Zig Ziglar, Fred Pryor, Tom Peters, Ken Blanchard, Mary Lou Retton, and Fran Tarkenton.

Even the most popular and busiest speakers in the country are generally represented by at least one bureau, to help them handle the massive amounts of marketing, contracting, and scheduling that come with being in demand. As a seminar promoter, using a speakers bureau can save you hours. You tell the bureau the topics you plan to present at your seminar, your guidelines for speakers (whether they should use your script or their own material, for instance), your budget, and when and where your program will take place. The bureau sends you a list of potential candidates, demo tapes and references, and so on. Generally speaking, it won't cost you any more to hire a speaker through a bureau than it would to hire the speaker directly, because the speaker receives a commission from the bureau, not from you.

You don't have to limit yourself to using speakers bureaus located near you; most bureaus represent speakers from across the country. Some even represent speakers based around the world. To locate speakers bureaus, you can start with organizations such as Meeting Planners International (MPI), in Dallas, Texas; the American Society of Association Executives (ASAE), in Washington, DC; or Toastmasters International, in Mission Viejo, California. Each of these organizations can provide guidance to you based on your specific requirements and budget. (Contact information for these organizations appears in Appendix A.)

Networking

A 1994 NSA survey of 10,000 corporate executives, association executives, and meeting planners shows that the top four ways respondents search for a speaker are: (1) word of mouth, (2) direct contact by the speaker, (3) industry magazines, and (4) brochures. Most professional speakers rely heavily on word-of-mouth referrals to keep busy. Robert Leiman, a member of the IPA and a noted expert on parliamentary procedures for the past 30 years, uses referrals almost exclusively today. The same can be said for a number of talented speakers who have become active within industry organizations and other speaker-support groups.

Take advantage of other people's experiences by joining as many industry groups as possible, and by learning who is a recognized authority on various topics. All of the groups mentioned above are great organizations for networking and building contacts; for keeping your speaking, marketing, and planning skills polished; and for keeping current on the world of seminars.

SELECTING SPEAKERS

A speaker can have a great resume, great references, and an outstanding brochure, but it's what that speaker can do in front of an audience—what you *see* happening—that makes the difference. Ask for a video of the speaker, preferably speaking before an audience, before you sign a contract. "It doesn't have to be a live conference," says Skill-Path co-founder Dudley of the videos she requests when previewing speakers, "but it helps. Even a small audience is OK."

For more than 5 years, video demonstrations have topped the list as the basis of hiring decisions. "We want to see naturalness," says Dudley. "We don't care if people are tall or short, fat or thin—that doesn't matter. What we really want is naturalness in front of a group." Noted speaker and author Eve Cappello remembers that when she first started speaking in front of groups nearly 20 years ago, "I started spouting off what I had learned in college, all the jargon, without knowing a darned thing." Yet, having been a professional singer-pianist for years before going back to school to get her PhD in psychology, she was very natural in front of groups.

"You were superb," a colleague told her in those early days. "But what did you say?"

She laughs. "I changed my material right then."

The best way to really "see" a speaker in action is to experience his or her presentation skills firsthand. If you cannot attend a meeting at which a potential speaker is featured, be sure to schedule a personal interview in addition to viewing the videotaped performance. The way people present themselves at interviews can say a lot about their style and their professionalism and can tell you whether this is the kind of person you had in mind for your target audience. In the NSA/ASAE *Guide to Professional Speakers,* six well-known speakers bureau owners from four states recommend asking the following questions when seeking to match a speaker with an intended audience:

- "What makes you a better speaker choice for this engagement than any other speaker?"
- "Whom have you worked for in this specific industry in the past two years?"

- "What steps will you take to customize this program?"
- "How flexible are you in meeting [our] needs?"
- "Can I call the last five people who used you, to get their reactions?"
- "What value-added services can you bring to this engagement?"

You should also ask about the speaker's willingness to negotiate fees, and, if you do not want any products offered for sale at your engagement, whether the speaker would have a problem with that restriction.

Be sure to ask about the length of time a speaker normally speaks on a topic, and how long his or her last 5 to 10 speeches have run. Many professional speakers believe it is hard to be effective in 30 to 45 minutes, because the time is too short to have the audience leave feeling that they have been given tangible tools to work with. On the other hand, it takes a special person to keep things going for four to six hours or more—even with breaks—and still be effective. Look at your seminar format and your material, and decide how much time your speaker will need to speak. Would you be better off with several speakers delivering short speeches, a main speaker with two guest speakers, or a single speaker presenting a fairly long speech? Be sure to ask your speaker for ideas regarding your format.

SPEAKERS' FEES

Top-name professional speakers such as Anthony Robbins and Zig Ziglar command fees of more than $25,000 per engagement. For sports celebrities or political figures like General Norman Schwarzkopf or former Los Angeles Lakers and New York Knicks coach Pat Riley, engagement fees can run from $20,000 to $65,000 and more.

When you are an established seminar promoter, such well-known speakers may attract large audiences to your seminars, but when you start out, you probably won't be able to afford them. Fortunately, you can find top-notch speakers to deliver a seminar for $300 to $2,000 per day, plus traveling expenses and accommodations.

Fees for professional speakers appear to be on the rise. Compared to a 1990 study, the 1994 NSA survey showed that many more professional speakers were in the $2,000-to-$5,000 and $5,000-to-$10,000 fee-per-engagement categories. Because fees paid to speakers vary so greatly, your best bet is to ask a prospective speaker what his or her standard daily fee is for a seminar on a given topic. If you are using a speakers bureau, be honest about what you can pay.

If you plan to host several seminars in the same general area or on the same topic, you can often cut your per-seminar costs by using the same speaker for a preset number of paid days per month. This can be tricky; the IRS carefully monitors any employer–independent contractor relationship. But if your speaker also speaks professionally for other companies or as an independent businessperson, then such an arrangement can work out quite well for both of you. At SkillPath, for example, speakers are paid $300 per day plus all transportation costs and a per-diem amount for meals, taxis, tips, and incidentals. In addition, they receive a percentage of all the product sales made during their seminar day. "This can be significant. It can even pass their base pay," says Dudley. "It depends on how good they are at knowing their products and at selling."

These same speakers may be able to charge more than $1,000 per speech on their own, but they are saving money on marketing costs, materials costs, and office time, and they are generally asked to speak a minimum of one week per month for the company. That's known income for at least one week per month. "We have to have a commitment of at least one week per month, and we need to know their availability about four to five months in advance, because that's when we're trying to do our planning," says Dudley. "They can give us more [time]. I think that almost everyone here works two weeks per month—that's the average— and some work three, but that's the most we generally let them do, even if they want more, because it's a really rigorous thing to do, to go out there and use your voice for six hours a day."

Negotiating with Speakers

Do speakers negotiate the fees they charge? "Many speakers do not negotiate fees, but virtually all speakers negotiate the services they provide for their fees," says 1995–1996 NSA president James F. Hennig, PhD, in the NSA/ASAE *Guide to Professional Speakers*. "Preparation time, in addition to travel and presentation time, are important factors for speakers in establishing their fees. Multiple presentations, particularly those requiring little or no additional preparation time, may justify a varied fee structure for some speakers." Some speakers, he notes, provide separate fee structures, depending on whether they can sell their books, audiotapes, videotapes, or other products at the seminar.

You may be able to save money by paying an "inclusive fee" to cover travel expenses. This means that instead of covering the speaker's exact travel expenses, you agree to pay the speaker a set fee to be spent as he or she sees fit on travel costs. This arrangement works only if you *and* the speaker agree to it. Even if a speaker ends up spending less for travel than you've allowed, your total travel costs for the seminar will be fixed and paid up front.

Here's another way for you to save money on travel expenses. If a speaker requests first-class travel, ask whether he or she has any frequent-flyer mileage saved. If so, would he or she be willing to use it on an upgrade to first class? Speakers travel often in the course of their work, and they build up mileage quickly. Trading some of the accumulated miles for a first-class upgrade may be attractive and will cost you less than a full fare. (Make it a stated policy *not* to pay first-class airfare. If it is an important point to a particular speaker, decide how much you want *this* speaker at the time of the negotiation. Use of frequent flyer miles is always worth a try, and it could save you money while still allowing the speaker to travel as he or she chooses.)

Regardless of whom you hire, most speakers will require a significant portion (and in some cases, all) of their fee up front. This, along with their contract, secures their time for a specific date. You might have a different payment arrangement if you have established a long-term, continuing relationship with a speaker who knows he or she can count on being booked for a set number of days each week, month, or quarter, and will collect payment on a fixed schedule. Keep in mind that some speakers, especially those well-known and in high demand, may need a year's notice before they will agree to speak at your program.

Speakers' Agreement

Your speakers' agreement, or contract, is a legal document outlining the obligations of all parties involved in a planned engagement—the seminar promoter, the speakers bureau, and the speaker. The contract should specify the date, time, and duration of your program, the expected number of attendees (if available), the suggested dress code, and the travel arrangements that are being provided. It should also specify the method, amounts, and times of payment. If there is a specific person to contact at the seminar site, such as yourself or an assistant, that person's name and phone number should appear on the document. Your contract should also cover the following items:

- Whether the speaker will be allowed to sell any products. If so, a specific statement should say who will pay for the inventory and who will get the proceeds. Will you, as the promoter, get a percentage of sales? Many speakers bureaus collect a commission on product sales, in addition to their standard commission, for the engagements they set up.

- A description of the independent contractor's status, and what that status entails in regard to tax responsibilities.
- Your rights regarding advance fees and substitution if the contracted speaker is unable to attend the seminar. This is a rare occurrence; any reputable speaker will make the utmost effort to honor any contract. In case of severe illness or emergency, however, even the most dedicated speaker will be unable to be present at the seminar. Your chances of finding a replacement are greater if you have as much advance notice as possible.

If you run a speakers bureau and are setting up an engagement, it is standard practice to stipulate that you will receive a commission, in the form of a specific percentage, on any future speaking engagements or other types of spin-offs, such as consulting or training, that result from your booking. The contract should state that, for this engagement, the speaker is representing XYZ Speakers Bureau and should work through you, making no separate or independent agreement for this or any future engagement.

OFFICE AND ON-SITE EMPLOYEES

Speakers are essential to your success, but you will also need to hire a good office manager or administrative assistant, plus sales and marketing staff, to grow your business and keep track of your various engagements. You will also need people at each of the actual seminars to welcome and direct attendees, staff sign-in and registration desks, collect payments from any "walk-in" attendees, make last-minute copies, pull in chairs and tables, and react appropriately to any unexpected occurrences.

Office Manager/Administrative Assistant

Although you may be able to live without an office administrator when you start your business, that's not likely to be the case for long. You will make the initial contacts with speakers bureaus, speakers, seminar sites, printers, salespeople, and the media, but you will find it hard to juggle all these contacts without another set of hands. You also need to have someone available to answer the phone and take registration information during business hours.

Dudley and partner Jerry Brown started SkillPath Seminars with a single employee, Linda Walker, and a company goal: to make sure that it is wonderful to work at SkillPath. Says Dudley, "I think that has been one of our secrets." When the phone rang, one of the three of them picked it up and helped the caller. Soon, Walker had hired four more employees and SkillPath was on its way.

Look for someone who is able and willing to handle many facets of your business. On top of routine tasks, like answering phones, sending out speakers agreements, confirming travel arrangements, and other daily activities, your administrator can coordinate rental times and fees with facilities, prescreen speaker resumes and videos, outline topics for future seminars, and supervise the collection of seminar enrollment fees. He or she can also help you communicate with the media by circulating press releases.

Depending on the level of experience and the amount of responsibility you want your administrator (office manager or administrative assistant) to have, expect to pay an annual salary of $20,000 to $40,000 per year. Always research salaries in your area well; this is not a place where you want to cut corners. Other than yourself and any partners you may have, your first employee/administrator will know more about your business than anyone, and can be instrumental in its growth or stagnation.

You should look for someone with a customer service background, strong writing skills, word processing and database management skills, negotiation skills, and the ability to manage many tasks and projects simultaneously. You'll also want someone who is capable of managing other people and scheduling their work.

Sales and Marketing Staff

Being a successful seminar promoter takes a full sales effort, says Key Seminars' Podolinsky. "The person who does that has to also be a full-time salesman and has to be a motivator in terms of managing people to get them to go out and do the selling. It's hard to do that *and* handle the production side of things." If you are comfortable with cold calling and sales, you can do much of this marketing yourself. If not, you had better get someone on your team who is. "I used to do a lot of cold calling in the beginning. I never hesitated to promote myself," says Cappello. Today, she teaches other speakers to "position, package and promote" themselves.

Although you will use direct mail to market your seminars, a sales representative can make a great difference in growing your business from day one. Most sales representatives are active members of many professional organizations, which gives them an automatic connection to one of your biggest target markets. They can also mass-market your less expensive offerings to large and small associations, clubs, and centers throughout the country (see Chapter 1). Finally, they can target large and small businesses in the cities where your seminars will take place and try to sell blocks of tickets to them.

Salespeople themselves comprise an excellent audience for public seminars. If one or more of your seminars is geared toward salespeople, then an effective sales representative can make cold calls to surrounding businesses and tell them about the sales-boosting motivation and skills training your seminars offer. He or she can also network with other salespeople and get *them* to persuade their sales managers to send them to your events. A sales representative can attract more attendees than other marketing methods would, if your seminars appeal to various segments of the population.

Depending on the number of seminars you will put on each year, you need to decide whether you want a dedicated sales representative or a professional salesperson who serves many clients. Generally, the former will want a base salary plus commission on sales (although one seminar producer we spoke with pays his salespeople a commission of 40 percent of the face value of the tickets they sell, with no base salary); the latter will likely accept payment in the form of straight commission. Devise a commission structure that rewards both large group sales and individual sales. Sell the idea of discounting your seminars to large groups. You might, for example, "sell" a 25 percent discount to the local Kiwanis Club, which has 630 members. Base salaries for salespeople range anywhere from $25,000 to $50,000 per year (and up), depending on their track record of sales, their experience in an industry, and their commission structure and perks.

You will also need a top-notch marketing staff. Dudley was a clinical psychologist and had been vice president of seminars and curriculum for another national seminar company before branching out on her own. Her partner, Brown, had a strong advertising and marketing background and had also worked with Dudley in the seminar industry. Without this kind of team at your company, success will not come easy. "I would say the biggest challenge we face is making sure that we can convince the person reading [our marketing] brochure that this is something they will benefit from," says Dudley. She and Brown actually produce the brochures for SkillPath, but not every successful entrepreneur has skills in this area. "Marketing is one of my weakest points, especially compared to speaking," says 30-year veteran Leiman.

To offset this area of weakness, retain a marketing company or a freelance marketing copywriter (with experience in promoting seminars), or hire an employee with strong marketing skills. As with hiring speakers, you want to *see* what these people can do, so be sure to get three to five samples of their best work along with their resumes and reference sheets. Because direct response mailing of brochures is the number-one type of advertising done in this business, strong, effective writing skills are the most crucial qualification for this job.

Freelancers will likely charge from $20 to $65 per hour to produce your marketing materials. Collect several competitive bids outlining the scope of services that each freelancer includes in his or her fee. An in-house marketing staffer will want anywhere from $25,000 to more than $50,000 per year—depending, as always, on the level of expertise.

TEMPORARY SEMINAR EMPLOYEES

In addition to the employees hired on a regular basis for the daily operation of your business, you will also need employees for each seminar: ushers, hosts and hostesses (or program managers), and cashiers for any product tables you have. You may also need to hire security guards, especially if your seminar attracts a large crowd of attendees or your speaker is a celebrity.

Program Managers/Assistants

At SkillPath, CareerTrack, and other major seminar companies, program managers or hosts/hostesses are hired in each city to facilitate the event when your seminar comes to their town. This can save you thousands of dollars on the travel costs you would incur (not to mention the wear and tear on your employees!) if you sent a staff member to every city in which you held a seminar.

If your seminars are held within a two-hour drive of your location, your marketing and office staff may be willing to work the seminars for extra money. This can be a great arrangement for you; these people are highly knowledgeable about your seminars and products. However, even someone unfamiliar with working at a seminar can usually handle the basic tasks of greeting attendees, giving out name tags or seminar workbooks, helping people find their seats, collecting money, and answering general questions about the day's events.

If you are putting on a seminar in a new city, consider hiring temporary employees through a temporary help agency. You can usually find these types of firms in large metropolitan areas by simply looking in the local Yellow Pages under the heading "Employment Agencies" or "Employment—Temporary," or you can contact large, national firms.

Agencies charge an hourly rate for employees (as little as $6 to $7 an hour, depending on the skill level needed), and they handle all related tax and other paperwork. They also prescreen their employees, provide them with directions to your site, and call to ensure that someone is there to serve you when needed.

Dudley says that SkillPath uses its seminar sites to solicit program managers in new cities. "What we generally do is we put a little flyer out on the table that says, 'Are You Interested in Being A Program Manager? Or Do You Know Someone Who Would Be?' Most of the time that's what does it," she says, though program managers are actually acquired in many different ways. "Somebody takes home that flyer, and they've got a retired mom who would just love to be a hostess, and we hear from them and acquire them that way."

You can also run an ad in a local newspaper for "Part-Time Host/Hostess" or "Part-Time Seminar Assistant" and conduct interviews yourself when you make your first trip to a new city. This is a good job for people who want to work only a few days per month, are retired from full-time work, or are pursuing freelance or other job opportunities that do not require a commitment to a five-day workweek. You might even talk with speakers in the cities where you are presenting a seminar. If they are not the right candidates for your particular topic or seminar series, but do seem like professionals you would enjoy working with and are available on the day(s) you will be holding your event, they may enjoy the opportunity to earn some extra money and talk with attendees. (Ask whether they might be a backup in case your featured speaker encounters an emergency.)

Expect to pay independent contractors anywhere from $50 to $150 per day to serve as program managers. The pay will vary, depending on the city where the event is being held, the number of attendees you expect, and the range of responsibilities you'd like them handle. Assistants for very large seminars—those drawing more than 100 attendees—can be paid hourly and should be paid at the market rate for that area. Expect to pay anywhere from $5 to $10 per hour. You might also consider paying your lead host/hostess a percentage of the receipts from product sales.

Bill Hill, manager of seminar operations at CareerTrack, says the company recently began hiring seminar program managers with previous sales experience to help increase product sales at their events. "I wouldn't say that it's a hard sell; I'd say it's more of a coaching and identifying-needs sell, but we have literally thousands of products and we're trying to match them with the customer," he says. These regional program managers are paid base salaries and commissions.

Ushers/Security

For very simple jobs like ushering, you can consider hiring high school or college students at minimum wage, to help seat your attendees as they arrive. One seminar promoter that *Entrepreneur* spoke with a few years ago said that he offers high school students free admission to his programs if they act as ushers. In this way, he gets free "employees" and the students see a free seminar. Be sure to communicate your dress code to the students you hire.

As for security guards, they won't be needed for every seminar. When they are, you have a few options. If your program takes place at a site often used for large gatherings or events, such as a hotel or arena, the facility may be able to provide security for you. If you use a local church hall or community center, you may need to look in the Yellow Pages under "Security Management Consultants." At these smaller events, a full security contingent may be unnecessary.

HIRING PERSONNEL

Some business owners find hiring intimidating. Some fear being cheated or ripped off, others fear that the job won't be done or will be done poorly. Businesses sometimes fail to move into high income and profit levels because the owners don't hire assistants. With common sense and preparation, though, you can minimize the risk and effort involved in hiring.

A small business's recruitment efforts are usually limited by geography and are sometimes further handicapped because the best local talent may prefer employment in larger, better-known companies. By paying competitive wages and stressing promotional opportunities or a better chance to learn the business, you can offset these handicaps. Promoting your company aggressively can also help you secure an adequate supply of qualified job applicants. Strive to create a public image of your seminar company as a good place to work.

Don't look for potential employees among your friends and relatives. Remember, if a friend or relative does not work out as an employee and you have to let him or her go, you lose both an employee and a good relationship.

Here are some general rules to remember when hiring employees:

1. *No employee is perfect.* Don't expect to find someone to work for you who fulfills your every business need. You must compromise and be satisfied with people who have most of the qualities you seek, and you should be prepared to interview them properly. Be sure to list the skills you are seeking, in the order of their importance, and be as specific as necessary. If you need someone who can operate your Microsoft Access database efficiently, then list that requirement. If you simply need someone who is familiar with computer spreadsheets, be more open.

2. *Pay what the market requires,* and give significant increases once employees have proven themselves. Two well-paid, motivated, capable employees will serve you better than three mediocre, apathetic, underpaid ones.

3. *Don't hold on to a bad match.* If employees fail to perform as you expect and you cannot get them to change through constructive management, let them go. Weak employees hurt the morale of others who do their work well.

Before hiring anyone, write down the following:

- A *job description,* outlining the objectives of the job, the responsibilities of the position, the working conditions, and the relationships of the position to other jobs.
- A *job analysis,* including a description of the qualifications required to fill the job—experience, education, special skills, and any physical requirements.

Once you have written out these documents, begin recruiting prospective employees who seem to match what you have written.

Recruiting

Don't limit your pool of applicants to people who happen to stop by the seminar registration table and ask for jobs. Go out and recruit—at schools and universities (which maintain job placement bureaus for their students and graduates), at established government and private employment agencies, and through referrals from friends and other business firms. Advertising in newspapers or trade publications can be effective, but usually only if the position requires very special training and the advertising expenses are reasonable. "We have rarely had to advertise for trainers," says Dudley. "Every now and then we'll [place] an ad for certain kinds of trainers. For a seminar called 'Project Management' it's really better to have a project manager, like an engineer, [lead the seminar]. But overall, we have no trouble getting applicants."

When writing a classified ad, remember whom you want for the job. In the ad, don't include requirements other than those related to education or experience, and be specific. Don't ask for certain personality characteristics. (After all, anyone considering working in the seminar industry probably considers himself or herself a "self-starter" or a "dynamic" individual.) *Do* say a word about your company (for example, that it is fast-growing or employee-focused). Tell the applicants about the excitement and challenge of the job, the money ("competitive salary scale"), and what they're going to get out of it, or how they'll feel working for you. You've got to sell people on the idea of coming to see you.

The title of the position is no less important. Advertising for a clerk/typist won't attract as strong a response as advertising for an administrative assistant. Stipulate "college education required" in your ad if you only want college graduates to respond. Be very specific about the experience you require; otherwise, you will attract as many unqualified applicants as qualified ones and will have time wasted on go-nowhere applications. Unqualified people will still call you, but they will be less likely to aggressively pursue you about the job.

Screening Applicants

Your time as owner of your own business is extremely valuable. Many of the people responding to an ad will not be qualified. To save yourself some time, screen applicants by phone. Question them about their qualifications. If they don't have enough experience, say very directly, "I am looking for someone more experienced. I can't train an inexperienced person." This will reduce the number of people you have to interview personally.

Another good screening device is to have applicants mail in their resumes along with a cover letter. By previewing the applicants' resumes, you will be able to pick the most qualified candidates for personal interviews. Pay attention to the cover letter when you're narrowing down your list of potential interviewees. A resume can be very general and straightforward; a good cover letter can tell you why an applicant wants to work for you.

If you are hiring a marketing copywriter or graphic artist, ask the candidates for samples of their work, or test them to see whether they have the skills needed to perform the work well. This is a very good way to screen applicants before proceeding to the interview.

Interviewing Applicants

Call the most qualified applicants for personal interviews. Require each applicant to complete a detailed application form and give references.

Keep the application in front of you during the interview, and be certain to give the interviewee plenty of time to present himself or herself thoroughly. Put the interviewee at ease; nervousness may distract you from effectively evaluating their capabilities. When the interviewee first enters the office, say something like: "Make yourself comfortable" or "May I get you a cup of coffee?" Be pleasant and courteous, but avoid too much small talk; it wastes time that you need for important discussion. You can help break the ice by speaking first. Describe the job and your business; give some of its history and discuss where it is headed. You must be enthusiastic about your business if you expect your employees to have enthusiasm for the position you are seeking to fill.

During the interview, concentrate on being observant. Look at the person's dress and mannerisms. If the person is reticent and answers questions with a single word such as "yes" or "no" or with stifled responses, you can assume his or her personality is incompatible with a job opening for a salesperson. On the other hand, a person who is very vocal, sociable, and outgoing might not be suitable for a detail-oriented position, such as a bookkeeper, who chiefly works alone. By being observant, you can read between the lines; you can often learn more from your observations than you can from direct questions.

Let the interviewee talk, and listen to what the person says and doesn't say. For example, if an applicant talks about what a lousy boss he has now, and complains about what poor bosses he has had in the past, it's possible he has trouble getting along with authority figures. If an applicant has gone from one job to another looking for "just the right thing," she may soon tire of working for you as well.

Candidates for jobs at the managerial level require a more extended interview; hourly employees need much less time. Direct the discussion into various channels to find out as much as possible about the person's interests. If not already known, discuss past wages or salaries and expected compensation. Keep salaries in line with the competition—or slightly better, if you can justifiably do so.

Make notes during the interview, or record the person's responses and your impressions as soon as possible afterward, before you forget details. Even if you make notes during the interview, you will probably want to amplify them with your impressions afterward so you don't forget what you discussed.

If you are uncomfortable with the interviewing process, ask your partner or manager to conduct the interviews with you or for you. You should remain involved, at least in the early days, because *your* company is really about you and whom you can work with. "I want somebody in my office that I'm going to enjoy working with. I find that goes a long way," says an entrepreneur whose company has grown to include 10 employees.

The Importance of References

If you are seriously interested in a candidate after you have conducted the interview, *check his or her references and employment history.* One of the worst mistakes that a business owner or manager can make is to hire without checking references and prior employers.

Will an applicant give you only names and phone numbers of people who will rave about his or her performance? Not always. Sometimes, an applicant just hopes that you won't call the references listed.

It is a very bad sign if the references you are given are no longer current. Many managers have called an applicant's former employer and asked for "Mr. or Mrs. So-And-So" only to be told that "So-And-So" left the company more than a year ago. People do change jobs, and an applicant can't always keep track of all former bosses or coworkers, but if someone is being listed as a reference, the applicant should be sure that the reference information is current and that the person you are calling will not be caught off guard by your call.

Be sure to call every company that is listed on an application, going back at least 5 years. A writer we know, who once typed resumes for a living, says she was aghast at how many people came in to "update" their resumes and changed their job titles, assigned duties, and even *companies' names* on their resumes. Approach hiring as though you are buying an expensive commodity: "Buyer, beware!"

With proper planning and effective execution, the hiring process can be quite successful and is crucial for your success. Just as you shop around for the best suppliers, spend equivalent time looking for the right employees. Some of the expenses of hiring new employees may be tax-deductible. For specific information, refer to IRS Publication 334, *Tax Guide for Small Businesses.*

TRAINING PERSONNEL

Training is one of those words that is quite foreign to many entrepreneurs. Small businesses often conduct their "training" by just throwing someone into the job.

You can't afford *not* to adequately train your employees. Even if their skills and background are exceptional, every company is different and you want your employees to embody what makes *your* company unique.

Luckily, the seminar and speaking industry is about training. If you don't understand the value of training—and if you're not focused here—your business may quickly be in trouble. Great training provides you with an advantage over other companies, and it allows you to compete with businesses much larger than yours. If training is not your specialty, or if training/management seminars aren't the mainstay of your business, attend some seminars yourself on this valuable topic. By providing your employees and managers with the special skills, knowledge, and procedures to do their jobs in the most productive and efficient manner possible, your business will soar. Instead of fighting their way through projects using equipment they barely understand and procedures that are foreign to them, they will have the knowledge to perform their jobs with a high degree of quality and proficiency. By making training an integral part of your hiring and promotion process, you will create a very competitive business.

Start by knowing your business extremely well. If you haven't sold tickets to customers, then you can't train someone to sell tickets. If you haven't explained your programs verbally to a new prospect, you probably won't be able to explain them well enough to get your new employees excited about your business and your services. Attend as many seminars as you can, and have your employees do the same. If possible, set up a training schedule that allows each new employee to handle, for at least half a day, all of the job functions involved in running the company—answering phones, processing enrollment forms, staffing the seminar table, selling products, working with vendors, booking a conference room, and so on. Not only will this kind of cross-training prepare your staff to handle a crisis if a valued employee gets sick or leaves (especially in the early days, when you will have the fewest employees), it also gives you a group of employees who understand and appreciate each other's contributions to the company.

Building Employee Morale

Employee morale and team spirit are important to the success of any business. Authorities on business leadership agree that a significant factor in a business owner's success is the ability to accept and use the ideas of the company's employees, giving them full credit if the ideas are successful. This encourages employee contributions and creates a true group spirit of aggressiveness and accomplishment. Here are some suggestions for building employee morale and team spirit:

1. Tell and show your employees that you are interested in them, and welcome their ideas on how working conditions might be improved.
2. Accept the fact that others may not see things as you do.
3. Respect differences of opinion.
4. Give explanations for management actions whenever possible.
5. Provide information and guidance on matters affecting employee security.
6. Make reasonable efforts to keep jobs interesting.
7. Encourage promotion from within.
8. Express appreciation publicly for jobs well done.

9. Offer criticism privately in the form of constructive suggestions for improvement.
10. Train supervisors to think about the people involved rather than just the work.
11. Keep your employees up to date on all business matters affecting them, and quell rumors with correct information.

PERSONNEL PROGRAMS

Besides considering what your employees want from their jobs and how you can foster an efficient, happy, and productive staff, you must recognize the legal framework within which all personnel policies must operate. Personnel programs are not left to the discretion of business owners. Even well-meaning policies that have proven successful may conflict with legal regulations.

Chief among government regulations for employers today are the minimum-wage laws, fair employment regulations, the rights of employees to engage in collective bargaining and to form unions, requirements for withholding income taxes and other items from employees' paychecks, and public policy regarding equal opportunity. Before you begin hiring, check the status of these regulations with your state employment department.

Fringe benefits, health and hospital insurance, profit-sharing plans, pensions, and paid vacations are all part of a complete personnel program. All business owners must recognize that having fair wages, attractive fringe benefits, desirable working conditions, and concern for employees are important ways to build a dedicated and efficient staff.

Group insurance is easy to acquire and will start at about $75 per month per employee. As owner, you can receive company-paid insurance and hospitalization if you provide them for your employees. Your insurance broker will handle your group insurance plan.

Performance Appraisal and Counseling

Good speakers always have their presentations evaluated by their audience. It is the only way to truly ensure that their presentation is effective and inspiring, and that it meets the needs of the groups they address. Likewise, good employers always provide feedback on performance so that the employees can constantly improve and flourish.

There are several methods of documenting employee performance:

1. *Numerical.* Workers receive scores reflecting their performance based on company expectations.

2. *Percentile.* Workers are appraised and categorized by percentage: the upper 25 percent, the lower 50 percent, and so on.
3. *Descriptive statement.* Counselors make a weak/strong judgment in response to prepared statements describing employee performance.
4. *Written report.* Appraisers write an outline of an individual's job performance.
5. *Performance/Objective.* Appraisers compare employee performance with goals set at the beginning of the evaluation period.

Although different companies have varying policies, most evaluate office employees on an annual basis, and speakers on an ongoing basis. Regular reviews are effective motivational instruments, but the most satisfactory and positive way to hold a person accountable is simply through periodic communication on how he or she is doing.

Speaker Performance Evaluations

The speaker performance evaluation will actually be a part of every seminar that you hold. Every attendee should be strongly encouraged to fill out the speaker/seminar evaluation in its entirety. Offer door prizes, a drawing for a free seminar, $5 off of their next seminar fee, or whatever you can to encourage this feedback.

Keep the evaluation form simple. If you ask for too much, your attendees may just decide not to fill it out. At the same time, ask the *right* questions. Questions recommended by our experts include:

- Do you think that the speaker was well prepared?
- Did the speaker address the topics that we promised we would address in our brochures? Did the speaker present the topics of greatest value to you?
- Do you feel you are leaving this seminar with tools that can help make a difference in your life/career/relationship?
- What would you like to see more of in a future seminar?
- What would you like to see much less of?
- What other seminars have you attended?
- What was your favorite portion of this seminar? Least favorite portion?
- What did you think of the facilities? The neighborhood?
- Would you attend one of our seminars again? What topics are of most interest to you?

To evaluate speakers, use a questionnaire asking for both multiple-choice and written responses. You might have attendees select a response from 1 to 5 or 1 to 10, and allow space for brief comments below each question. These questionnaires not only provide great feedback on the effectiveness of your speakers, they are also invaluable market research tools.

Group Life and Health

Group life insurance policies provide your employees with the type of benefits that attract and keep productive, sound workers. These policies are generally figured on some multiple or fraction of the worker's yearly salary. An employee making $20,000 per year may be insured for $10,000; a $50,000 executive may have a $100,000 policy. Some group policies are tax-deductible. A very small firm might consider purchasing inexpensive individual term life insurance instead.

Group life insurance is available in a number of different packages. Group paid-up plans offer a combination of accumulating units of single premium whole life insurance, and decreasing amounts of group term life insurance. Level premium group permanent insurance is a form of permanent life insurance with premiums payable to a specified age, say 65. Upon leaving the firm, the employee may retain the paid-up portion of the policy or continue self-payment to the insurer. Both of these types of policies are fairly uncommon.

Survivor income plans provide a monthly income payable to surviving dependents after the death of the employee. Elective group coverages begin with the employee's signing up for a basic group term life insurance plan. Thereafter, elective plans consist of more group term, group survivor income, and, more recently, group universal life plans.

An insured employee normally has the right to convert the face amount of the insurance to an individual policy of permanent insurance. The real benefit, though nonfinancial, is that the employee has the right to convert the policy within one month, without evidence of insurability—that is, without a medical exam to prove fitness. Informing your employees of these hidden benefits is bound to increase the caliber of worker you attract.

Group life insurance often comes with group health insurance in economically attractive packages. Standard indemnity health insurance generally includes hospitalization, regular medical/surgical, and major medical coverage. Employees must pick up the initial deductible expenses and pharmaceutical costs on their own. Coinsurance arrangements will pay for 80 or 90 percent of major medical costs, leaving the rest to the employee. Optical and dental packages are optional, but worth including if your firm can afford them.

Explore the wide range of options available in health care coverage today: traditional indemnity, HMOs, PPOs, and hospital service associations.

Some national insurers have begun offering hybrid plans (in limited areas) in which regular indemnity health insurance is combined with an HMO or PPO. Known as dual- and triple-option plans, respectively, these offerings combine the best features of each of the three types of coverage into one easily administered package.

Flexible benefits, a generic term referring to a variety of programs that enable employees to choose from different fringe benefits, have gained in popularity. These "cafeteria plans" allow trade-offs among specific health, dental, and optical plans.

Because of the travel and long hours inherent in the seminar business, your employees may appreciate a health program that includes some sort of fitness program. Some health programs have more liberal coverage, such as treatment for alcohol and substance abuse.

The best-designed plan in the world will fail you if it is poorly administered. Ask about the plan. Ask claims representatives specific questions about costs for a typical claim: ambulance service, outpatient services, and rehabilitation (if any).

Note: A provision of the Omnibus Budget Reconciliation Act of 1993 requires employers to report information about their employees' health care coverage status to the Health Care Financing Administration (HCFA) on an attachment to the employees' W-2 tax forms.

COBRA

The Consolidated Omnibus Budget Reconciliation Act (COBRA) was enacted to extend health insurance to employees and dependents beyond the point at which coverage traditionally ceases. For employees, COBRA means an extension of up to 18 months of coverage under a company's plan even after they quit or are terminated (provided the reason for termination isn't gross misconduct). Employees' spouses can obtain COBRA coverage for up to 36 months after a divorce, and children can receive 36 additional months of coverage when they reach the age at which they cease to be classified as dependents.

Despite what you may expect, however, extending COBRA benefits shouldn't cost your company a penny. Employers are permitted by law to charge recipients 102 percent of the cost of extending the benefits (the extra 2 percent covers administrative costs).

The federal COBRA plan applies to all companies with more than 20 employees, and many states have similar laws that pertain to much smaller companies.

Family and Medical Leave Act of 1993

A relatively new law on the books is the Family and Medical Leave Act of 1993, which provides qualified participants the option to take up to 12 weeks of unpaid time off to care for a newborn child or an ill family member. The precise wording of the Act allows covered employees who have been employed for at least one year, working over 1,250 hours in that 12-month period, to elect for 12 weeks of unpaid, job-protected leave, for certain family and medical reasons. There must be at least 50 employees working within a 75-mile radius for the company to become eligible, and the employee must give at least 30 days' advance notice in order to take the leave.

Pension Plans

Pension plans help attract and retain top-notch employees. But with these benefits come responsibilities—specifically, the fiduciary responsibility to make sure your plan is run wisely and complies with federal Employee Retirement Income Security Act (ERISA) requirements. You can shift part of the trustee responsibility to investment managers or brokerage firms that manage your company's retirement assets. For example, Merrill Lynch, Pierce, Fenner & Smith Inc. serves as a trustee for companies using its Simplified Employee Pension (SEP) Plan. The benefits to the companies include ease of establishing the retirement plan and use of a seasoned investment professional to safeguard assets.

CPAs and pension administration companies can give you details of various programs if you tell them you have a business and are interested in setting up a plan. Typically, they will counsel you for free because they want to sell you a plan. This is a confusing topic, but, under the right circumstances, a pension plan can be a valuable source of tax deductions for you.

There are three types of retirement plans: (1) the Individual Retirement Account (IRA), (2) the SEP, and (3) the Keogh plan. All three plans allow you to add money and earn interest tax-free until you retire, but each has distinct requirements, advantages, and disadvantages.

IRA Option

The great advantage of the IRA is simplicity. The paperwork and tax-reporting requirements are minimal, and you are not obligated to cover any of your employees. You can set up or contribute to an IRA account any time up to the date your annual federal income tax re-turn is due—April 15 of the following year.

The biggest drawback is that your maximum annual contribution is limited to the lesser of $2,000 or your taxable earnings. Another stumbling block: If you or your spouse is covered by a retirement plan, then neither of you can make a tax-deductible contribution to an IRA, though you may still benefit from an IRA since the interest it earns is tax-free.

Even if you are not covered by another retirement plan, you may be disqualified from receiving a tax deduction for your contributions because you make too much money. The $2,000 deduction is phased out for single taxpayers making between $25,000 and $35,000; for married couples, the phase-out range is between $40,000 and $50,000.

Simplified Employee Pension Program

If you don't have any employees and hate paperwork, consider the Simplified Employee Pension plan (SEP). The SEP is essentially a glorified IRA that allows you to make a contribution of 13.0435 percent of net earnings, up to a maximum of $30,000 per year. The paperwork is minimal, and you have until April 15 to set up the plan and make a contribution that will be tax-deductible on your current year's federal income tax return. You are not required to make a contribution each year.

Yet, unlike Keogh plans, which allow you to exclude employees who work fewer than 1,000 hours per year, SEPs require that you include all employees over the age of 21 who have worked for you for 3 out of the past 5 years—including part-time employees.

Who pays for the contributions depends on the type of SEP you set up. Under a regular SEP, you pay the full cost of the plan, and you must contribute, for all eligible employees, whatever percentage you contribute for yourself.

If your business has 25 or fewer employees, you can choose a "salary reduction arrangement" SEP. With this type of plan, employees can opt to have you place a portion of their pretax pay into the SEP. This arrangement has other requirements and contribution limitations that differ from those of the regular SEP.

Keogh Plans

The most common type of Keogh retirement plan is a profit-sharing plan. This plan permits you to determine the amount you contribute each year, based on the profits of your business as shown on your tax return prior to deducting the Keogh plan contribution. The Omnibus

Budget Reconciliation Act of 1993 lowered the maximum amount of annual compensation (from $235,840 down to $150,000) that may be considered for computing benefits and contributions to qualified employee benefit plans. The change is effective for plan years beginning after January 1, 1994. Top executives participating in profit-sharing plans will no longer be able to obtain the $30,000 maximum contribution under the plan, but will be limited to a contribution of $22,500 (15 percent of $150,000). You can also adopt a "defined contribution" plan that allows a flat contribution each year of up to 10 percent of your net profits.

Another option is a "defined benefit" plan. With this option, an actuary determines the contribution to be made each year. The actuary calculates the contribution that must be made in order to yield a certain amount on retirement, based on the participant's remaining years and the expected earnings of the contributions. This type of plan is usually the most expensive to administer, because of the additional cost of the actuary.

You must sign all the papers to open your Keogh plan on or before December 31 of the year you open it. However, you need not make the actual cash contribution until the due date of your tax return. Many stockbrokers and insurance companies and some banks offer Keogh plans for nominal installation charges (less than $200) and with modest or no yearly administration fees (up to $100 per covered individual). These institutions administer the plan while you direct them, as trustee of the plan, concerning its investments. The earnings of the Keogh plan are tax-free until withdrawn by the participants.

Generally, the plan must cover all employees who are at least 21 years of age and who have one year of service with the employer. You can usually exclude part-time employees from your plan. Benefits of the plan must be nondiscriminatory.

If your business is incorporated and you wish to install a corporate pension plan, you must adopt the plan before the end of your fiscal year. You can integrate the plan with employees' Social Security benefits, so that higher-paid executives may receive more benefits than other employees.

The same maximum contribution rules that govern Keogh plans also govern corporate plans. The maximum contribution for an employee cannot exceed 25 percent of his or her earnings. Ten percent of that can go toward a defined contribution plan, and 15 percent can go toward a profit-sharing plan. The alternative is a defined contribution plan in which an actuary determines the maximum allowable contribution per employee.

Other types of plans are available to corporations, including Employee Stock Ownership Plans, in which the contributions are the employer corporation's stock, and Section 401(k) plans, in which an employee may elect to defer up to $9,500 of his or her earnings (after 1986) per year tax-free. Generally, with a 401(k) plan, the employee has the option to choose the type of investments in which the deferred amount goes.

How do you protect yourself if your plan is managed by an outside investment expert, or if your plan allows employees to make their own investment decisions? Under new regulations issued recently, fiduciaries of participant-directed individual account plans, such as many 401(k) plans, can protect themselves against liability for investment losses incurred by participants by meeting certain requirements set by the Department of Labor under ERISA. To protect yourself against liability, according to Richard J. Maturi in *Entrepreneur* magazine,[1] you must:

- Provide plan participants with enough information to allow them to make informed investment decisions.
- Allow participants to exercise control.
- Permit participants to choose from a broad range of at least three investment alternatives.
- Allow participants to make investment choices regarding each investment alternative with a frequency appropriate to that investment's market volatility.

With any type of qualified retirement plan, the Internal Revenue Service (IRS) watches closely to be sure the plan does not discriminate against certain employees or plan members. Only a nondiscriminatory plan can achieve tax-qualified status, postponing tax liability until the participants receive their retirement contributions.

A plan is considered nondiscriminatory if it passes either one of two coverage tests—the ratio percentage test or the average benefit percentage test. It must also pass a minimum participation test and a contribution or benefits nondiscrimination test.

To meet the ratio percentage test, the number of nonhighly compensated employees (NHCEs) benefiting from the plan must equal at least 70 percent of the number of highly compensated employees (HCEs) benefiting from the plan. At press time, highly compensated employees are those who meet at least one of four criteria:

1. They own 5 percent or more of the company.
2. They will receive compensation from the employer in excess of $96,368 for the year (indexed to the Consumer Price Index).

3. They will receive straight compensation in excess of $64,245 for the year and are among the top 20 percent of paid employees for the year.

4. They will receive compensation in excess of $57,821 for the year and are officers of the company.

If you do not pass the ratio percentage test, you must pass the average benefit percentage test. This has two parts: the classification requirement and the average benefit percentage requirement. To meet the *classification requirement,* your plan must cover a "reasonable" classification of employees. For example, the IRS considers classifications by specified job categories or nature of compensation reasonable. This means you could make your plan available only to specified jobs, or only to salaried employees and not hourly workers. However, this classification must also be objective, which generally means NHCE participation must equal at least 50 percent of HCE participation.

The *average benefit percentage requirement* demands that the average benefit for NHCEs must equal at least 70 percent of the average benefit for HCEs.

In addition to passing either the ratio percentage test or the average benefit percentage test, your retirement plan must pass a minimum participation test. This means it must benefit at least 50 employees or at least 40 percent of all your employees (certain exclusions are allowed). Finally, in addition to the prior two tests, a plan must satisfy a general nondiscrimination test that proves it doesn't discriminate in favor of HCEs.

The IRS is trying to ease the administrative burden on employers. Proposed changes to Treasury Department regulations would allow employers whose plans fall short of the prescribed benefit or contribution levels and percentages by a small margin to argue their case with the IRS.

REGULATION OF WAGES AND HOURS

The Fair Labor Standards Act requires minimum hourly wages for the employees of most firms. The minimum wage for employees covered by this act, set by Congress, is $4.75 at the time of this writing. The act also requires employers to compensate employees at a time-and-a-half rate for hours worked in excess of 40 per week.

Not all firms engage in interstate commerce, but all employees of such firms are covered by the federal Fair Labor Standards Act. Those not covered include employees of retail stores and service establishments that have annual gross sales or receipts of less than $250,000;

outside salespeople; and executive, administrative, and professional personnel.

Small businesses not covered by the federal act are most likely subject to similar minimum-wage requirements in their respective states. Currently, Puerto Rico, the District of Columbia, and a large majority of states have minimum-wage laws that come close to meeting federal standards. A smaller majority of states have attempted to regulate the number of working hours by imposing overtime wage premiums.

Most states limit working hours for children and for workers in hazardous occupations. Many states now have time-off-for-voting laws, usually providing paid time, particularly if employees can't vote before or after work.

REGULATION OF WORKING CONDITIONS

Various states also regulate working conditions, especially in regard to industrial safety and health. At the federal level, employee safety and health are regulated by provisions of the Occupational Safety and Health Act of 1970 (OSHA). Many states have taken over the administration of OSHA in their jurisdictions.

Federal law requires employers to provide employees with a workplace that is free of hazardous conditions, such as exposure to toxic materials or other physically harmful agents. In retail and service establishments, according to OSHA, the most frequent violations are improperly marked or unmarked exits, fire extinguishers that are not mounted and/or are not easy to spot, and fall-hazard debris in storerooms.

Safety inspections of business premises can be made at any time and without advance notice. Firms found in violation of OSHA's safety and health standards may incur severe fines and other penalties.

THE HIDDEN COSTS OF EMPLOYING

Employees will cost you between 15 and 30 percent above the amount of their wages or salaries, depending on the benefits you offer. If you're paying an employee a salary of $25,000 per year, your actual cost could be more than $30,000. Figure that 15 percent of the total wages will cover payroll taxes, worker's compensation, and paid vacation, and 30 percent above total wages will cover all taxes and a full slate of benefits.

You must match every dollar of federal Social Security taxes that you deduct from your employees' checks. You must pay 6.2 percent for Social Security tax and 1.45 percent for Medicare tax. You must also pay state and federal unemployment taxes. Federal unemployment tax will range from 0.8 percent to 6.2 percent, depending on how high the state tax is. State taxes will vary from one state to another. Social Security and unemployment tax rates can change from year to year. In some states, the employer also pays a portion of the state disability insurance premiums.

Your success will often depend on your employees. Develop effective interview techniques to ferret out smart, diligent workers. More information on finding top employees appears in guide No. 1801, *Managing Personnel in a Small Business.*

5

LEGAL REQUIREMENTS

LEGAL FORM OF OPERATION

One of the first things to consider when starting a seminar promotion business is the legal form under which it will operate. Small businesses commonly operate as one of the following:

1. Sole proprietorship.
2. General partnership.
3. Limited partnership.
4. Corporation.
5. Limited liability company.

Sole Proprietorship

"Sole" means only one owner—not even silent partners are allowed. A sole proprietorship is the easiest form under which to start a business. Legal papers aren't required, except for a business license (or licenses, if you have locations in more than one jurisdiction), and federal and state payroll identification (I.D.) numbers if you plan to hire employees or if entities with which you plan to do business require them. (You can secure the federal employer identification number by filing Form SS-4 with the Internal Revenue Service.) You also need to submit a fictitious name filing or dba (doing business as) with the county clerk if you plan to do business under a name other than your own. No separate income tax returns are necessary, unlike other forms of business. FICA taxes for the owner are lower than they are under other forms as well. You report all your income and expenses on Schedule C or C-EZ of IRS Form 1040. Schedule C is the long form for sole proprietors and you must fill it out if you have gross receipts of more than $25,000 and expenses of more than $2,000.

Schedule C-EZ, a simplified version of Schedule C, has just three lines for reporting:

1. Gross receipts.
2. Total expenses.
3. Net profit (line 1 minus line 2).

To qualify, you must have gross receipts of $25,000 or less, report expenses of $2,000 or less, use the cash method of accounting (discussed in Chapter 6 below), have had no inventory during the year, own only one business as a sole proprietor, and not have a net loss from that business. A sole proprietorship has one major disadvantage. Creditors of your business can attach your personal property, bank account, and other items. You can be harassed for years after you abandon a business, and your personal credit can be ruined.

General Partnership

A partnership is even more dangerous than a sole proprietorship, because each partner is liable for the other's actions. In any legal or creditor action, each partner will be sued personally, and the property and bank accounts of each will be attached. Also, when an individual contributes assets to a partnership, he or she doesn't retain a claim to those specific properties, but merely acquires equity in all assets of the firm. The partner with the most to lose usually gets hit the hardest.

A lawyer's charge for drawing up a partnership contract is about the same as for forming a corporation. Forming a partnership on a handshake and verbal agreement, without a formal contract, is very unwise. You can buy partnership agreement forms at just about any stationery store, or you can purchase books like *The Partnership Book: How to Write a Partnership Agreement* or software such as *Nolo's Partnership Maker* for DOS, both available from Nolo Press, 950 Parker St., Berkeley, CA 94710-9867; (800) 992-6656.

A partnership must secure a federal employee identification number from the IRS, using Form SS-4. Then it must file Form 1065 each year as its tax return, and send Schedule K-1 to each partner. Generally, IRS regulations require that a partnership use a calendar-year end. Each partner reports his or her share of partnership profits or losses on an individual tax return and pays the tax on those profits. The partnership itself does not pay any taxes with its tax return.

Choosing a partner is one of the most important steps you'll take in your venture, so proceed with caution. To ensure that you have a successful relationship, consider these factors:

- *Dividing responsibility.* Don't assume it's clear who will do what; clearly divide your responsibilities to prevent any misunderstandings.
- *An exit strategy.* In case one partner decides to sell out later on, talk about a buy–sell agreement early on.
- *Life insurance.* If you or your partner dies, a "key man" insurance policy ensures that the surviving partner will be able to buy the deceased partner's share from his or her heirs.
- *Consulting outsiders.* Just because you've split responsibilities, that doesn't mean you've covered all the bases. Make sure to consult an attorney, an accountant, or another business expert on matters outside your expertise.

Limited Partnership

In many ways, a limited partnership is like a corporation. The investors become limited partners and are personally liable only for the amount of their investment. The general partner, usually the operator of the business, can be either a sole proprietor or a corporation. There is also the classic "silent partner" situation—one or more limited partners put up money and the other general partners run the business. A limited partnership in this case serves to protect the assets of wealthier silent partners and acts as a conduit to pass current operating profits or losses to them as well as to preserve the special tax character of certain items.

Limited partnerships are commonly used for real estate syndications. The legal costs of forming a limited partnership can be even higher than those of forming a corporation because, in some states, they are governed by securities laws. In some lines of business, the limited partner (also called the passive investor) may be subject to special tax liabilities that can offset tax-shelter advantages. The IRS tends to look at these facts on a case-by-case basis.

The 1986 Tax Reform Act limits the amount of losses a limited partner can deduct on a personal tax return. If your partnership is expected to generate tax losses in its early years, consult your accountant to determine whether those losses will benefit you.

Corporation

A corporate structure is perhaps the most advantageous way to start a business because the corporation exists as a separate entity. It alone is legally responsible for its actions and debts. You are personally protected in most situations because you will only be an employee of the corporation, even though you may own all or most of the stock.

Shareholders forming a corporation can divide ownership into shares, they can define responsibilities in the corporate minutes, and they can accommodate a shareholder who wants to leave without much legal difficulty. You can use stock as collateral. The death of one shareholder doesn't stop the business. (In a partnership, it sometimes does.) Also, you can enjoy many executive privileges that are difficult to justify in a sole proprietorship or partnership. Until your corporation has operated successfully for many years, however, you will most likely still have to accept personal liability for any corporate loans made by banks or other financial institutions.

Use a shareholders' agreement that provides for the purchase of a deceased shareholder's shares by the surviving shareholders. Such an agreement usually provides a method of determining the price of a selling shareholder's shares, if the remaining shareholders wish to purchase them, or it might grant the other shareholders the right of first refusal.

The only disadvantage is potential double taxation: the corporation must pay taxes on its net income, and you must also pay taxes on any dividends you may receive from the corporation. Business owners often increase their own salaries in order to reduce or wipe out corporate profits and thereby prevent those profits from being taxed twice (once as income to the corporation and again as income to shareholders upon receipt of dividends).

Subchapter S Corporations

You can avoid potential double federal taxation by filing a Subchapter S election with the IRS. (Be aware that many states do not recognize a Subchapter S election for state tax purposes and will tax the corporation as a regular corporation.) Qualifications for electing Subchapter S changed when the Subchapter S Revisions Act of 1982 liberalized many of the old rules and gave new flexibility to these corporations, now popular with small and medium-size businesses. Subchapter S allows profits or losses to travel directly through the corporation to shareholders. If you earn other income during the first year and the corporation has a loss, you can deduct against the other income, possibly wiping out your tax liability completely—subject to the limitations of the 1986 Tax Reform Act.

Subchapter S corporations elect not to be taxed as corporations. Instead, the shareholders of a Subchapter S corporation include their proportionate shares of the corporate profits and losses in their individual gross incomes. Subchapter S corporations are excellent devices for allowing small businesses to avoid double taxation. If your company produces a substantial profit, forming a Subchapter S corporation would be wise, because the profits will be added to your personal income and taxed at an individual rate, which may be lower than the regular corporate rate on that income.

To qualify under Subchapter S, the corporation must:

- Be domestic.
- Not be a member of an affiliated group.
- Not have more than 35 shareholders (all of whom are either individuals or estates).
- Not have a nonresident alien as a shareholder.
- Not have more than one class of outstanding stock.

The new rules allow an unlimited amount of passive income from rents and royalties. A passive activity is one in which a taxpayer does not materially participate. Material participation requires involvement in operations on a regular, continuous, and substantial basis.

Under the 1986 Tax Reform Act, losses and credits from a "passive" business activity will be deductible only against passive income. You will not be able to use passive losses and credits against nonpassive income, which includes compensation and portfolio income. However, you can deduct rental losses and credits against up to $25,000 of nonpassive income.

If a shareholder of a Subchapter S corporation does not actively participate in the operation of the business, it is considered a passive activity. If the Subchapter S corporation produces a loss during the year, that shareholder's deduction for his or her portion of the loss will be cut back dramatically. However, if income is accrued from the Subchapter S corporation, it can be offset by losses and credits from other passive activities.

For more information on the rules that apply to a Subchapter S corporation, call your local IRS office.

Forming a Corporation

In the past, it was sometimes advantageous to file documents of incorporation in states or countries other than those in which the corporation operated. Tax advantages in some places meant large savings to new companies. In recent years, however, many states have plugged these loopholes because they didn't have control over corporations operating within their borders and were losing filing fees and taxes.

If you locate in any state other than the one in which you incorporate, that state will require you to file corporate papers as a foreign corporation. The fees are higher than those for a domestic corporation. Lawyers charge from $350 to $2,000 to file corporate papers, with $700 being the average. Unless you have more than 10 stockholders or a very complicated partnership arrangement, you don't need a lawyer. Incorporation fees are the easiest money an attorney makes. The forms required are no harder to complete than an average credit application.

For more information on self-incorporation, Entrepreneur Magazine Group publishes *The Entrepreneur's Incorporation Kit* (#7100), which details the complete incorporation process and provides samples for you to refer to while filling out the forms.

Limited Liability Company

A new business form called the limited liability company (LLC) has sprung up in 48 states (all but Hawaii and Vermont). The LLC arose from the desire of business owners to adopt a business structure permitting them to operate like a traditional partnership. This structure distributes the income and income tax to the partners (reported on their individual income tax returns), but protects them from personal liability for the business's debts, as though they had a corporate business form. In an ordinary enterprise, the owner and partners (if any) assume complete liability for all debts of the business unless a separate corporation is established. Under the LLC concept, an individual is not responsible for the firm's debt.

The LLC offers a number of advantages over S corporations. For example, S corporations can issue only one class of company stock; LLCs can offer several different classes with different rights. In addition, S corporations are limited to a maximum of 35 individual shareholders (who must be U.S. residents); an unlimited number of individuals, corporations, and partnerships may participate in an LLC.

The LLC also carries significant tax advantages over the limited partnership. For instance, unless the partner in a limited partnership assumes an active role, his or her losses are considered "passive" losses and are ineligible for use as tax deductions against active income. But if the partner does take an active role in the firm's management, he or she becomes liable for the firm's debt. It's a Catch-22 situation. The owners of an LLC, on the other hand, do not assume liability for the business's debt, and they can use any losses as tax deductions against active income.

In exchange for these two considerable benefits, however, the owners of LLCs must meet the "transferability restriction test," which means the ownership interests in the LLC must not be transferable without some restrictions. These restrictions make the LLC structure unworkable for major corporations. For corporations to attract large sums of capital, their corporate stock must be easily transferable on the stock exchanges. However, this restriction should not pose a problem for the typical entrepreneurial business, in which ownership transfers take place relatively infrequently.

A number of quirks in current state LLC legislation require tricky maneuvering and plenty of advance planning. For example, LLC legislation in Colorado and Wyoming does not allow for continuity of the business. In those states, the business is dissolved upon the death, retirement, resignation, or expulsion of an owner. While the same is true for both sole proprietorships and partnerships, you must still plan accordingly.

In Florida, the state's corporate tax also applies to LLCs. And with state shortfalls in tax revenues and strained budgets, other states may look to LLCs for additional tax revenues, even though similar businesses such as S corporations are typically exempt from state and federal income taxes.

Because the LLC is a relatively new legal form for businesses, federal and state governments are still looking at ways to tighten the regulations surrounding this business tool. The attempts to tighten regulations governing LLCs come from a concern that some investment promoters are using this legal form to evade securities laws. Although most LLCs are legitimate, the Securities and Exchange Commission (SEC) is moving quickly to tighten control of those firms engaged in irregular activity.

If this form of business sounds like it would fit your needs, explore new and pending legislation concerning LLCs in your area.

FICTITIOUS NAME (DBA)

Sole proprietorships and partnerships have the option of choosing a distinctive name or *dba* ("doing business as") for their businesses. If you want to operate your business under a name other than your personal name (for instance, Irene Adler doing business as "Training Team Seminars"), you may be required by the county, city, or state to register your fictitious name.

In many states, you need only go to the county offices and pay a registration fee to the county clerk. Some states, however, will require you to place a fictitious name ad in a local newspaper. Procedures vary from state to state. Generally, the newspaper that prints the legal notice for your business name will file the necessary papers with the county for a small fee.

The cost of filing a fictitious name notice ranges from $10 to $100. Call your bank and ask whether it requires a fictitious name registry or certificate in order to open a business account. If so, inquire where you should go to obtain one.

Fictitious name filings do not apply to corporations in most states unless the corporations do business under names other than their own. Documents of incorporation have the same effect for corporate businesses as fictitious name filings have for sole proprietorships and partnerships.

LICENSES AND PERMITS

Most cities and counties require business operators to obtain various licenses and permits to comply with local regulations.

Business License

City business license departments operate as tax-collecting bureaus and do not perform any public service. You simply pay a fee to operate your business in that city. Some cities also claim a percentage of your gross sales.

The planning or zoning department will process your license application and check to make sure the zone covering your property allows the proposed use and that there are enough parking places to meet the code. You should not encounter many problems if you are opening your business in a structure that previously housed a similar business.

You will not be allowed to operate in an area that is not zoned for your business unless you first have a variance or conditional-use permit (explained below in "Zoning Ordinances"). But before you make the effort to obtain this authorization, be sure the zoning really prohibits your type of business. Remember that many bureaucrats may not be genuinely familiar with the laws they administer. Ask the same question of three license clerks, and you may receive three different answers.

Fire Department Permit

The fire department may require you to obtain a permit if your business uses any flammable materials or if your premises will be open to the public. (If you hold your seminars in a facility that is normally open to the public, like a hotel or convention center, this will not pertain to you.) In some cities, you must secure a permit before you open for business. Other jurisdictions don't require permits. Instead, they schedule periodic inspections of the premises to see whether you meet regulations. If you don't, they will issue a citation.

Sign Permit

Recently, many cities and suburbs have instituted sign ordinances that restrict the size, location, and sometimes the lighting and type of sign you can use in front of your business. Landlords may also impose their own restrictions. To avoid costly mistakes, check local regulations and secure the written approval of your landlord before you invest in a sign.

County Permits

County governments often require essentially the same types of permits and licenses as cities. These permits apply to commercial enterprises located outside city limits. Learn about county ordinances that apply to your business if you locate outside a city's or town's jurisdiction. County regulations are often less strict than those of adjoining cities.

State Licenses

Many states require persons engaged in certain occupations to hold licenses or occupational permits. Often, these persons must pass state examinations before they can conduct business. States commonly require licensing for the following workers: auto mechanics, building contractors, collection agents, electricians, insurance agents, plumbers, real estate brokers, repossessors, and those providing personal services (barbers, cosmetologists, doctors, and nurses). Recently, some states have also begun regulating persons engaged in financial planning and investment advisory services, including people who offer seminars on these topics. Your state government offices can provide a complete list of occupations that require licensing.

Federal Licenses

A few businesses and businesspeople require federal licensing: meat processors, common carriers, radio and television stations, and investment advisory services. The Federal Trade Commission can tell you whether your business requires a federal license.

Zoning Ordinances

If you want to run your seminar promotion business legitimately from your home, you will have to investigate the zoning ordinances for your area. Don't go to the zoning officer for advice. Go to the city/township clerk's office and ask for a copy of any ordinances concerning home-based businesses. Then find out, if you don't already know, exactly how your residence is zoned.

Once you know how your area is zoned, you'll have a good idea whether your planned business is permitted there. To be certain, consult an attorney who can interpret the fine points of the ordinance. There is often a substantial difference between what an ordinance says and the way it is enforced.

If you locate your seminar promotion business in a structure previously used for commercial purposes, zoning regulations will not be a problem in most cases. However, if you intend to construct a new facility, use an existing building for a different purpose, or perform extensive remodeling, you should carefully check local building and zoning codes. If zoning regulations do not allow operation of the type of business you wish to open, you may file for a zoning variance, a conditional-use permit, or a zone change.

A variance or conditional-use permit grants you the conditional privilege of operating a business on land that is not zoned for that purpose. The filing fee may be as high as $1,200, and it may take 90 days or more before you get a decision. A zone change, on the other hand, amounts to a permanent change in the way a particular area is zoned—and in the way it will be used long into the future. It involves a lengthy procedure of six months or more, in which you must file a petition with the city planning commission, issue notice, present your case at public hearings, and get the city council or other governing body to make a decision.

In some cases, a change in land use—whether permanent (by zone change) or temporary (by variance or conditional-use permit)—will require environmental clearance. Local planning or zoning departments can tell you whether your project is exempt from the law or whether you should seek a negative declaration from its regulations. If your project will displace residents, generate a lot of traffic, or affect natural habitat, some municipalities will require you to prepare an environmental impact report. This can be a costly and time-consuming procedure for which you will need expert help.

If the city approves your request for a zoning variance or change, many restrictions still apply. In addition to meeting local building codes, you will probably have to comply with regulations specifying minimum setbacks at the front, side, and rear of the structure; maximum floor space in relation to land area; maximum heights; minimum provisions for parking; and other factors. We cannot enlarge on this subject since each government entity has its own policies.

Essentially, zoning ensures that different kinds of developments are properly located in relation to each other; that adequate space is available for each type of development; that the density of construction in each area is in proper proportion to the availability of such facilities as streets, schools, recreational areas, and utility systems; and that the development is sufficiently open to permit light, air, and privacy for persons living and working within the area.

Other Regulations

In addition to licenses and permits, other regulations may apply to your business. Federal and state laws designed to encourage competition (antitrust laws) prohibit contracts, combinations, and conspiracies in restraint of trade. They also prohibit price discrimination between different purchasers of commodities similar in grade and quality that may injure competition. And they make unlawful "unfair methods of competition" and "unfair or deceptive practices."

The term *deceptive practices* refers to false advertising, misrepresentation, simulation of competitive products, and the slandering of competitors.

The Federal Trade Commission (FTC) regulates any firm conducting business across state lines. Any business that advertises in more than one state is subject to FTC regulations. Even the smallest mail-order business comes under FTC jurisdiction.

Additional federal regulations apply to home-based businesses. Under the Fair Labor Standards Act, home-based operators cannot hire employees for homework involving the production of women's apparel or jewelry that requires a production process defined as too hazardous for homework. To legally employ workers making other regulated products (gloves, mittens, buttons, buckles, handkerchiefs, embroidery, and knitted outerwear), employers must obtain a certificate of authorization and homework handbooks from the U.S. Department of Labor.

Remember that the Fair Labor Standards Act is federal legislation; individual states may have differing or additional legislation regarding homework. Because of the complexities of these regulations and the severe penalties imposed for violations, you must consult a lawyer if your business may be subject to them.

IDEA PROTECTION

The scope of idea protection laws extends to just about every form of original invention or creation, provided that the idea can be presented in some tangible, physical form. It can be a design, a model, or a write-up. Two methods of idea protection offered by the United States government may apply to your seminar promotion business: copyright and trademark registration. If you ever release a recording (either audio or video) of a seminar, it would be a good idea to copyright it first. (See a lawyer for more details on who would hold the copyright in such a case. It might be you, the speaker, or both.) Trademark registration might be used to protect a unique name, logo, or symbol for your business, if you come up with one. Each of these types of idea protection is discussed individually below.

You need to be aware of idea protection laws not only because they can protect your work, but also because they apply to other works that you may want to use in your seminars. Just about any musical composition is protected by copyright, and you may need to pay a royalty before you can play any music at any time during the seminar. You may, for instance, want to play some pleasant background music while attendees enter the seminar site. Your speaker, furthermore, may include music in her presentation. In both cases, you may be obligated to pay a royalty to the holder of the copyright on the music you plan to use. If you use music without paying a licensing fee for it, you may be charged a fine, based on your attendance. For more information on music licensing, contact the American Society of Composers, Authors and Publishers (ASCAP) at (800) 627-9805, and Broadcast Music Inc. (BMI) at (800) 669-4264.

Copyright

If your idea is an original work of authorship in written form, you can obtain protection under an American copyright. You can copyright cartoon characters, sculptures, paintings, plays, maps, songs, scripts, photos, books, and poems. Until recently, you had to publish a work before you could copyright it. But now, as long as you have fixed the material in some kind of tangible form, even if it's just a handwritten or typed manuscript, you can obtain this kind of protection.

All you need to do is include a copyright notice on the material. Three elements make up the copyright notice:

1. The word "copyright," the copyright symbol (©), or the abbreviation "copr."
2. The name of the owner of the copyright.
3. The year of first publication.

Here is an example of a typical copyright:

Copyright © by John Doe, 1996

There are five classes of copyrights:

1. Class TX: *Nondramatic Literary Works.* This broad category covers all types of published and unpublished works written in words or other verbal or numeric symbols. Some of the types of works included in this class are fiction, nonfiction, poetry, advertising copy, periodicals, textbooks, and reference works.
2. Class PA: *Works of the Performing Arts.* These are published and unpublished works created for the purpose of being "performed" before an audience, whether this performance is live or "by means of any device or process." Included in this category are drama, music, choreography, motion pictures, and audiovisual works.
3. Class SR: *Sound Recordings.* This category can apply in two instances: where the claimant seeks to copyright a sound recording alone, and where the claimant seeks to copyright a sound recording in addition to the musical, dramatic, or literary work embodied in the sound recording. This does not apply to the audio portion of a motion picture or other audiovisual work.
4. Class VA: *Works of the Visual Arts.* Pictorial, graphic, and sculptural works are protected under this category. Two-dimensional and three-dimensional works such as models, globes, and works of fine art are included, in addition to photography, technical drawings, maps, and advertisements.

5. Class RE: *Renewal Registration.* This category covers renewal of registration for works originally copyrighted before January 1, 1978. Extending copyright protection for an additional 47 years, this class applies to all classes of copyrights.

The typical procedure for filing is to send a copy of the work, with an official form, to the Copyright Office, Library of Congress, Washington, DC 20540; (202) 707-3000. There is a $20 fee for each application.

You should register your copyright even though a work is automatically copyrighted upon creation. In cases of infringement, it is always good to have a public record of your copyright and the date it went into effect. In fact, you may have to register your copyright with the Copyright Office to take an infringement suit to court.

Remember, the copyright protects only the uniqueness of the form in which you express your idea—not the idea itself.

Disclosure Document Program

You can protect an idea during the development stage through the Disclosure Document Program. This protection is valid for only two years. If you haven't filed for a patent during this time, your file will be destroyed. However, if you file for a patent within two years, the Patent Office will maintain your disclosure document in its files for the duration of the patent. This can be helpful in the event of a dispute or infringement suit.

To file, all you do is send the Patent Office the following five items: (1) a transmittal letter requesting that the enclosed disclosure be accepted under the Disclosure Document Program; (2) one photocopy of that letter; (3) a check to cover the filing fee; (4) a copy of your invention disclosure; and (5) a self-addressed, stamped envelope.

Your invention disclosure should be a signed document describing your invention's use, function, and structure, in addition to how it differs from similar inventions. Your document must be either a written explanation or a drawing of your invention. You may need to send photographs in duplicate and sign them to complete your file.

Some important details:

1. Number your pages and use paper that folds to less than 8 by 13 inches.

2. Sign and date two copies of the document, and have each copy witnessed by two people.

3. Send both copies to the U.S. Patent and Trademark Office, Washington, DC 20231. The commissioner will return one copy to you.

Trademark Registration

A trademark is any name, word, or symbol with which a business identifies its products, services, or organization. Legal protection for trademarks depends on how distinctive the law considers the trademark in question. Marks that describe a product's function or characteristic usually aren't granted protection because these names resemble everyday words and the government guarantees everybody's right to use them. Generally, names that are not in common usage—arbitrary, fanciful, or coined terms—receive protection.

Because you cannot register a mark with the Patent and Trademark Office before you use it in conjunction with some product or service, you must protect your mark during the development stage by means of a trade secret. Any information, design, process, formula, technique, device, or composition that is kept secret and gives a company a competitive edge in the market constitutes a trade secret.

Make sure your mark is not descriptive and that it is not already in use. Before you register your mark, use the trademark symbol properly on your product. To do so, you must insert the superscript "TM" or "(T)."

Once you have used your trademark, you should register it with the Patent and Trademark Office. After it is registered, you must indicate this protection by placing the symbol ® or "Reg. U.S. Patent & TM Off." on your trademark.

Four elements make up the trademark application. First, you will need a written application, including your name, citizenship, address, proof of prior use of the mark, the product on which you use the mark, and the class of merchandise. If you don't know which class your product falls into, you can contact the Patent and Trademark Office.

Second, you must submit a drawing of the mark. If you seek protection for a word, a number, or a combination thereof, you do not need to submit a drawing. You can simply type the word unit in capital letters on paper.

Third, five facsimiles or specimens of your trademark must accompany your application. The five specimens you submit must be duplicates of the actual trademark, but they must not exceed 8 by 13 inches. Specimens must be flat, not bulky or three-dimensional. If your trademark isn't flat, you can submit five photographs in place of the specimens.

Fourth, to complete your application, you must include the filing fee. For more information about trademarks, consult the following publications, produced by the Patent and Trademark Office: *Basic Facts About Registering a Trademark* and *Official Gazette—Trademarks*. Check with your library to see whether it has these publications. If it does not, you can order them from the U.S. Government Printing Office by calling (202) 512-1800.

ATTORNEYS

Finding the right lawyer, early in the formation of your business, is critical. Lawyers who can meet your needs should possess several key qualities. Among the most important traits are honesty, experience in your field, and availability. Keep looking until you find a lawyer you can trust and with whom you are comfortable.

Good, honest lawyers will tell you whether you are out of their principal line of practice and may refer you to another attorney who can do a better job for you. Choose a lawyer who has the time and willingness to sit down and talk with you, or to discuss a legal problem over the telephone when you need advice. If you keep calling your lawyer only to hear that "We'll get back to you" (and you don't hear anything until days or weeks later), find another practitioner who appreciates your business and has the time to do justice to your needs. A great lawyer you can't reach is worthless.

Closely related to availability is dependability. Make sure your lawyer can follow through on your problems. Lawyers are selling services. If your attorney can't provide services on time and satisfactorily—at a price consistent with their value—find one who will.

Make certain you understand your attorney's fee schedule; this is the biggest area of misunderstanding between clients and lawyers. It is best to have your agreement in writing. Generally, lawyers who are experts in business cannot be retained inexpensively. If you want excellent legal advice, you must be prepared to pay for it.

Once you have established a firm relationship with a good lawyer, you will have found an invaluable tool.

Searching for a Lawyer

Compile a list of prospects, beginning with those recommended to you by friends and relatives. Your accountant or banker may also be able to suggest a lawyer. Other sources include the telephone directory and the *Martindale-Hubbell Law Directory*, available in many public libraries and all law libraries. Most local bar associations also have referral services.

When Do You Need a Lawyer?

According to Richard D. Bank in *Business Start-Ups*,[1] there are certain situations in which you should consult a lawyer:

- Complying with regulations and licensing requirements.
- Preparing, negotiating, and executing contracts, franchise agreements, leases, letters of intent, and other legal documents.
- Buying or selling a business.
- Obtaining patents, copyrights, and trademarks.
- Extending warranties to the public.
- Extending credit to the public.
- Establishing employee relations policies, including hiring, discipline, evaluations, promotions, and termination.

Many entrepreneurs prefer to have one general lawyer handle all their needs. You can then rely on that lawyer to refer you to someone in a more specialized practice if the need arises.

INSURANCE: MANAGING RISK

Knowing what kind of insurance to carry, and how much, is an important aspect of good risk management. Consider: (1) the size of the potential loss; (2) the probability of the loss; and (3) the resources available to meet the loss if it should occur.

There isn't a single business that can possibly eliminate or transfer all of its risks. You must assume some of the risks of your venture. To decide whether you should transfer a particular risk to an insurance company, figure the maximum potential loss that might result. If the loss would force your company into bankruptcy or cause serious financial damage, don't assume the risk.

Contrary to popular opinion, a high probability of loss doesn't mean you should insure against the risk. In fact, the greater the probability, the less appropriate the purchase of insurance.

Losses that occur with relative frequency (such as bad-debt losses) are predictable and typically small, and you can assume them without too much financial difficulty. They are often budgeted as part of the normal costs of doing business and are figured into the prices charged to customers. Also, where the probability of loss is high, a more effective method of controlling the loss is to adopt appropriate precautionary measures. The key to purchasing insurance (and all risk management) is: *Do not risk more than you can afford to lose.*

Insurance Planning

Begin by considering the insurable risks your business faces. In general, insurance can cover the following risks:

1. Loss or damage of property—including merchandise, supplies, fixtures, and building.
2. Loss of income resulting from interruption of business caused by damage to the firm's operating assets.
3. Personal injury to employees and the general public.
4. Loss to the business caused by the death or disability of key employees or the owner.

A standard fire insurance policy pays the policyholder only for losses directly due to fire. Other indirect losses, known as consequential losses, may be even more important to your company's welfare. You can protect yourself against these losses by obtaining business-interruption insurance. Some consequential losses are:

1. Loss of use of a facility.
2. Continuing expenses after a fire—salaries, rents paid in advance, interest obligations, and so on.
3. Extra expenses of obtaining temporary quarters.
4. If you are a landlord, loss of rental income on buildings damaged or destroyed by fire.

The basic business package, many experts agree, consists of four fundamental coverages—(1) general liability, (2) workers' compensation, (3) auto, and (4) property/casualty—plus an added layer of protection over them, often called an umbrella policy.

Under common law, as well as workers' compensation laws, you as an employer are liable for injury to employees at work caused by your failure to: provide safe equipment and working conditions, hire competent fellow employees, or warn employees of an existing danger. In every state, an employer must insure against potential workers' compensation claims. However, employee coverage and the extent of the employer's liability vary from state to state.

Overall, commercial general liability coverage insures a business against accidents and injury that might occur on its premises, as well as exposures related to its products. In some cases, this liability may even extend to trespassers. As a business owner, you may also be liable for bodily injuries to customers, pedestrians, delivery people, and other outsiders—even in cases where you have exercised "reasonable care."

The real trick with general liability is to determine how much coverage you need. The soundest approach is to figure out how much you can be sued for and buy the appropriate coverage.

Cars and trucks are sources of liability. Even if you own no vehicles, under the "doctrine of agency," a business can be liable for injuries and property damage caused by employees operating their own or some-one else's car while on company business.

The company may have some coverage under the employee's own liability policy, but the limits might be grossly inadequate. If it is cus-tomary or convenient for employees to operate their own cars while on company business, as with salespeople on the road or covering a route, you should acquire nonownership liability insurance. You can insure five or more motor vehicles, operated as a fleet for business purposes, under a low-cost fleet policy.

Auto insurance is fairly straightforward, yet there are opportu-nities to save money here. The primary strategy is to increase your deductible. Also, pay attention to policy limits. Many states set mini-mum liability coverages that may be well below what you need. Some insurance experts recommend carrying at least $1 million in liability coverage.

When you purchase property/casualty coverage, some insurance experts recommend that you purchase all-risks coverage. Also, care-fully review the policy's exclusions. All policies cover loss by fire, but what about crises like explosions or hailstorms? You may want to con-sider buying coverage for all these types of risks. Whenever possible, consider replacement-cost insurance, which will replace your property at current prices, regardless of the cost when you bought the items. This offers protection from inflation. But make sure that your total re-placements do not exceed the policy cap.

Types of Coverage

You can purchase insurance to cover almost any risk. The following types of coverage are most common:

1. *Fire and general property insurance*—covering fire losses, van-dalism, hail, and wind damage.
2. *Plate glass insurance*—covering window breakage.
3. *Consequential loss insurance*—covering loss of earnings or extra expenses when business is suspended due to fire or other cata-strophe.
4. *Burglary insurance*—covering forced entry and theft of mer-chandise and cash.
5. *Fraud insurance*—covering counterfeit money, bad checks, and larceny.
6. *Public liability insurance*—covering injury to the public, such as a customer or pedestrian falling on the premises.

7. *Product liability insurance*—covering injury to customers arising from the use of goods purchased through the company.

8. *Workers' compensation insurance*—covering injury to employees at work.

9. *Life insurance*—covering the life of the owner(s) or key employee(s).

10. *Boiler insurance*—covering damage to the building premises caused by boiler explosion.

11. *Business-interruption insurance.*

12. *Malpractice insurance*—covering against claims from clients who suffer damages as a result of services you perform.

13. *Errors and omissions insurance*—covering against claims from customers who suffer injury or loss because of errors you made or things you should have done but failed to do.

If you choose to operate your business from home, consult your insurance agent or company to determine whether you need to obtain additional coverage. Your homeowner's policy may be sufficient, but if you plan to store or use expensive machinery, such as a computer, you may require additional coverage.

Obtaining Coverage

After listing your insurable risks and the types of insurance available to cover them, decide how much of a loss you can afford to bear yourself and the possible losses that you would prefer to transfer, and then look at an insurance company's premiums for assuming part of the risk. Seek cost estimates from at least two reliable insurance agents and carefully evaluate them before buying any coverage. Explore package insurance policies at discounted rates.

Look in the Yellow Pages under the "Insurance" heading to find companies that specialize in business insurance. If your business is unusual in any way, having the services of a company that specializes is most important. Look for an insurance agent who can assist you in planning risk management as your business grows.

6

RECORD KEEPING AND TAXES

There are two reasons to keep records of a business operation: (1) records are required by law, and (2) they are useful to you as a manager. Maintaining accurate records is vital to the day-to-day operation of your seminar business. Information about your business's financial condition will help you identify and correct income or expense problems before they become major catastrophes.

You must also keep records to determine your tax liabilities. Regardless of the type of bookkeeping system you use, your records must be permanent, accurate, and complete, and they must clearly establish income, deductions, credits, employee information, and anything else specified by federal, state, and local regulations. The law does not require that you keep particular kinds of records, but they must be complete and separate for each business.

When you start in business, establish the type and arrangement of books and records most suitable for your operation, keeping in mind when your tax liabilities fall due. If you are not competent in this area, seek the aid of a professional accountant. Your system for good record keeping is set up only once, for the life of your business. Doing it efficiently makes things easier later.

ACCOUNTING METHODS

Business owners typically use one of two accounting systems for record-keeping purposes: cash basis or accrual basis. The better choice for your seminar business depends on your sales volume, your business's legal form, and whether you extend credit.

Cash Basis

In cash basis accounting, you conduct business and pay taxes according to your real-time cash flow. Cash income begins as soon as you ring up a sale on the register or receive payment in a check. You pay expenses as they occur. Cash income and expenses are put on the books and charged to the period in which they are received or paid.

With a cash basis system, you can defer income to the following year as long as you haven't actually or constructively received it in the present year. A check you receive in the present year but do not cash until the following year is still income to you for the present year. If you want to shift income to the following year, you will have to delay billing until the following year or bill so late in the present year that a present-year payment is unlikely.

If you want to accelerate expenses to the present year, you should pay the bills you have received and log them as the present year's expenses. An expense you charge to a credit card will count as an expense in the year you charged it, not when you pay the card company. Be careful about paying next year's expenses in advance. Generally, expenses prepaid in excess of one month have to be prorated over the specified payment period. However, you can currently deduct dues and subscriptions if they are prepaid for the forthcoming year.

Accrual Basis

With accrual basis accounting, you charge income and expenses to the period to which they (should) apply, whether you have paid or received money or not. You report income when you bill. You deduct expenses when you are billed, not when you pay. This accounting method offers more tax benefits to a company with a small amount of receivables and large amounts of current liabilities. Advance payments to an accrual basis taxpayer are considered taxable income in the year in which they are received.

A contractor, for instance, would record all expenses related to a project during the period in which the contract was to have been paid, even if the client has not yet paid the billed amount. If an employee works for you this month but you haven't paid for the work done, you still take the deduction for that expense because the person has earned the money.

The accrual method is mandatory for purchases and sales when and where inventories are used in the business. Under the Tax Reform Act of 1986, if your gross sales receipts exceed $5 million per year and your business is a corporation, partnership, or trust, the IRS will not permit you to use the cash method. You must use the accrual accounting method. Some businesses can use the cash method of accounting no matter how large the gross receipts are: farms, partnerships without corporate partners, sole proprietorships, and "qualified" personal service corporations (those in the fields of health, law, accounting, actuarial science, or consulting). In addition, shareholders who perform services for the corporation must own 95 percent of the stock.

If you choose accrual basis accounting, you must use it for all reports and credit purposes. If you run two or more businesses at the same time, you may use different accounting methods for each business. One business can be on the cash basis and the other, on the accrual basis.

RECORD KEEPING

Keep your record-keeping system as simple as possible. Your time is valuable, and if your records are too complex, you will spend too much time maintaining them. If complicated records are unavoidable, hire an accountant or bookkeeper to maintain them. The data you enter into your records should have a direct bearing on the financial condition of your seminar promoting business. Don't maintain irrelevant records.

Bookkeeping Systems

Double-entry bookkeeping, which makes use of journals and ledgers, is the usual method of keeping business records. The bookkeeper first enters transactions in a journal, and then posts monthly totals to the appropriate ledger accounts. The five categories of ledger accounts are: (1) income, (2) expense, (3) assets, (4) liabilities, and (5) net worth. Income and expense accounts are closed each year; asset, liability, and net worth accounts are maintained on a permanent and continuous basis.

Although it is not as complete as the double-entry method, you may use single-entry bookkeeping effectively in a small business, especially during its early years. The single-entry system can be relatively simple. The bookkeeper records the flow of income and expense through a daily summary of cash receipts, a monthly summary of receipts, and a monthly disbursements journal (such as a checkbook). This system is entirely adequate for the tax purposes of many small businesses.

Records to Keep

Four basic records that your seminar business will generate and must account for are:

1. Sales records.
2. Cash receipts.
3. Cash disbursements.
4. Accounts receivable.

Sales records include all income derived from the sales of products (at your seminars, through catalogs, and so on) or from the seminars themselves. You can group them into one large category called *gross sales,* or into several subcategories that depict different product/service lines, so you know what's doing well and what isn't.

Cash receipts account for all income generated through cash sales and the collection of accounts receivable. This is actual collected income and doesn't include earnings from your sales records unless you operate a cash-and-carry business. In a cash-and-carry business, your cash receipts theoretically match your sales records.

Cash disbursements are sometimes called operating expense records, or accounts payable. You should make all disbursements by check if possible, so you can document business expenses for tax purposes. If you must make a cash payment, you should include a receipt for the payment—or at least an explanation of it—in the business records. File all canceled checks, paid bills, and other documents that substantiate the entries in the business records in an orderly manner, and store them in a safe place. Breaking the cash disbursement headings into different categories, such as rent, maintenance, and advertising, may simplify your expense records.

Establish a petty cash fund to cover expenses that are immediate and small enough to warrant payment by cash. The Small Business Administration suggests that you account for petty cash by cashing a check for the purpose of petty cash and placing the money in a safe or lock box. Record items purchased from the petty cash fund on a form that lists the date, amount, and purpose of the purchase. When the petty cash fund is almost exhausted, total the cost of all the items and write a check for the resulting amount to replenish the account.

Accounts receivable are sales stemming from the extension of credit, such as when you bill a corporation for a seminar put on exclusively for its employees and present an invoice at the conclusion of the event. Maintain these records on a monthly basis so you can age your receivables and determine how long your credit customers are taking to pay their bills. If an account ages beyond 60 days, investigate why the customer is taking so long to pay. We will cover the extension and collection of credit in Chapter 7.

OTHER RECORDS YOU SHOULD RETAIN

Keep any records that support entries on a federal tax return until the statute of limitations expires (usually, three years after the return is due). Keep copies of your federal income tax returns forever; they may even be helpful to the executor of your estate. Maintain careful records for three other important items: (1) capital equipment, (2) insurance, and (3) payroll.

Capital Equipment

Keep records of major equipment purchases so you can determine your depreciation expenses for tax purposes. Don't keep records on small items like staplers, tape recorders, and answering machines. Don't list leased equipment in this section; maintain it under cash disbursements instead (you do not own it). Leased equipment is a liability that is payable each month.

Maintain records only on capital equipment you have purchased, whether outright, on a contract, or through a chattel mortgage. Major equipment you have purchased is considered an asset even though you may have financed it. As you pay off your loan obligation, you build equity in the equipment which you can list on your balance sheet as an asset.

Your equipment records should include the purchase date for each piece of equipment, the vendor's name, a brief description of the item, how you paid for it, the check number if appropriate, and the full amount of the purchase.

Insurance

Keep all records pertaining to your company's insurance policies. Include any special coverage you may obtain to decrease the risk of liability in a specific area. List the carriers of the policies and the underwriting agents who issued the coverages. Maintain records on any claims made against your policies, to resolve any misunderstandings that may arise.

When updating your records, enter all information about the payment of premiums: the date a check was written, the amount, and the policy (description and number) for which it was written. This will help with payment disputes and tax preparation.

Payroll

Any employer, regardless of the number of employees, must maintain all records pertaining to payroll taxes (income tax withheld, Social Security, and federal unemployment tax) for at least four years after the tax becomes due or is paid, whichever is later.

Under a payroll tax law that went into effect in January 1993, companies need to look back at the payroll taxes they paid from July 1 to June 30 of the following year. If the accumulated taxes are less than $50,000, employers remit taxes monthly; if they are more than $50,000, employers remit semiweekly. If you accumulate or owe more than $100,000 in payroll taxes during any semiweekly or monthly period, then you become a semiweekly depositor for the balance of the year, and for all of the following year.

New deposit rules have also tightened the "safe harbor" for underpayments. Under the old rules, employers were not penalized if their deposit was within 5 percent of the amount owed. Now, the safe harbor is 2 percent or $100, whichever is greater. For monthly depositors, the shortfall is due on the date the employer files the quarterly Form 941; for semiweekly depositors, the due date for shortfalls is the first Wednesday or Friday following the 15th of the following month. After these grace periods, the penalties start to apply. There are 20 different kinds of employment records that you must maintain just to satisfy federal requirements. These records are summarized as follows:

Income Tax Withholding Records

1. Name, address, and Social Security number of each employee.
2. Amount and date of each payment of compensation.

3. Amount of wages subject to withholding in each payment.
4. Amount of withholding tax collected from each payment.
5. Reason why the taxable amount is less than the total payment.
6. Statements relating to employees' nonresident alien status.
7. Market value and date of noncash compensation.
8. Information about payments made under sick-pay plans.
9. Withholding exemption certificates.
10. Agreements regarding the voluntary withholding of extra cash.
11. Dates and payments to employees for nonbusiness services.
12. Statements of tips received by employees.
13. Requests for different computation of taxes withheld.

Social Security (FICA) Tax Records

1. Amount of each payment subject to FICA tax.
2. Amount and date of FICA tax collected from each payment.
3. Explanation for the difference, if any.

Federal Unemployment Tax (FUTA) Records

1. Total amount paid during calendar year.
2. Amount subject to unemployment tax.
3. Amount of contributions paid into the state unemployment fund.
4. Any other information requested on the unemployment tax return.

A good pegboard or "one-write" system simplifies payroll for a small firm. Any office supply store can show you samples of different one-write systems. A good accounting clerk can learn how to use one in about 15 minutes. Most accountants recommend these systems because they reduce errors and save time in making payroll entries.

Business Papers

Carefully preserve all purchase invoices, receiving reports, copies of sales slips, invoices sent to business firm customers, canceled checks, receipts for cash paid out, and cash register tapes. These are not only essential to maintaining good records but may also be important if legal or tax questions ever arise.

How Long Should I Keep These Records?

Price Waterhouse, an international accounting firm, offers the following guidelines:

- Income tax, revenue agents' reports, protests, court briefs and appeals: Retain indefinitely.
- Annual financial statements: Retain indefinitely.
- Monthly financial statements used for internal purposes: Retain for three years.
- Books of account, such as the general ledger and general journal: Retain indefinitely.
- Cash books: Retain indefinitely, unless posted regularly to the general ledger.
- Subsidiary ledgers: Retain for three years. (Ledgers are the actual books—or the magnetic tapes, disks, or other media on which the ledgers and journals are stored.)
- Canceled payroll and dividend checks: Retain for six years.
- Income tax payment checks: Retain indefinitely.
- Bank reconciliations, voided checks, check stubs, and check register tapes: Retain for six years.
- Sales records, such as invoices, monthly statements, remittance advisories, shipping papers, bills of lading, and customers' purchase orders: Retain for six years.
- Purchase records, including purchase orders, payment vouchers authorizing payment to vendors, and vendors' invoices: Retain for six years.
- Travel and entertainment records, including account books, diaries, and expense statements: Retain for six years.
- Documents substantiating fixed asset additions, such as the amounts and dates of additions or improvements, details related to retirements, depreciation policies, and salvage values assigned to assets: Retain indefinitely.
- Personnel and payroll records, such as payments and reports to taxing authorities, including federal income tax withholding, FICA contributions, unemployment taxes, and workers' compensation insurance: Retain for four years.

- Corporate documents, including certificate of incorporation, corporate charter, constitution and bylaws; deeds and easements; stock, stock transfer, and stockholder records; minutes of board of directors' meetings; retirement and pension records; labor contracts; and licenses, patents, trademarks, and registration applications: Retain indefinitely.

Recording Transactions

A manual or a one-write system automatically records financial transactions in the cash disbursements journal. This system is popular with many small businesses because it saves time. If you are only writing two dozen checks per month, it makes sense to use a manual or one-write system. Maintaining your general ledger on a regular basis should give you all the financial information you need to make good business decisions. This type of system works well with personal service businesses. An accountant, for example, pays the rent and some miscellaneous bills, perhaps writing only 20 checks per month. Although CPAs use computers for many clients, they often do their own books manually because their practice requires very few checks.

If you write a lot of checks each month, consider changing to batch processing of your general ledger postings. A data processing service will handle this for you. First, develop expense codes for the types of checks you write. Make an adding machine tape of the checks, showing their codes and payable amounts, and send the tape to the data processing center. You will get back a computer printout of your general ledger, with all of your checks listed according to their expense codes.

If you are spending a lot of cash rather than paying by check, list your cash expenditures on an expense report form. On the form, which is readily available at stationery stores, are designated categories: travel, entertainment, office supplies, and so on. Attach the relevant receipts to the page of the form where the expenditure is entered. Your bookkeeper adds the expense codes and writes you a check for the reimbursement of expenses. Ultimately, therefore, all cash disbursements—even out-of-pocket expenses—are handled by check. If you spend $200 out of pocket, for example, fill out an expense report and pay yourself for what you spent. In this way, you know you entered those expenses into your bookkeeping system.

It is essential that you try to pay as much as you can by check, to have a record of all debits to your company. Most bookkeepers agree that it is best to work out of one checkbook for the business. Nothing bothers an accountant more than interaccount transfers—the source of many financial problems with businesses. You risk recording an investment in the business as income, or making a similar mistake.

In some lines of business, legal restrictions prevent the owner from running the business out of one checkbook. Lawyers and collection agents are usually required by law to maintain trust accounts on behalf of their clients. These accounts represent money held in trust on the client's behalf until it is disbursed in the form of client receipts (like court-awarded damages or collection moneys) or, ultimately, service fees.

ACCOUNTANTS

A good accountant will be your single most important outside adviser. The services of a lawyer and consultant are vital during specific periods in the development of your business or in times of trouble, but your accountant will have the greatest impact on the success or failure of your business.

Once you are in business, you will have to decide whether your volume warrants a full-time bookkeeper, an outside accounting service, or merely a year-end accounting and tax-preparation service. Even the smallest unincorporated businesses employ outside public accountants to prepare their financial statements.

When you borrow money, your bank manager will want to see your balance sheet and your operating statement. If they have been prepared by a reputable public accountant, they will be more credible than if you prepared them yourself. (If you are borrowing less than $500,000, most banks will accept unaudited financial statements prepared by a public accountant.)

Public accountants must meet certain proficiency levels in order to be licensed by the states in which they practice. This does not ensure that an independent business accountant will do a good job for you, but it does reduce your chances of running into an unqualified accountant.

If you are organizing a corporation, your accountant should counsel you during start-up to determine how to manage your taxes. If you are starting a sole proprietorship or a partnership, you'll want the accountant to set up a bookkeeping system you can operate internally.

Experienced independent accountants will usually be familiar with the accounting problems peculiar to your business, and will be able to direct you wisely. Before the calendar year ends, always ask your accountant to organize your records for that tax year.

An accountant should, ideally, help organize the statistical data concerning your business, assist in charting future actions based on past performance, and advise you on your overall financial strategy regarding purchasing, capital investment, and other matters related to your business goals. Today, however, accountants spend much of their time keeping clients in compliance with shifting interpretations of laws and regulations.

Because accountants specialize in knowing the legal requirements you must meet, you need their services if you expect to succeed. If you spend your time researching answers to perplexing questions—questions that accountants can answer more efficiently—you will not have the time to manage your business properly. Spend your time doing what you do best, and leave the accounting to the experts.

To find a good accountant, ask other small business owners, your banker, or your lawyer for recommendations. Accountants' fees, like those of lawyers, doctors, and other professionals, vary widely. Small-town accountants in business for themselves may charge $60 and up per hour; some of the large, nationally known firms might charge $100 to $250 per hour or more.

TAXES

As a business owner and employer, you will be responsible for collecting various state and federal taxes and remitting them to the proper agencies. You will also have to pay certain taxes yourself.

The tax information given here reflects current law at press time. Congress has been passing tax legislation at the rate of one major act every two years. Therefore, check for any major tax changes before making a decision that will affect the tax structure of your business.

Employer Tax Identification Number

You are required to withhold income tax and Social Security tax from each employee's paycheck and to remit these withheld amounts to the proper agencies. File IRS Form SS-4 to request an employer tax number from the federal government. If your state has an income tax, get a number from the state as well. Call the local offices of the IRS and your state's tax department and place your request. The federal agency will send you your number as well as charts for calculating payroll tax deductions, quarterly and annual forms, W-4 forms, tax-deposit forms, and an instruction manual explaining how to fill out the forms. No advance fees or deposits are required.

All corporations and partnerships are required to have an Employer Identification Number (EIN), whether or not they have employees. Sole proprietorships, however, don't need an EIN unless they have employees or a Keogh retirement plan.

If you are a sole proprietor and plan to hire an employee, call the IRS at (800) TAX-FORM and ask for a copy of Form SS-4.

Income Tax Withholding

The amount of pay-as-you-go tax you must withhold from each employee's wages depends on the employee's wage level, the number of exemptions claimed on the employee's withholding exemption certificate (Form W-4), the employee's marital status, and the length of the payroll period. The percentage withheld is figured on a sliding basis, and IRS percentage tables are available for weekly, biweekly, monthly, and other payroll periods.

Call the IRS at (800) TAX-FORM and ask for a copy of *Circular E: Employer's Tax Guide.*

Social Security (FICA) Tax

The Federal Insurance Contributions Act (FICA) requires employers to withhold two different kinds of taxes: Social Security and Medicare. You need to know the difference between the two taxes because the rates are different.

As of 1997, the FICA tax (for both employers and employees) is 6.2 percent for Old-Age, Survivors', and Disability Insurance (OASDI), commonly known as Social Security, for wages through $62,700, and 1.45 percent for Medicare (on all earnings; there is no limit). For self-employed individuals, the 1997 OASDI tax rate is 12.4 percent on wages through $62,700 and 2.9 percent for Medicare (on all earnings; no limit).

As an employer, you have two responsibilities in regard to FICA: (1) you must withhold 7.65 percent of your employees' wages for FICA; (2) you must pay another 7.65 percent, matching the amount withheld as Social Security tax.

Both the federal withholding tax and the full 15.3 percent FICA tax are reported on Form 941, Federal Payroll Tax Return. You need to file Form 941 quarterly, and as long as total taxes due per quarter are less than $500, you can pay the entire amount when you file the return. The returns are due the last day of the month following the end of the quarter.

As a new employer, if you don't fall under the less-than-$500 quarterly exemption, you qualify with the IRS as a monthly depositor.

You must deposit FICA and federal withholding for every calendar month by the 15th day of the following month. You must deposit January taxes, for example, by February 15. You must make monthly deposits with Form 8109, Federal Tax Deposit (FTD) Coupon. If you are a new employer, the IRS will send you an FTD coupon book five to six weeks after you receive your EIN.

Charts and instructions for Social Security deductions come with the IRS payroll forms. Be aware that Congress has recently accelerated the requirements for depositing FICA and withholding taxes. Failure to comply subjects a business to substantial penalties.

You must file four different reports with the IRS district director in connection with the payroll taxes (both FICA and income taxes) withheld from your employees' wages:

1. Quarterly return of taxes withheld on wages (Form 941).
2. Annual statement of taxes withheld on wages (Form W-2).
3. Reconciliation of quarterly returns of taxes withheld with annual statement of taxes withheld (Form W-3).
4. Annual Federal Unemployment Tax Return (Form 940).

Federal Unemployment Tax

In addition to the FICA taxes withheld, the Federal Unemployment Tax Act (FUTA) requires payment under certain conditions. If during the calendar year you paid total wages of $1,500 or more in any quarter or had any employee who worked at least one day during 20 different weeks, you must pay FUTA tax on behalf of your employees.

The FUTA rate is 6.2 percent of the first $7,000 of wages. Any state unemployment tax rate you pay is subtracted from your federal rate, up to 5.4 percent. If you qualify for the full 5.4 percent credit, your FUTA rate could drop to 0.8 percent. You pay your employee's FUTA tax when you file Form 940, Employer's Annual Federal Unemployment Tax Return, or Form 940EZ with restrictions. Form 940 is due on or before January 31st of the following year.

W-2 and W-3 Forms

Form W-2 gives the employee and the government a record of the employee's earnings and the sums withheld for federal income tax, state income tax, and FICA taxes. The form must also contain the employee's full name, address, and Social Security number.

Form W-2, Wage and Tax Statement, is a five-part form that must be mailed or delivered to each employee by January 31st of the following tax year. The employee gets three copies, the fourth copy is for the company's records, and the fifth copy is to be mailed to the Social Security Administration (SSA). The SSA's copies of Form W-2 must be summarized on Form W-3, Transmittal of Income and Tax Statements, and mailed to the SSA by February 28.

State Payroll Taxes

Almost all states have payroll taxes of some kind that employers must collect and remit to the appropriate agencies. Most states have an unemployment tax that is paid entirely by the employer. The tax, figured as a percentage of a company's total payroll, is remitted at the end of each year. The actual percentage varies with the state and the employer.

Some states impose an income tax that must be deducted from each employee's paycheck. As an employer, you are responsible for collecting this tax and remitting it to the state. A few states have a disability insurance tax that you must deduct from employees' pay; in some states, this tax may be split between employer and employee.

Most states have patterned their tax-collecting systems after the federal government's. They issue similar forms, employer numbers, and instruction booklets. As discussed above, you may apply for the employer number and request various forms and booklets by calling the local office of the appropriate state agency.

Independent Contractors

If you hire individuals as independent contractors, you have to file an annual information return (Form 1099) to report payments totaling $600, or more, made to any individual in the course of trade or business during the calendar year. If you do not file this form, you will be subject to penalties. Be sure your records list the name, address, and Social Security number of every independent contractor you hired, along with pertinent dates and the amounts paid to each person. Every payment should be supported by an invoice submitted by the contractor.

Other than licensed real estate agents, very few people who perform services on your premises qualify as independent contractors. The IRS uses 20 criteria to determine whether a worker is an employee or an independent contractor. If a person performs services for more than one firm, determines how the work is to be done, uses his or her own tools, hires and pays his or her own employees, and works for a fee rather than a salary, the person is an independent contractor. If the IRS feels a worker whom you treated as a contractor should have been treated as an employee, you will be liable for payroll taxes that should have been withheld and paid, plus penalties and interest.

An independent contractor must have:

1. A business license.
2. Business cards, stationery, and a real business address.
3. A business bank account.
4. Various customers he or she regularly services.

To support the position that a worker is an independent contractor, businesses should describe the method of payment as based on a job rather than on time worked, and avoid establishing hours of work; avoid non-compete or exclusivity clauses, and indicate the person can work for anyone else; allow the independent contractor to determine who will perform the work and how it is to be done; provide for termination of service under specified conditions but avoid employment-at-will language; permit the independent contractor to provide supplies, tools, and equipment; and indicate that the independent contractor is responsible for any damage, errors, or losses in connection with the engagement.

Personal Income Tax

Operating as a sole proprietor or partner, you will not receive a salary; therefore, no income tax will be withheld from the money you take out of your business for personal use. Instead, you must estimate your tax liability each year and pay it in quarterly installments, using Form 1040 ES. Your local IRS office will supply the forms and instructions for filing estimated tax returns. When applying for the forms, also request the *Tax Guide for Small Business* (Publication 334).

At the end of the year, you must file an income tax return as an individual and compute your tax liability on the profits your business earned during that year.

Corporate Income Tax

If your business is organized as a corporation, you will be paid a salary like other employees. Any profit the business makes will accrue to the corporation, not to you personally. At the end of the year, you must file a corporate income tax return.

Corporate tax returns may be prepared on a calendar-year or fiscal-year basis. If the tax liability of the business is calculated on a calendar-year basis, you must file the tax return with the IRS no later than March 15.

Reporting income on a fiscal-year cycle is more convenient for most businesses because they can end their tax year in any month they choose. Pursuant to the 1986 Tax Reform Act, a corporation whose income is primarily derived from the personal services of its shareholders must use a calendar-year end for tax purposes. Most Subchapter S corporations also have to use the calendar-year end.

Sales Taxes

Sales taxes are levied by many cities and states, at varying rates. Most provide specific exemptions for certain classes of merchandise or particular groups of customers. Service businesses are often exempt altogether. Contact your state and/or local revenue offices for information on the law in your area so you can adapt your bookkeeping to the appropriate requirements.

You will need to distinguish tax-exempt sales from taxable sales. You can then deduct tax-exempt sales from total sales when filing your sales tax returns each month. Remember, if you fail to collect all taxes, you can be held liable for the full amount of uncollected tax.

Advance Deposits

Many states will require you to make an advance deposit against future taxes. In lieu of the deposit, state tax bureaus may accept a surety bond from your insurance company. If you have a good credit record, the bond is usually simple to obtain. The cost varies according to the amount and the risk; 5 percent is the norm, but 10 percent is not unusual for small dollar amounts.

If your state requires a deposit or bond, you can keep the amount down by estimating sales on the low side. This is wise because most new business owners tend to overestimate early sales.

The Reseller Permit

In many states, wholesalers or manufacturers will not sell to you at wholesale prices unless you can show them your sales tax permit or number, also called a reseller's or seller's permit. You will usually have to sign a tax card, to put your signature in their files.

Different agencies issue these permits in different states, but generally an Equalization Board, a State Sales Tax Commission, or a Franchise Tax Board will be the issuer. Contact the entity responsible for governing taxes in your state, and apply for your resale tax or wholesale permit. You will have to provide documentation to prove you are a retailer; your business permit will usually be acceptable.

A resale permit allows you to avoid paying sales tax on merchandise at the time you purchase it from suppliers. This does not mean you won't be remitting taxes on the merchandise; you are only deferring them until you sell the merchandise to your customers. You will add the sales taxes (where applicable) to their purchases. You will then remit the taxes with the appropriate forms.

When conducting business across state lines, you are not required to collect taxes for any other states except those in which you maintain offices.

STANDARD BUSINESS DEDUCTIONS

G & A Expenses

Among the deductible *general and administrative (G & A) expenses* of your business are *all* office expenses: telephone bills, utilities, office rent, salaries, legal and accounting expenses, professional services, dues, and subscriptions to business publications.

Many people working out of their homes want to claim a home office expense. That deduction was severely limited by the 1986 Tax Reform Act, which stated that a person could claim a home office deduction only if that office was the sole and primary place of doing business. If you have another office somewhere, you will not be able to deduct the cost of a home office. You might still deduct the cost of some business-related telephone calls made from your home, as well as the cost of business equipment and supplies, but you will not be able to deduct any part of your rent or depreciate any part of the property as a business expense.

A deduction is allowable for that portion of your home which you use exclusively and regularly as your principal place of business. Normally, you must use this portion of your residence to meet clients, to store inventory, and to perform your work. If you perform the majority of your work somewhere else, the home office may not be deductible.

Eligible home-office expenses include all normal office expenses plus interest, taxes, insurance, and depreciation on the portion of your home you use exclusively as your office. The total amount of the deduction is limited by the gross income you derive from that business activity, minus all of your other business expenses apart from those related to the home office. You cannot use a home office to produce tax losses for an otherwise profitable business. You can carry over any disallowed losses and use them in a year in which you do not exceed the limitation.

Home-office expenses are generally based on the ratio of the square footage used exclusively for business to the total square footage of the residence.

The Deficit Reduction Act of 1984 severely limits the conditions under which you can use computers in the home to limit tax liability. A home computer used for business more than 50 percent of the time can qualify for appropriate business deductions or credits. Business owners using home computers have to document business and personal use of the machine in writing.

Section 179

The biggest tax break for start-up entrepreneurs is the newly revised rule on depreciation for equipment purchased in 1993 and after. As explained in Chapter 3, the government allows you to take a depreciation deduction based on the usable life of equipment purchased for your business. One such depreciation deduction, Section 179, allows you to deduct up to $17,500 for equipment you use in the course of business. This deduction had previously been $10,000.

Therefore, if you purchased equipment on or after January 1, 1993, you are allowed a one-time deduction up to $17,500 for each piece of equipment, provided that (1) your total does not exceed $200,000 and (2) the amount is less than or equal to your taxable income. If the amount exceeds your taxable income, you would then carry the excess forward to the next tax year.

Automobile Expenses

Almost everybody doing business in the United States has to drive an automobile to conduct that business. At this writing, business-related automobile mileage is deductible at $0.31 a mile. Keep abreast of any changes the IRS may make.

Calculating your straight mileage deduction is very simple. Suppose you drive a car 20,000 miles a year, and 12,000 of those miles are for business purposes. Your deduction is $0.31 × 12,000 miles, or $3,720.

The distance you drive from your home to your place of business is not deductible, but mileage you drive from your place of business to any other location for business purposes is. Business miles accumulate when you drive for the purpose of either *doing* business or *seeking* business. Distances covered when you go to talk to a potential customer, or you do something to promote your business, would be considered business mileage. Keep in mind that you have to maintain a log of your business miles for tax purposes. Enter your mileage on your appointment calendar at the end of each day.

Another method of deducting the cost of driving uses actual operating expenses. The deductible expenses are depreciation, garage rent, gas, insurance, lease fees, licenses, oil, parking fees, rental fees, repairs, tires, and tolls. For example, let us assume that you are going to take a depreciation deduction of $3,120. Add to this the following expenses for operating your car: insurance, $400; maintenance, $500; gasoline, $1,600. You have $5,620 in deductions. Take this number and multiply it by the fraction of business miles over total miles driven: 12,000 business miles divided by 20,000 total miles, or 60 percent. Sixty percent of $5,620 is $3,372. If you elect the second method, you get a deduction of $3,372 for the same mileage versus $3,720 for the straight mileage calculation. These are hypothetical amounts. Figuring your expenses one way won't necessarily give you a greater deduction than the other.

If you use this second method, you must stay with it for the life of the vehicle. If you sell the car for a profit, you have to take the depreciation off its cost to determine its tax basis. If you sell it for more than its base, you'll have a gain that will result in a tax at your regular income tax rate.

Generally, straight mileage is best if you are driving an older car for many miles. If you are driving a fairly new car with a fairly high cost (more than $10,000), the operating expenses/depreciation method might offer you more deductions.

Entertainment and Travel

If you entertain clients for promotional purposes, you have to maintain a log of the entertainment, travel, and related expenses you are entitled to deduct. Use a standard appointment calendar to record whom you were entertaining, the nature of the business, where you were, and how much money you spent. Contrary to popular belief, you do not need receipts for entertainment expenditures of less than $25—but you must record those amounts in your log. In certain instances, you can even claim business-related home entertainment as a deduction. Have clients or prospects sign a guest log. If you prepare a meal or serve drinks, your expenses are deductible as part of the expense of doing business.

Since 1994, the limit on business meals and entertainment dropped from 80 percent to 50 percent. You can deduct 50 percent of entertainment expenses.

For entertainment expenses, you must prove all of these elements:

1. Amount of expenditure.
2. Date of expenditure.
3. Name, address, and type of entertainment.
4. Reason for entertainment and the nature of the business discussion that took place. (General "good will" is *not* accepted by the IRS.)
5. Occupation of the person entertained.

A deduction is no longer permitted for travel, food, and lodging expenses incurred in connection with a conference, convention, or seminar related to investment activities such as real estate investments or stock investments. However, the cost of the actual seminar is still deductible.

Business travel deductions range from the cost of air, rail, bus, or auto fares and hotels and meals, to such incidental expenditures as dry cleaning, tips, and taxis. The rule is: You must stay overnight *on business* in order to claim travel/incidentals deductions.

The things you do to expand your awareness of and expertise in your field of business are tax-deductible. Accordingly, deductions are allowed for convention expenses. Rules limiting the amount that you can deduct for attending conventions in foreign countries have been toughened. Also, there are limits to the deductibility of conventions held on cruise ships.

The cost of getting to and from the convention and the cost of your stay there are deductible. If you stay three days after the convention ends, the expenses you incur during those three days would not be deductible. Deductions for your spouse are not allowed unless he or she is active in the business.

Dues and Subscriptions

Although prior law allowed a tax deduction for dues to clubs that the taxpayer could prove were used primarily to further a trade or business, the new tax act eliminates the deduction for club dues. You can, however, deduct subscriptions to professional, technical, and trade journals addressing your industry.

TAX ADJUSTMENTS

If the IRS wants to audit one of your tax returns, it must do so within three years of the time you filed it. The exception is that if the IRS alleges fraud for any reason, it may look at tax returns that you have filed at any time. Many cases involve deductions claimed with the intent to defraud the government out of tax revenues, or unreported income.

Assuming that you are doing a proper job of tracking your tax credits and liability, the IRS has three years to look at your records. The statute of limitations for assessment of taxes starts from the date you file your tax return. If you fail to file your tax return, the statute does not start to run.

This means you have three years to straighten out tax matters as they arise. If you discover something that results in a change in your taxable income in any of three previous years, you may file a one-page amended return, known as a Form 1040X, indicating any changes. It may mean you'll pay more taxes. On the other hand, if you were entitled to business deductions that you didn't take, you can file an amended return and claim a refund—plus interest.

TAX PLANNING

Good tax planning does more than minimize your taxes; it provides more money for your business or investments. As an entrepreneur, you should view tax savings as a potential source of working capital. There are two important rules to follow in your tax planning. First, don't incur an additional expense solely for the sake of getting an extra deduction. For instance, your accountant may tell you that you are in the 33 percent tax bracket and need more deductions. To get an extra $1,000 interest/expense deduction, you incur $1,000 in finance charges from credit card purchases. You do not incur these finance charges because of a cash-flow problem or for business reasons, but solely for the benefit of writing off $1,000. If you think you'll come out ahead because you saved $330 in taxes, think again. You actually lost money. In effect, you avoided paying one party $330 by giving another party $1,000. You just spent $670 out of your pocket.

The second rule to remember is that immediately deferring taxes allows you to use your money interest-free before paying it to the government. Interest rates may justify deferring taxes, though doing so may cost you more taxes in a later year.

Net Operating Loss Provision

According to the IRS, the goal of the net operating loss provision is to average out your tax liability. If your business is a C corporation, it can opt for various treatments. It can take its loss in the current year and apply it to previous years' tax returns to get a refund, or it can apply the loss forward 15 years to reduce future tax liabilities. A company can also apply the loss back 3 years, then take any leftover loss forward.

Taking advantage of this provision is fairly easy, but recently there have been some questions about the best way to use the net operating loss provision.

Under the rules governing the net operating loss provision, so-called "loss corporations" can first take their losses backward, against the previous years. Then, if any loss is left over, they can take it forward for up to 15 years. (If a company has any "unused" loss after 15 years, it may no longer apply it to any income and loses it.)

On the other hand, a company may elect to carry a loss immediately forward, in hopes of sheltering future income against higher tax rates. Be aware that this strategy could backfire if rates don't increase or if net income doesn't materialize. Once you make the election to carry it forward, you can never reverse it. Therefore, your seminar promotion business would give up the certain refund it would get at the time by applying the loss to last year's gain in return for uncertain tax savings that it won't realize for at least one year.

Estimated Tax Underpayments

If you have not paid sufficient amounts of estimated income tax, you may be able to avoid or reduce penalties for underpayment by arranging to increase the amounts withheld from the paychecks remaining in the present year. All withheld income tax is treated as if spread equally over the calendar year, even when a disproportionately large amount is withheld in December. Individuals required to make estimated tax payments should pay special attention to other techniques that may be beneficial, especially if their income is irregular or seasonal.

Any small business must carefully plan and analyze required tax payments because of the high nondeductible penalty rates in effect.

Equipment Purchases

Due to a $10,000 expensing deduction, the year's end is the time to buy business equipment. Under Section 179 of the Internal Revenue Code, this deduction is not prorated for the period of the year in which you hold and use the equipment. Consequently, you will get the same deduction whether you buy and use the equipment at the beginning or the end of the year.

You can only take this deduction for tangible personal property used in your business; you cannot take it for real estate or automobiles.

You can deduct up to $10,000 in equipment costs incurred in trade or business. You may take the expensing deduction in full even though you acquire and use the property in the last days of the year. But if you purchase the equipment in the present year and don't use it until the following year, the expensing deduction won't be allowed for the present year. You must reduce the cost basis for the equipment in computing its depreciation by the amount of the deduction.

Inventory Valuation

You don't automatically get a deduction for purchasing inventory for your business. You must reduce the amount paid for inventory purchases by the value of the inventory at the end of the year. For example, if you paid $10,000 for merchandise in one year, and your inventory at the end of the year was worth $7,000, you could deduct only $3,000 for purchases.

Changing how you value your inventory can save a substantial amount in taxes. Given the current inflationary trend, a switch to LIFO in a typical year will give your company a one-shot loss deduction for the price increase of your inventory. You can switch to LIFO by filing Form 970 with your tax return. Once you adopt the LIFO method, you will have to obtain IRS approval if you want to return to FIFO.

Postponing Income

If you are employed by someone else and expect to receive a year-end bonus or other additional compensation, you may want to defer receipt until the forthcoming year, especially if you will then be in a lower tax bracket. This is often the case with first-time entrepreneurs who quit their jobs without securing the steady sources of income they need until their new business breaks even. If your employer uses the accrual method of accounting, the bonus should still be deductible in the current year, provided it is fixed by year-end and paid shortly thereafter and the employer is legally obligated to pay it.

You may also want to negotiate with your employer an agreement to have part of your earnings deferred and paid in either one or several future years. Because the employer will have the use of the funds during the deferral period, you may add an interest factor. If certain requirements are met, deferred compensation will generally not be taxed to you and will not be deductible by your employer until actually paid.

You must compute projected tax liability to evaluate the desirability of postponing compensation. Any potential tax advantage of deferring compensation will be offset, at least in part, by the loss of interest or other income unless the deferred compensation is increased. Credit risk is another important factor to consider.

You should seek consultation prior to entering into deferred-compensation agreements. Deferring compensation may reduce your retirement or other benefits by reducing the base-period figure used in calculating the benefits. Also, special rules apply to employees of state and local governments and tax-exempt organizations.

Postponing the reporting of taxable investment income, if possible, is almost always advantageous because it enables you to defer taxes and use funds for an additional period of time. However, you must evaluate tax-rate prospects for future years.

Several methods are commonly used to defer income:

- *Treasury bills and bank certificates.* Investors in short-term securities can shift interest income forward into a succeeding year by buying Treasury bills or certain bank certificates with a term of one year (or less) that mature in the next year. This applies both to businesses and to individuals.

- *Savings bonds.* United States savings bonds have become more viable investments for some purposes. Bondholders may elect to postpone the tax on the interest until they cash in the bonds, which may be 30 or more years later if the Treasury continues to extend maturities as it has in the past. Alternatively, you can reduce or avoid the income tax by giving the bonds to children in low tax brackets at the time of purchase and have them elect to report the interest currently. This election, once made, applies to all savings bonds owned now or in the future, and the election cannot be reversed. The election by the children will not be considered an election by the donor. If you have accumulated untaxed savings bond interest for many years and now require current funds, you can extend the tax postponement if you exchange the bonds for Series HH bonds, which pay interest semiannually.

• *Deferred annuities.* You can postpone taxes on earnings from capital put aside for long-range goals by purchasing a deferred annuity. Annuities are arranged by contract with an insurance company. There is no tax deduction for the amount contributed, but all interest earned and compounded will be tax-free until it is withdrawn, which may be as late as age 70 for some plans. You may purchase deferred annuities in installments or with a single payment. Early withdrawals will be deemed taxable to the extent that the cash value of the contract exceeds the investment in the contract. It will only be possible to make a nontaxable early withdrawal of principal after any excess has been withdrawn as taxable income.

7

FINANCIAL MANAGEMENT

How you manage your financial assets will often determine whether you succeed or fail. Your capital is not merely a collection of money and property; it is a powerful business tool that deserves your careful attention. Because going into business for yourself is such a risky proposition, this capital should yield a higher rate of return than an ordinary investment would.

Making capital work for you requires careful management of your business, especially your current and future assets. This attention to assets is something many small business owners neglect. They get so caught up in their business that they fail to manage their finances. The responsibility of managing their finances then falls to their accountants, who diligently prepare the proper financial statements at least once a year but do not contribute the creativity and money market awareness needed to make assets grow. As long as their businesses make money, most entrepreneurs are content to continue the arrangement.

There is more to effective financial control than just generating financial statements. Financial control starts with a comprehensive record-keeping system that produces thorough accounting records on a daily basis. (See Chapter 6 for more information on forming a good accounting and record-keeping system.) Your accounting records will form the basis of your financial statements. You need to produce and update three key financial reports to manage your finances: (1) the income statement, (2) the balance sheet, and (3) the cash-flow statement.

Using these three reports, you can track assets, liabilities, the various components of working capital, and equity, in order to evaluate your business's financial performance, which these reports express in terms of dollars and percentages. By tracking the financial performance of your company, you can evaluate past performance and current performance, calculate financial ratios, and compare them to industry standards. This type of financial analysis can reveal your business's strengths and weaknesses as well as any recurring trends that will help you manage your finances better.

This chapter discusses the major tools used in financial planning, such as the financial statements each business should produce, financial analysis, working with banks, and credit management and collections.

Careful financial planning is necessary throughout the life of your business. You must efficiently manage your money so that you can:

1. Avoid an excessive investment in fixed assets.
2. Understand banking relationships better.
3. Maintain receivables and net working capital in proper proportion to sales.
4. Avoid excessive inventories.

All financial difficulties of all firms, regardless of size, can be traced to the violation of one or more of these principles of financial management.

FINANCIAL STATEMENTS

Financial statements are to business what scorecards are to athletic events. There are three important statements with which you should be familiar. They are integral for planning and for attracting start-up or expansion capital, and they will help you form your business plan—the blueprint that will guide your business. These statements are the *balance sheet*, the *profit and loss* or *income statement*, and the *cash-flow statement*.

The Balance Sheet

A balance sheet is a tabulation of a business's assets and liabilities, as well as its capital, at a given point in time (Table 7–1). A balance sheet

Table 7–1   Balance Sheet

This balance sheet shows the assets and liabilities of two hypothetical seminar promotion businesses. The low-end business has gross sales of $194,400 per year, while the high-end business grosses $954,624 per year. Both businesses are homebased. Because attendees must buy tickets before they can participate in a seminar, these businesses do not have any accounts receivable. The liabilities of both businesses consist of various expenses associated with the production and staging of the seminars.

Assets

Current Assets	Low	High
Cash	$16,200	$ 79,552
Inventory	0	8,352
Supplies	200	575
Total Current Assets	$16,400	$ 88,479

Fixed Assets	Low	High
Equipment	4,734	14,568
Total Fixed Assets	$ 4,734	$ 14,568
TOTAL ASSETS	$21,134	$103,047

Liabilities & Equity

Current Liabilities	Low	High
Seminar Expenses	$ 3,850	$ 45,388
Accounts Payable	815	4,007
Salaries	2,700	5,250
Utilities	400	5,250
Taxes	25	1,380
Total Current Liabilities	$ 7,790	$ 61,275

Equity/Capital	Low	High
Owner's Equity	$13,344	$ 41,772
Total Equity	$13,344	41,772
TOTAL LIABILITIES & EQUITY	$21,134	$103,047

is typically generated monthly, quarterly, or annually when the company's books are closed. The top portion of the balance sheet lists your company's assets—any items of wealth, economic utility, or value. Anything that contributes to the total value of your business is an asset. Assets can be classified as current assets or long-term (fixed) assets. Current assets are those assets that you will convert to cash or otherwise use within one year or less.

- *Cash.* All income derived from cash sales, as well as any assets that you have converted to cash during the accounting period. This term generally refers to all cash in checking, savings, and short-term investment accounts.
- *Accounts receivable.* Income generated through the extension of credit which you have yet to collect at the end of the accounting period, less an allowance for bad debt.
- *Inventory.* Supplies, and any items that you hand out or sell during your seminars/speaking engagements. When you determine the value of your inventory, allow for inventory loss.
- *Marketable securities.* All the company's short-term investments in items like stocks and bonds, which you can easily convert into cash in a period of one year or less.

Other assets that appear in the balance sheet are called long-term or fixed assets, because they are durable and will last more than one year. Following are examples of fixed assets:

- *Equipment.* The book value of all equipment, less depreciation.
- *Buildings.* The appraised value of all buildings the business owns, less depreciation.
- *Land.* The appraised value of all land the business owns.
- *Long-term investments.* Any of the company's investments that cannot be converted into cash in less than one year. Most companies just starting out will not have any long-term investments.
- *Miscellaneous assets.* All other long-term assets that do not fit into capital, plant, or investment categories. They might include patents, trade investment, or even good will, at least to the extent that you purchased it. These types of assets are generally known as intangible assets.

The bottom half of the balance sheet lists the liabilities of the business and the amount of equity or capital you have accumulated. Liabilities are a business's debts, its obligations to creditors. Like assets, liabilities may be classified as current or long-term. If the debts are due in one year or less, they are classified as current liabilities. If they are due in more than one year, they are long-term liabilities.

Current liabilities indicate the company's short-term cash requirements; you must pay for them *with cash* within a year. Following are some examples of current liabilities:

- *Accounts payable.* Amounts owed to suppliers of goods and services, which are due and payable in a year or less.

- *Accrued liabilities.* Expenses like operating costs, sales commissions, and property tax, which will be incurred by the business but haven't been billed by the close of the reporting period.
- *Notes payable.* All promissory notes that the business has taken out that are due and payable within one year. If you must pay a note in full in more than one year, you should classify it as a long-term liability.
- *Taxes.* Amounts you still owe for business income, taxable sales, real property, and employee withholding.

Long-term liabilities are obligations of the business that will not be due for at least a year. They include:

- *Mortgage payable.* The amount you owe to a bank or lending institution on real property. The mortgage payable is the amount still due at the close of books for the year.
- *Long-term notes payable.* All promissory notes taken out by the business that are payable in a year or more.
- *Bonds payable.* Publicly held debts that the company has offered for sale. At the end of the year, you should list all bonds that are due and payable over a period of more than one year.

Capital, also referred to as owner's equity, comprises the claim that the business owner has on the assets of the business. Capital is not money in an accounting sense. Capital is equal to net assets, or the total value of assets minus the liabilities.

Example: If a person has a car worth $5,000 (asset), and that person owes the bank $3,000 (debt), then the equity in the car (the capital claim) is $5,000 – $3,000 = $2,000. The $2,000 is not cash money. It is the monetary value of the owner's claim on the car.

The basic structure of a balance sheet is as follows:

$$\text{Assets} = \text{Liabilities} + \text{Capital}$$

We know that an asset is anything of value. The liabilities and capital represent claims on those items of value. The asset side of the equation tells us what we have and what it's worth. The other side tells us how the assets were financed and to whom they belong. For example, if you start a business by investing $10,000, then the business has $10,000 in assets, and you have a capital claim of $10,000. Should you decide to borrow an additional $20,000, the business would have $30,000 in cash (assets), and liabilities of $20,000, and a capital claim of $10,000.

Income Statement

The income statement (or profit and loss statement) is a simple and straightforward report on the proposed business's cash-generating ability (Table 7–2). It illustrates how much your company makes or loses during the year by subtracting the cost of sales and expenses from revenue to arrive at a net result—either a profit or a loss.

Whatever the primary purpose of a projected income statement—to obtain a bank loan, to estimate cash requirements, or to provide information for management planning—you should create such a statement before you start your business. Later, as operating data become available, you can update and refine your projections regularly.

The steps for estimating monthly sales and profits are as follows:

1. Estimate how many of the people in your target market you can reasonably hope to attract as customers.
2. Estimate the average revenue you will generate from each customer.
3. Calculate the total annual sales volume: Dollars per customer × Number of customers = Total sales.
4. Estimate the seasonal sales patterns for the business, attributing varying percentages of the total volume to each month of the year.
5. Allocate the total annual sales calculated in step 3 to months: Annual sales × Monthly percentage = Monthly sales.
6. Adjust these normal monthly sales totals to reflect the start-up period.
7. Deduct from the monthly sales totals all your seminar costs and overhead expenses. What's left is your net profit before taxes.

Cash-Flow Statement

The cash-flow statement summarizes the operating, investing, and financing activities of your seminar-based business as they relate to the inflow and outflow of cash. This statement is necessary for determining (1) positive and negative cash flows and (2) whether your investment and financing endeavors are building or depleting your cash resources.

Just like the balance sheet and income statement, the cash-flow statement charts your business's performance over a specific accounting period—a month, a quarter, six months, or a year. Most companies will

Table 7-2   Monthly Income Statement

This income statement depicts two hypothetical seminar promotion businesses. The low-end business has gross sales of $194,400 per year, while the high-end business grosses $954,624 per year. The owner of the low-end business operates out of his home, but holds seminars in rented meeting rooms in hotels. The owner also serves as the speaker. He produces highly specialized seminars which emphasize one-on-one follow-up sessions, which an employee conducts. Each seminar costs $450 to attend and the business holds 20 seminars per year, with an average of 18 attendees per seminar.

The owner of the high-end business also operates from home and holds seminars in various locations across the country. This business offers four different seminars, and puts on each one once a week for 50 weeks a year. It costs $89 to attend each of these seminars. Each seminar attracts an average of about 50 attendees. This business employs a receptionist, an assistant, and a part-time marketing employee.

The owners of both businesses take a percentage of their net profits as their income, and do not have a salary. Both businesses use direct mail and word of mouth to obtain most of their new business. The low-end business hands out extensive workbooks to all attendees. The high-end business sells videotapes and books related to the seminar at each show, averaging 18 sales per event.

The low-end seminar expenses reflect the costs of producing two seminars, while the high-end seminar expenses represent the costs of producing 16 seminars. Within this category, product costs reflect the costs of duplicating tapes and printing books.

Item	Low	High
Income		
Ticket Sales	$16,200	$71,200
Product Sales	0	8,352
GROSS SALES	$16,200	$79,552
Seminar Expenses		
Site Rental	$ 200	$ 4,160
Refreshments	280	2,240
Workbooks	2,600	6,400
Speaker(s)	0	5,600
Program Manager	0	1,520
Assistant to Program Manager	0	800
On-Site Material/Equipment Costs	0	1,120
Advertising/Promotion	770	23,040
Product Costs	0	508
TOTAL SEMINAR EXPENSES	$ 3,850	$45,388
Overhead Expenses		
Phone/Utilities	$ 400	$ 1,600
Postage/Delivery	270	1,000
Licenses/Taxes	25	280
Employees	2,700	5,250
Benefits/Taxes	0	1,100
Legal Services	80	1,200
Accounting	50	500
Supplies	200	575
Transportation	250	950
Subscriptions/Dues	80	120
Insurance	25	107
Miscellaneous	60	130
TOTAL OVERHEAD EXPENSES	$ 4,140	$12,812
TOTAL EXPENSES	$ 7,990	$58,200
PRETAX NET PROFIT	$ 8,210	$21,352
Net Profit as a % Gross Sales	51%	27%

Table 7–3 Low-End 6-Month Cash-Flow Projection for Business Guide 1071

Item	January	February	March	April	May	June	Total
Cash Sales	$2,504	$4,988	$7,473	$9,957	$12,519	$14,946	$52,387
Total Income	$2,504	$4,988	$7,473	$9,957	$12,519	$14,946	$52,387
Material/Merchandise	$ 0	$ 595	$1,185	$ 1,776	$ 2,366	$ 2,975	$ 8,898
Direct Labor	0	0	0	0	0	0	0
Overhead	124	346	567	788	1,012	1,233	4,071
Marketing & Sales	1,080	1,080	1,080	1,080	1,080	1,080	6,480
Research & Development	270	270	270	270	270	270	1,620
General & Administrative	1,350	1,350	1,350	1,350	1,350	1,350	8,100
Taxes	36	72	108	144	182	217	760
Loans	0	0	0	0	0	0	0
Total Expenses	$2,861	$3,713	$4,561	$5,408	$ 6,260	$ 7,125	$29,928
Net Cash Flow	($357)	$1,275	$2,912	$4,548	$ 6,259	$ 7,821	$22,458
Cumulative Cash Flow	($357)	$ 918	$3,830	$8,379	$14,638	$22,458	$22,458

prepare monthly cash-flow statements and summarize them through an annual report for year-end meetings (Table 7–3).

Don't underestimate the importance of the cash-flow statement; it shows the heartbeat of your business. It reveals your sources and uses of money and indicates whether you have a cash surplus or deficit. By observing trends in the cash flow, you can compare the influx of cash from operating activities (e.g., cash sales, accounts receivable, and interest from investments) with the outflow for operating expenses, and determine your business's liquidity. If you find a trend in which operating revenue does not generate enough income to meet expenses, then your liquidity is threatened. You will have to obtain additional revenue either through financing or from the sale of investments.

The cash-flow statement doesn't reveal a profit or a loss. Just because your company has a positive cash flow, it didn't necessarily generate more income from operating activities than it spent meeting its obligations. You may have obtained additional revenue from investment and financing activities, both of which add to the business's cash position but not to its profitability.

On the other hand, a negative cash flow doesn't mean your business is *not* profitable. You may very well produce a net profit for that accounting period, but may have additional obligations that do not affect the profitability of the company, but do alter its cash position.

The three sections of the cash-flow statement, in order, are:

1. Income.
2. Expenses.
3. Cash flow.

The income section shows all the influx of revenue into the company. Entries will include the following:

- *Cash sales.* Income derived from sales paid for in cash.
- *Receivables.* Income derived from the collection of payment for sales made on credit (i.e., billing statements to clients).
- *Investment income.* Income derived from investments, interest on loans that you have extended, and the liquidation of any assets.
- *Financing income.* Income derived from interest-bearing notes payable.

The second section includes all cash disbursements. These expenses include:

- *Material/Merchandise.* The cash outlay for inventory during the accounting period.
- *Overhead.* All fixed and variable expenses required for the operation of your seminar business.
- *Marketing and sales.* All salaries, commissions, and other direct costs associated with publicizing and selling your seminar program.
- *Research and Development (R&D).* All the labor expenses required to support the research and development operations of the business.
- *General and Administrative (G&A).* All the labor expenses required to support the general and administrative functions of the business.
- *Taxes.* All taxes, except payroll, paid to the appropriate government institutions.
- *Capital.* The money required to obtain any equipment that you need to generate income.
- *Loans.* The total of all loan payments made to reduce long-term debts.

The third section deals with the net and cumulative cash flow of your business. Net cash flow is the difference between income and expenses. You carry this amount over to the next reporting period through cumulative cash flow. To determine your cumulative cash flow, add the net cash flow of the current period to the cumulative cash flow from the previous period. (See Tables 7–3 and 7–4.)

ANALYSIS METHODS

Over the years, a great many financial analysis techniques have developed. They illustrate, as ratios, the relationship between values drawn

Table 7–4 High-End 6-Month Cash-Flow Projection for Business Guide 1071

Item	January	February	March	April	May	June	Total
Cash Sales	$12,295	$24,494	$36,697	$48,893	$61,478	$73,395	$257,251
Total Income	$12,295	$24,494	$36,697	$48,893	$61,478	$73,395	$257,251
Material/Merchandise	$ 0	$ 7,015	$13,975	$20,937	$27,895	$35,076	$104,898
Direct Labor	0	0	0	0	0	0	0
Overhead	564	1,539	2,510	3,481	4,465	5,444	18,002
Marketing & Sales	2,540	2,540	2,540	2,540	2,540	2,540	15,240
Research & Development	645	635	635	635	635	635	3,810
General & Administrative	3,175	3,175	3,175	3,175	3,175	3,175	19,050
Taxes	178	355	532	709	891	1,064	3,730
Loans	0	0	0	0	0	0	0
Total Expenses	$ 7,092	$15,259	$23,367	$31,477	$39,602	$47,934	$164,731
Net Cash Flow	$ 5,203	$ 9,235	$13,330	$17,415	$21,875	$25,461	$ 92,521
Cumulative Cash Flow	$ 5,203	$14,438	$27,769	$45,184	$67,060	$92,521	$ 92,521

from the balance sheet and the income statement, and they are usually more informative than if dollar amounts were used instead.

Financial ratio analysis enables the small business owner to gauge the business's financial weaknesses and strengths and take the appropriate action. It also allows you to compare the performance of your company with that of similar businesses in your industry.

Financial ratio analysis will generally measure two areas within a company: (1) *liquidity* (the amount of liquid assets your business has at any given time to meet accounts or notes payable) and (2) *profitability* (the ability of the business to generate revenues, net income, and an acceptable return on investment).

Don't assume, however, that ratio analyses will tell you everything you need to know about the financial performance of your business. They won't. They provide a great deal of illumination, but they have limitations. According to Jack Zwick, in *A Handbook of Small Business Finance*,[1] those limitations are:

- *Not all businesses are the same.* When comparing ratios with industry averages, keep in mind that many businesspeople prepare their financial statements differently from others, resulting in financial ratios that may not present an accurate accounting of the average business in your industry.
- *Ratios are developed for specific periods.* If you operate a seasonal business (perhaps giving seminars on preparing for college), ratios may not provide an accurate measure of financial performance.
- *The analyses are based on the company's past performance.* They don't necessarily offer any indication of present or future performance.

Even with these limitations, financial ratio analyses will be of great help to you in managing your financial situation.

Measures of Liquidity

The various measures of liquidity will tell you how much cash you have on hand, the value of assets that you can readily turn into cash, and, generally, how quickly you can do so. A good rule of thumb for determining your financial health is: The more liquid you are, the better.

Perhaps the best-known ratio analysis is the *current ratio*—the ratio of your current assets to your current liabilities, plus a safety margin for miscellaneous losses like uncollectible accounts receivable. As discussed previously, you can find current assets and current liabilities on your balance sheet. For instance, suppose your current assets are $90,000 and your current liabilities are $30,000. The current ratio would be:

$$\$90,000 \text{ divided by } 30,000 = 3$$

Generally, if your current ratio of assets to liabilities is at least 2:1, your business is in good condition. If you feel that your current ratio is too low after you evaluate it and compare it to other averages in the industry, you may be able to increase it in a number of ways. For instance, you may be able to add to your current assets by raising capital through equity or debt financing. If you choose to borrow money through debt financing, make sure the loan will mature at least one year in the future. You can increase your current ratio by paying off some of your debts that appear as current liabilities, or by turning some of your fixed or miscellaneous assets into current assets. As a last resort, you may have to funnel profits back into the business.

Another common ratio is the *acid-test* or *quick ratio*. Like the current ratio, the acid-test ratio measures the liquidity of your business. To find it, total all your liquid assets such as cash on hand plus any government securities and receivables, then divide these assets by your current liabilities. For example, suppose your current liquid assets are $30,000 in cash, $50,000 in receivables, and $20,000 in securities, for a total of $100,000. You've determined your current liabilities are $50,000, so you would have a quick ratio of:

$$\$100,000 \text{ divided by } 50,000 = 2.0$$

For most businesses, a quick ratio of 2.0 or better is more than sufficient. If, however, there are factors that will slow payment of receivables, or if your payables are due before your receivables are, then you will need a higher ratio than 2.0.

An acid-test ratio is a measure of exactly where you would be if you faced a crisis and had no way to correct your financial position. Try to keep your quick ratio at a level sufficient for your needs. Remember, good financial management allows the best use of your assets and increases the profitability of your business. If you have cash, receivables, and inventories that exceed your needs and are lying idle, you are not using them to your greatest advantage. You have to walk a tightrope between too much liquidity and not enough liquidity.

To determine what the right degree of liquidity might be for your business, conduct an evaluation of the average collection period for your receivables. Start with your net sales figure, found on your profit and loss or income statement. Divide this amount by the number of days in your fiscal accounting period. The resulting figure is your average sales per day. Now divide your average sales per day by your accounts receivable, shown on your balance sheet. This will result in your average collection period.

For example, say your annual net sales are $150,000, your fiscal accounting period is 365 days, and your accounts receivable are worth $20,000. The calculations would be:

$150,000 divided by 365 days = $410.96 average sales per day

$20,000 divided by $410.96 = 48.7 days average collection period

The average collection period in this example is 48.7 days, or 49 days. If your credit terms are 60 days, then your accounts—the people to whom you extended credit—are very dependable. However, if your average collection period is 30 days, you might need to review your credit policies and institute a more effective credit collection strategy.

Another measure to determine the correct amount of liquidity you should maintain is *inventory turnover*—how much capital you invest in inventory to meet your operational requirements. Turnover represents the number of times per year your inventory investment revolves.

Inventory Turnover = Net Sales (or Cost of Goods) divided by the Average Value of Inventory on Order and on Hand

This ratio measures the efficiency of funds invested in materials and inventory and how often inventory is liquidated.

To illustrate inventory turnover, let's say your cost of goods sold is $60,000 and the average value of inventory is $12,000. To arrive at your inventory turnover, you would divide $60,000 by $12,000. This results in an inventory turnover of 5.0.

If inventory turnover is low in comparison to the average for the industry (or in comparison to the average ratio for other speakers/seminar promoters with similar topics and items), there is a possibility that you are carrying some obsolete or otherwise unsalable inventory items. On the other hand, if the turnover is unusually high compared to the average, your business may be losing sales because of lack of adequate stock on hand.

It will be helpful to determine the turnover rate of each stock item so that you can evaluate how well each is moving. You may want to evaluate your inventory turnover more frequently than once a year.

Profitability Measures

Throughout your business's lifetime, you'll rely on your business for several things. Making money, of course, is the highest priority; after all, it is the reason you went into business in the first place. If your company isn't profitable, why put yourself through the headaches and long hours that usually come with owning your own business? You could work for someone else, secure in the knowledge that you will receive a weekly paycheck, benefits, and more free time.

Making money is what being in business is all about. In this section, we will discuss several methods that measure just how profitable your business is. These measures are:

1. Asset earning power.
2. Return on owner's equity.
3. Net profit on sales.
4. Investment turnover.
5. Return on investment (ROI).

Using these profitability measures, you'll learn how much money you are making, whether you are using your present resources to maximize the profit potential of your business, and whether you are losing money or just breaking even.

Asset earning power measures how well your assets are performing for you. We are interested in the earning power of your *total* assets, not just your liquid assets. To calculate your asset earning power ratio, divide your earnings before taxes and interest by your total assets. For instance, if you had total earnings before taxes and interest of $100,000 and total assets of $300,000, you would have an asset earning power of .33 or 33 percent. In other words, your total assets are earning you 33 percent of their present marketable value.

The ratio known as *return on owner's equity* determines what return your business is giving you on the amount of money you've invested in it. Equity in a company is usually based on capital investment and includes both initial and ongoing capitalization. You can also include any intangible assets such as patents or trade secrets that have been contributed to the business in exchange for equity. If you are the only investor in your company, you control the total equity.

To compute your return on owner's equity, you first have to calculate what your average equity investment in the business has been over a 12-month period. You can find this figure on the balance sheet. Next, divide your net profit by the equity and you will have computed your return on owner's equity. For example, if you have $75,000 equity in the business and your net profit is $50,000, your return on owner's equity would be .66 or 66 percent.

Net profit on sales is one of the most common ratios used to determine the profitability of a business. It measures the difference between your net sales and what you spend to operate your business. To determine the net profit on sales, you have to divide the net profit by the net sales. If we use the net profit of $50,000 from the above example and have net sales of $300,000, your net profit on sales would be .16 or 16 percent.

Most experts agree that if your ratio of net profit to net sales doesn't exceed the amount of money that you could earn from interest or dividends in securities, then you are not utilizing your assets to your best advantage. In the above example, you are earning 16 cents on every dollar your company spends. This is a very good return for most businesses. Check the average ratios of similar businesses within your industry and compare your net profit on sales against theirs. If your net profit on sales is substantially lower, you should reevaluate the areas in your business that could be reducing your earning power. Those areas might be high operating costs, high shrinkage, or a price point that may not produce sufficient profit or might not be competitive enough.

Like inventory turnover, *investment turnover* determines the number of times per year that your total investments or assets revolve. To calculate your investment turnover, divide your total annual net sales by your total assets. If your net sales are $500,000 and your total assets are $300,000, your investment turnover would be 1.6.

Compare your investment turnover with those of similar businesses within the industry. Investment turnover may be lower in businesses requiring large investments than in firms that don't require heavy capitalization.

Return on investment is the most common ratio used to determine a business's profitability. There are several ways to determine ROI; but the easiest and most popular is to divide the net profit by the total assets. For example, if net profit were $100,000 and total assets were $300,000, your ROI would be .33 or 33 percent.

Return on investment is not necessarily the same as profit. ROI deals with the money you, the owner, invest in the company and the return you realize on that money, based on the net profit of the business. Profit, on the other hand, measures the performance of the business. Don't confuse ROI with the return on owner's equity. This is an entirely different item as well. Only in very few enterprises, most of which are sole proprietorships, does equity equal the total investment or assets of the business.

You can use ROI to measure the profitability of your business in several different ways—as a measure of the performance of your pricing policies, your inventory investment, your capital equipment investment, and so forth. Some other ways to use ROI within your company are:

- Divide net income, interest, and taxes by total liabilities to measure a *rate of earnings of total capital employed.*
- Divide net income and income taxes by proprietary equity and fixed liabilities to produce a *rate of earnings on invested capital.*
- Divide net income by total capital plus reserves to calculate the *rate of earnings on proprietary equity and stock equity.*

Break-Even Analysis

A break-even analysis is important when you are in the planning stages of your business start-up. It is an essential piece of information that you will need to include in your business plan, which Chapter 10 discusses in more detail. A break-even analysis tells you how much money you need to make—daily, weekly, or monthly—in order to pay all of your expenses.

To put together a break-even analysis, you first have to separate variable costs from the fixed costs of your business. For the analysis, the only true variable costs are those directly related to putting on each seminar. Remember that the total overhead of any company will equal the sum of the fixed and variable expenses.

The detailed break-even analysis in Table 7–5 is based on the high-end seminar promoting business described in Table 7–4. First, determine your monthly fixed and variable costs.

Once you've determined your monthly operating expenses, you are ready to take the next step in your break-even calculation—the price of each ticket. The ticket price is determined by calculating all the expenses associated with a given seminar, adding overhead, and then

Table 7–5   Break-Even Analysis

Fixed Costs	
Rent	$ 0
Phone/Utilities	1,600
Postage/Delivery	1,000
Licenses/Taxes	280
Owner/Manager	0
Employees	5,250
Benefits/Taxes	1,100
Legal Services	1,200
Accounting	500
Supplies	575
Transportation	950
Subscriptions/Dues	120
Insurance	107
Miscellaneous	130
Total	$12,812
Variable Costs	
Seminar Facility/Refreshments	$ 6,400/month
Seminar Workbooks/Equipment	7,520/month
Speakers' Fees	5,600/month
Seminar Employees	2,320/month
Marketing/Promotion	23,040/month
Product Costs	508/month
Total	$45,388/month
Total	**$2,837/seminar**

applying a profit factor or markup to the sum of those items. For instance, the subtotal of operating expenses in the example in Chapter 9 is $3,631, and the desired net profit is 20 percent. To determine the profit factor that corresponds to this desired net profit, first refer to the markup table in Chapter 9 and locate "20 percent" in the "Net Profit—Percent of Selling Price" column. Now, multiply the subtotal of operating expenses (also called the cost of service) by the corresponding percentage in the "Markup—Percent of Operating Costs" column, which turns out to be 25 percent. Therefore:

$$\$3,631 \times 25\% = \$908$$

Your total ticket sales needed to cover your costs and make the desired profit would equal:

$$\$3,631 + \$908 = \$4,539$$

Assuming that your market research indicates you can attract an average of 51 people to each seminar, you would need to charge:

$$\$4,539 \times 51 \text{ tickets} = \$89 \text{ per ticket}$$

The next step in computing break-even is to take the various components in our example and determine at what point, in terms of tickets sold, you will pay all of your expenses and begin to make a profit each month. Using the break-even equation:

Break-even = (Fixed expenses + Variable expenses) / Ticket price,

and inputting our data from Table 7–5:

Break-even = ($12,812 + $45,388) / $89.00 = 654 tickets.

According to this break-even analysis, if you don't change price or reduce expenses, you will need to sell 654 tickets per month (or somewhat less, if you can successfully sell products at your seminars) in order to pay all expenses and start making a profit. (See Table 7–3.)

BANKS

You need a business bank account. Do not just use the most convenient bank; it may not offer the financial services your business demands. Different businesses have different needs. To find the best bank for your business, interview bank managers in your area by phone.

Using this professional approach will give you an opportunity to establish a relationship with the bank manager. Ordinarily, when you just walk in to open an account, you will deal with the new accounts clerk and never come in contact with the bank executives. The closer the relationship you develop with the bank manager, the better your chances are of obtaining loans and special favors in marginal situations.

Don't be afraid to discuss your difficulties with your banker. No matter how small the problem may be, he or she may know just how to handle it. And don't pretend to know everything, in an effort to impress your bankers. You may be an expert in your field; they are definitely experts in theirs. Learn to talk to bankers in their language, on their terms. It will help your present situation and improve your position the next time you require their services.

In a branch-bank state, you will probably do business with a large bank that has many branches. Managers change frequently. Watch for changes and introduce yourself to each new manager to maintain that all-important relationship.

Independent banks without branch offices, or the small chains capable of meeting your needs, will provide the most personalized service. In a small bank, your account may be important; in a large bank, you may never be noticed.

Take time to find the most suitable bank, and then avoid moving your account if at all possible. If you move your account constantly, it will be hard to get a good bank reference if you need credit from your suppliers.

When You Open the Account

When opening your business account, the bank will need your Social Security number or your federal employer identification number, your driver's license, and (for partnerships and sole proprietorships) a fictitious name certificate. If you have formed a corporation, bring your corporate seal as evidence of your status. You will need a financial statement when requesting a VISA or MasterCard franchise.

Ask for Money Before You Need It

Practically every growing business experiences some rough financial periods and a few growing pains, and requires financing of some type sooner or later. Watch for signs of developing problems so you and your banker can deal with them in advance.

Plan your growth program and presell your banker. Foresight demonstrates that you are an astute professional manager who is on top of every situation. Your chances of obtaining a loan under marginal conditions will improve greatly if you can anticipate your needs.

BANK SPECIALTIES

Some banks specialize in certain types of businesses or have departments to handle different types of trade. Some banks only go for big money. You can usually tell which banks are interested in attracting loans from small businesses by their eagerness to obtain your account. Ask your prospective banker these questions, to help you make a judgment:

1. Is it necessary to maintain certain minimum balances before the bank will consider a loan?
2. Will the bank extend a line of credit? If so, what are the requirements?

3. Does the bank have limitations on the number of small loans it will grant or the types of businesses to which it will grant loans?
4. What is the bank's policy regarding the size or description of checks deposited to be held for collection?
5. Will checks under that size be credited immediately to the depositor's checking account balance? (This question is very important, and you must press for a definite answer.)

If you do not have a previous business account to serve as a reference, some banks will hold all checks for collection until they develop experience with you. Whether the bank exercises this precaution may depend on your personal credit rating.

BUSINESS CONSULTANTS

Many people jump headlong into a business venture—often pouring in their life savings—without submitting their business plans (if they even have such plans) to a competent business consultant for analysis. They are often so caught up with their ideas that they see only the goal, not the hazards along the way.

Enthusiasm is dangerous because it encourages people to rush ahead. Careful planning is necessary in any business venture. Such planning should be based on an unbiased analysis designed to uncover potential failure factors. Keep enthusiasm in check and follow a cautious, rational path.

Entrepreneur Magazine Group strongly believes in the value of seeking qualified outside opinions and demanding that consultants tear apart a business person's plans in every possible way. Only in this way can entrepreneurs objectively see the pitfalls and promise in their ideas.

Finding a Qualified Consultant

Business and management consultants are not licensed like doctors and lawyers. For this reason, you should demand proof of a consultant's expertise before retaining his or her services. Look for professionals. Ask for bank references, and confirm them. Make sure the consultant can prove that he or she has practical experience in managing and operating businesses—the more varied, the better.

Although highly paid consultants are available in many specific areas affecting your business, the consultant who will be able to advise you the best is probably already successful in the same business. Find a successful business in another part of town or a nearby city—one that will not be in direct competition with you—and ask the owner or manager to analyze your plans.

Because poor location and ineffective advertising are among the most common reasons for business failure, you will want these features of your plan examined with particular care. Offer a good fee in keeping with your geographic area, the experience of the consultant, and the complexity of the problems requiring attention.

Consulting fees vary widely. In 1995, the National Bureau of Professional Management Consultants, based in San Diego, California, surveyed its members to assess certain characteristics of their practices. The survey yielded much information about the hourly billing rates of consulting firms with 1 to 10 consultants. Six percent of the respondents had average hourly billable rates of $50; 22.2 percent charged $51 to $100 per hour for their services; 32.9 percent had rates of $101 to $150 per hour; 22.9 percent billed at a rate of $151 to $200 per hour; 4.6 percent had hourly rates of $201 to $250 per hour; and 11.6 percent had billable rates of $250 or more per hour.

A consultant's hourly fee will depend on his or her experience, location, and field of expertise. In addition to this fee, you can expect to pay related out-of-pocket costs such as travel or telephone bills.

If your start-up capital is limited, and you can't afford the high cost of a consultant, consider hiring an MBA student. Although lacking the practical expertise of highly paid professionals, he or she can easily research your competition, run a cash-flow projection, and perform other basic preparations.

Don't neglect to hire a consultant before you start any business. Remember to ask for a negative-stressed analysis with key success factors clearly stated.

8

ADVERTISING
AND PROMOTION

Whether you grow your seminar company to the point where you are representing or showcasing some very big-name speakers, or whether you become a big-name speaker yourself, you will be able to attract attendees simply by getting the word out. In fact, a handful of promoters spend relatively little on advertising. They employ a number of salespeople who make cold calls to local businesses to sell tickets when a big name comes to town.

Anyone in this business, however, will tell you that at least 90 percent of new business comes from one of three areas: (1) personal contact, (2) word-of-mouth referrals, and (3) direct mail advertising. The majority of companies continue to test radio, newspaper, and sometimes television advertising, but most say the return has not proven to be worthwhile. Instead, speakers use television and radio as public relations tools—they host a show, offer expert advice as guests, and so on—and seminar promoters try to garner free media publicity through the use of press releases.

Before you start planning your advertising campaign, go back to your market research to learn as much as possible about the market you will target. Start with the most basic questions to determine your relationship to your clients and your marketing goals.

1. Who are my potential customers?
2. How many are there?
3. Where are they located?
4. Where do they now find the knowledge or services I want to provide?
5. Can I offer them anything they are not getting now?
6. How can I persuade them to come to my seminars?

Having already applied that market information to your site selection and topic choices, you can now use it to plan a campaign that will reach and persuade potential attendees to come to your seminars.

Know Your Product

The key to success in advertising is understanding exactly what you're selling. Identify the best points of your product so you know what to emphasize. Ask yourself:

1. What knowledge, skills, or services am I offering?
2. What quality service do I sell?
3. What kind of image do I want to project?
4. How do I compare with my competition?

Remember, before you simply send out 50,000 direct mail pieces, you must consider what your market is looking for, and how your seminars address what is wanted.

Your advertising should immediately address your market's needs (even before your company's needs or your need to find clients). Doing so takes both talent and an in-depth understanding of your market and your offering.

Your Advertising Budget

Most companies devote a percentage of projected gross sales—generally, 2 to 5 percent—to their annual advertising budgets. This approach is known as the *cost method,* which theorizes that an advertiser can't afford to spend more money than he or she has. Thus, a business that projects $300,000 in gross sales in a given year and plans to spend 5 percent on advertising, would have $15,000 for that year, or about $1,250 a month, to work with.

Other companies base their advertising budgets on the amount of money they need to move their products or attract their customers. This is called the *task method,* and it is the method you will employ to create an advertising budget. You cannot, after all, make money until people first attend your seminars. To be successful, you must employ all means of advertising necessary to get out the word about your seminars and bring people in.

SELECTING THE RIGHT MEDIA

Advertising accomplishes the following:

- Points out the need and creates a desire for your seminars.
- Announces new programs.
- Draws customers to your business.
- Convinces customers that your company's seminars are the best.

Many consumers will not perceive a *need* for your seminars until advertising shows them how they can benefit from them. This is the number-one challenge for seminar promoters—persuading people that the benefits they will receive from hearing the speakers and learning their methods are real, tangible, and long-lasting—and it explains in part why advertising expenses for a new business are higher during the first few years.

Effective advertisements must be simple, easily understood, truthful, informative, sincere, and customer-oriented. Good advertising causes action. It persuades the prospective customer to give one of your seminars a try.

Advertising has a cumulative effect. Response will initially be slow but it will increase with time. Intermittent splurges rarely pay off. It is better to advertise on a small scale regularly and continuously than to invest money in larger advertisements infrequently.

The advertising media generally used in this business are personal selling and direct mail. In addition, catalogs, handouts, and brochures are used regularly and, on a much more limited scale, some local print media and advertising specialties (monogrammed calendars, telephone pads, T-shirts, and similar giveaways).

In smaller cities and towns, the local radio station and newspaper may cover the market of the small firm very well. However, because yours is a product that most consumers need to be convinced they *need,* these spots rarely give enough time to relay your message.

To decide which advertising media will be most effective for *you*, you must compare their effectiveness, considering the following factors:

1. *Cost per contact.* How much will it cost to reach prospective attendees?
2. *Frequency.* How frequent should these contacts or message deliveries be?
3. *Impact.* Does the medium in question offer full opportunities for appealing to the appropriate senses, such as sight and hearing, in presenting design, color, or sound?
4. *Selectivity.* To what degree can the message be restricted to those people who are known to be the most logical prospects?

Cost Per Contact

Considering cost per contact when evaluating advertising media is especially important for helping to determine your task-based ad budget. For example, if your research shows it will cost you $4,200 to mail 5,000 seminar brochures to potential attendees in Milwaukee, Wisconsin, your cost per contact is 84 cents. Now let's say other seminar promoters who promote topics similar to yours tell you that you can anticipate a return on your mailing (i.e., number of paid enrollees vs. number of pieces mailed) of 1.5 percent. This means that you can anticipate having 75 enrollees for your seminar, based on mailing 5,000 pieces. Is this enough attendance to cover the costs of the seminar and make the profit you desire? If not, you will have to raise your price, cut your costs, refocus your topic, find a new city, or take another look at advertising media that may be more effective.

Frequency

Frequency is important because it takes a while to build up awareness and break through the consumer's screening process. People are always screening out messages that aren't personally relevant, picking up on only those things that are important to them. *Persistence* is the key word here. It is much better to advertise regularly and frequently by mailing smaller, less glitzy brochures, than to spend money on a huge four-color catalog that only goes out sporadically to your prospects. Though they may not call and sign up for your seminar the first two or three times they receive a persuasive mailer, your prospects are likely to give at least one seminar a try, to see if what you're selling is true.

PERSONAL SELLING

As we mentioned in Chapter 4, a number of seminar promoters hire salespeople to make cold calls on local businesses that fit the target audience of the seminar. This kind of personal selling is useful because it lets you present your program, including the benefits to be received, directly to those most likely to gain from it. The more tickets one of your sales staffers sells, the higher will be his or her commission and your income. Group ticket sales are definitely goals that you and your staff members should try to meet.

At the same time, personal selling relies a lot on *you*, especially during the start-up phase. "Almost 95 percent of our clients come from referrals—almost everything is word of mouth. Just about every enrollment I get is because 'Oh, I heard about you from so-and-so,'" says Laura Lodato of Priority Management in Tampa, Florida. "Obviously, it makes sense for us to go to a company and try to draw up a contract that says 'We want to be your productivity partner and enroll your entire company over the next 12 months to go through a series of our programs.' In real life, or at least in my real life, that's just the start."

From that point on, Lodato and her program make the difference. "For example, I might break into CIGNA Health Care, and we may train a whole department within their company, and then that department comes back from the workshop all revved up and excited," she says. "Then, a week later, I might get a call from a series of individuals who say, 'I work with Jane Doe, and she went to your program, and I want to come. When is your next workshop?'"

"So it might start out as a group of people coming from one company, but then the fallout of that is we'll have a number of individuals calling us who know someone from that company and want to enroll."

Eve Cappello, PhD, a professional speaker and author, remembers going to mall grand openings and walking around introducing herself and talking to people about her workshops. "I used to do a lot of cold calling in the beginning. I never hesitated to promote myself," she says. Today, 97 percent of her speaking engagements come from referrals.

PRINT MEDIA

If your seminar appeals to a broad enough audience, you can consider running ads in local print media such as newspapers and other small publications. The majority of people interviewed for this book, however, say that such advertising rarely results in increased attendance.

If you do run any newspaper ads, you should keep them fairly simple. Michael Frank, owner of Speakers Unlimited, a speakers bureau in

Columbus, Ohio, and an experienced promoter, says that he only advertises if he has a well-known speaker on his program. If you have a speaker unknown to the general public, Frank says, it would cost too much to sell the speaker through advertising. For a better-known speaker, Frank says he might run an ad saying that "Zig Ziglar Is Coming To Columbus In Person." The ad would include his phone number so that readers of the ad could contact him for more details. He could either send callers a brochure or have a salesperson pay them a visit. Instead of running one big ad, he would run a number of smaller ads—say, two or three a day for three to four weeks.

If your seminar does not feature a "name" speaker, you can test local publication ads in the various cities where your seminars will be held. In most cases, however, your money would be better spent highlighting the content of the presentation in printed brochures you send directly to potential attendees.

DIRECT MAIL

The best advertising medium for your seminar is a personal direct-mail package. Through direct mail, companies can take the time to explain the actual benefits that attendees will receive—and why their seminars are far and away the best in the industry—and they can do so clearly, succinctly, and relatively inexpensively.

To make your direct mail campaign a success, you must produce high-quality, well-written marketing pieces, and you must target them to the most appropriate people within your market. In fact, doing so is the greatest challenge facing seminar promoters. "Our biggest challenge is making sure that we can convince the persons reading the brochure that this is something they will benefit from," says SkillPath co-founder Denise Dudley. Both she and co-founder Jerry Brown stay directly involved in developing all seminar brochures.

"There are a couple of challenges," agrees Bill Hill, manager of seminar operations for CareerTrack. "One is time—people have difficulty pulling time away from their jobs to give to a seminar. And the second thing is finding the right people to mail to."

Mailing Lists

Lists are available for almost any imaginable category of consumer. You can rent them from list brokers or lease them from other companies, like SkillPath and CareerTrack. Magazines related to your topic area can be a good list source, as can associations whose members fit your target market profile. The one-time rental fee for these names is usually between $100 and $150 per thousand. Less expensive lists can be purchased, but you want your lists to be very focused so that you are not wasting money printing and mailing materials to people who do not fit your profile. Should you decide to use a list broker—and many are very good—look in your local telephone Yellow Pages under "Advertising—Direct Mail." The majority can focus the lists they carry to fit the specifications you give them. Some will require a minimum rental (for example, 5,000 names), but most will simply charge for the list customization and include it in your per-thousand price quote.

Use the RFM formula to select a list: R stands for recency, F for frequency, and M for money. Because people and businesses move and their economic status changes, recency is vital to the success of a list. Frequency refers to how many times the people on the list responded. Money refers to how much they spent. Investigate the list as thoroughly as possible. Buy only from established groups or services. Ask how many times the list has been sold in the previous six months, and obtain the names and telephone numbers of some of the buyers. Call them to find out about the list's response rate, how many pieces were returned because of old addresses, and whether they thought the list was worth the cost.

Once you are established, you can use your own customer lists, and trade them with other established businesses.

Brochures, Catalogs and Sales Letters

In your direct mail campaign, you may use mailers that fall into one of the following formats:

1. *Solo mailer.* This format usually includes a sales letter, a brochure, and a reply card or enrollment form.
2. *Self-mailer.* An advertising and promotional piece, such as a postcard or company newsletter, mailed by itself.
3. *Catalog mailer.* Usually used to highlight various items sold in conjunction with seminars, such as books, videotapes, and audiotapes.

A brochure can convey the impression of a serious, established, high-quality business, even if you just opened yesterday. Professional speakers and speakers bureaus use brochures to highlight the accomplishments and skills of the speaker(s). Seminar promoters use them to outline the key benefits enrollees will gain by attending a specific seminar. Most brochures are 17×11-inch sheets, folded in half to create four-page 8½ × 11-inch booklets or, if desired, 8-, 12-, or 16-page booklets that are stapled or saddle-stitched at the fold.

Your brochure does not have to be a four-color masterpiece, especially if you want to keep costs down. Choose a light-colored card stock and one or two bold, professional colors that entice the recipients to read. Information should be presented in a compelling yet factual fashion. Photographs of notable speakers (especially in speakers bureau brochures) are essential. Be sure that any photos you use are sharp and clear. If you use a celebrity speaker, emphasize his or her name. If your speaker is not a celebrity, then emphasize the seminar's title and content. Give detailed information on the contents of the seminar, and say who should attend it. Most importantly, the brochure should outline the benefits that attendees will receive. If your seminar is on public speaking, for instance, your copy may highlight the following points: "Conquer stage fright. Learn how to hold your audience in the palm of your hand. Organize your thoughts for effective communication."

Your brochure should also include complete information on when and where the seminar will take place, as well as how much it will cost to attend. Mention any discounts for group purchases, students, spouses, and so on. Include any terms or restrictions on attendance in your brochure. If all tickets must be purchased in advance, say so in the brochure. Similarly, if you don't permit any attendees to carry recording devices, say so. Clarify your policy on refunds and credits.

If possible, use four-color printing and slightly heavier card stock on the cover of your brochure. If you are a professional speaker, invest in a smaller brochure (one 17 × 11-inch sheet, folded in half to create a four-page 8½ × 11-inch booklet) on heavier card stock, using four-color printing. Include a few photographs of yourself, and very focused copy. If you have any doubt about your ability to do a first-rate job on your brochures, entrust the writing and the design to marketing professionals.

The typeface should be easy to read—no smaller than 10 point. It shouldn't take more than a minute for anybody to scan your brochure, but those 60 seconds should be packed with memorable information. Enrollment forms and a phone number to call for more information should be included in the brochure, either on the back page or bound into the middle. Many brochures even feature on the front cover the phone number to call for enrollment.

Catalogs are usually printed on glossier paper, and they are at least 16 pages long. You can use a catalog to advertise your seminar-related products in an informative and entertaining fashion. Although most catalogs are between 20 and 36 pages long, your catalog can be smaller if you don't have enough products to fill the pages. As with seminar brochures, catalogs are generally 8½ × 11 inches, but digest-sized catalogs are also popular. When producing your first catalog, you may want to make it digest size by printing it on 8½ × 11-inch paper and folding it in half.

Because these are direct-sales pieces, most catalogs use four-color art; however, incorporating professionally drawn sketches of your products or using black-and-white photos can save you money. Ask your printer for recommendations.

Again, if you don't have strong copywriting skills, you may want to hire a freelance writer who is experienced in catalog production. The copy should be concise and compelling. Headlines throughout the catalog should point to the benefits of the products it contains ("Improve Your Career," "Take Charge of Your Life"). Finally, your catalog should make it easy for customers to order. Bind an order form and an envelope in the middle of the catalog, and/or include instructions for ordering by telephone or fax. Be sure to specify the acceptable methods and timing of payment.

Sales letters allow you to add a unique touch to your direct mail advertising. The letter should be personal, informal, and selectively directed. If you word your letter thoughtfully, you can create an impression of individualized attention to each recipient.

Start your letter with something that really grabs the prospect's attention—a description of the offer, or the benefits of attending a single seminar. The lead may even flatter the client, or tell a story. If you are pitching a seminar entitled "How Working Mothers Manage Stress," for instance, your sales letter might start off with: "I have been a working mother for six years, and there were times I was sure that I was going to lose my mind . . . ."

The body of your letter should tell the prospect what you have to offer and what the personal benefits will be. If you use a headline in the letter, describe the main benefit you are selling ("You *Can* Have More Time for Yourself and Your Family"). Emphasize that point, using different descriptions, throughout the body copy. Reiterate that specific benefit as often as you can, so that the reader remembers it.

To add credibility, qualify any claims you make in the letter by citing sources or offering endorsements. Describe what the reader will lose by not taking action, and lead into your closing, where you summarize the main benefits. Finally, conclude the letter with a call to action.

Here are some sales letter tips:

- Choose the most enticing special offer you can make potential enrollees, and include it or refer to it in your sales letter.
- Grab your reader's attention by mentioning something he or she wants. Relate it either to the special offer, or to the benefits of the seminar.

- Use proven winning words and phrases like "secret" and "free." They outpull bland words every time.
- Headlines of 10 or more words sell better than short ones, and long letters often yield higher returns than short ones.
- Don't write for millions of readers. Write for only one, as though you're speaking to him or her personally.
- Don't focus only on the features of your seminar. Tell the reader the benefits of attending.
- Use a personal touch like a hand-addressed envelope to get the reader to open the letter.
- Use the classic "A.I.D.A." formula: Attention, Interest, Desire, and Action.
- Letters with indented paragraphs, underlined words, and a second color outpull plain letters.
- Don't strive for eloquence. Use everyday language and address the average person.

Envelopes can be important components of your mailings. Frank suggests using envelopes imprinted with an announcement of your seminar. A message like "Zig Ziglar Is Coming To Town" or "Boost Your Productivity" on the outside of the envelope can increase the likelihood that people will actually read your mailer, instead of discarding it as junk mail. (If you use such envelopes, you will be printing custom envelopes for each seminar you put on.)

Reply Cards

Think about including a reply card with solo and catalog mailers. If you send a sales letter with a brochure, for instance, you can include a reply card that offers several responses from which the recipient can choose, like "Perhaps Next Quarter" or "Send More Information." The idea is to reinforce the idea of enrollment, now or at a later date.

Company Newsletters

A great way to position yourself and your company in an authority niche is to send out a company newsletter on topics related to your seminars. The newsletter can inform existing clients about your upcoming events and possibly attract new enrollees. If the newsletter is done well, it will be more informative and will contain less sales hype than most items your clients receive, creating more interest in your business. Many clients will actually read a newsletter rather than pitch it in the trash with all the other ads.

Your newsletter should inform your clients about developments in your industry and share information that could affect them. Your newsletter doesn't have to be all news, though. Including a coupon or special offer can move people from reading to buying. Always give upcoming events a prominent place in your newsletter.

When producing your newsletter, concentrate on the following points:

- *Recognition.* Your clients may already know you, but they may share the newsletter with others. Thus, your newsletter should tell people who you are, what you do, and where they can find you. If consumers have to read through two pages of solid text to find the name of your company, you're not doing much to increase your name recognition. Use your company logo prominently on the newsletter pages.

- *Image.* Your newsletter is an extension of your company's image. If it is interesting and professional, customers will think well of your expertise and of your company. If it looks shoddy and amateurish, they may doubt your credibility. "Professional-looking" doesn't necessarily mean "incredibly expensive." With today's advances in desktop publishing, most people can create their own newsletters on a computer, or have freelancers do them cheaply.

- *Specifics.* Give your readers specific reasons why they should choose your seminars and products above all others. Vague assertions like "We're the best" don't work nearly as well as matter-of-fact details.

- *Enactment.* Make the reader take action by picking up the phone, mailing in a reply card, or mailing or faxing an enrollment form for your next event.

Investigate the possibility of using a mailing service to organize your direct mail campaign. Check your Yellow Pages. A direct mail service can assist you in compiling your direct mail package, do all the printing, labeling, sorting, and mailing of your package to the names on your mailing list, and organize all the responses that come in.

Bulk versus First Class

Uncle Sam will get his cut in the form of postage. "Our mailing is a big cost—it's huge. I don't even know exactly how much we spend," says

Hill. Depending on the size of your company, postage alone could run $5,000 to $500,000 per year.

There are two ways to go. Bulk rate requires filing an application with the U.S. Postal Service and paying a one-time application fee (which remains in force as long as you use the service at least once a year). There's also an annual fee, good from January through December. If you pay your fee on December 10 and want to do a mailing in January, you will have to pay another annual fee when the new year begins. At this writing, the cost per letter runs at a discount of about 45 percent below the current first-class rate. Minimum mailing is 200 pieces or 50 pounds.

Sending in bulk requires bundling the mail according to ZIP codes, and any nondeliverable pieces are tossed unless you state on the face, "Return postage guaranteed." Bulk is slow; local delivery can take five to seven days, and to get from one coast to the other may take two weeks or more. Postal workers deliver bulk mail only when they have room, after taking all other classes of mail.

Bulk mail has the advantage of being relatively cheap; a 45 percent discount is nothing to dismiss out of hand. But it has some important shortcomings—typically, slowness and unpredictability. Also, bulk is generally perceived as junk mail. If image is important in your business, it makes sense to use first-class mail. You need to leave a strong and favorable impression on customer prospects. The Postal Service also has first-class bulk rates at a discount for those mailers who bundle their mail. Stamping bulk mail with precanceled bulk mail stamps makes your mail look more like first-class material, and is likely to give you a better response than "plain" bulk mail.

DESIGNING YOUR MAILER

To put together an effective advertisement, you first have to analyze the type of customers you want to appeal to in the ad. Next, you have to design an appeal—that is, something that will benefit the target audience—and incorporate it into your ad copy. Here are some guidelines that, if followed, will help you create strong, response-getting ads:

- *Create a sense of immediacy.* Because response diminishes over time, advertising relies on getting people to act immediately. Most people like to be led—particularly when they're in unfamiliar territory. Tell your audience what response you want. At different points throughout the ad, and especially at the conclusion, ask for a physical response: "Limited Seats Available," "Early Enrollment Discount," "Call Now." Offer an incentive to encourage a quick response. You might even reserve seats in different sections of your seminar sites, and assign seats (or sections) in order of ticket purchase.

- *Repetition sells.* Keep weaving and reweaving the same sales pitch throughout the ad, each time giving a slightly new slant to the significant features and benefits of your seminar. Repetition sells because the more times someone hears or reads something, the more believable it becomes. Repetition is particularly important in advertising (as in speeches), because you normally don't have the full attention of your audience. For a lot of people, writing repetitiously is difficult because they were taught in school to avoid redundancy at all cost. When writing ad copy, forget this training and repeat, repeat, repeat.

- *Hit the "hot buttons."* Different people will be attracted to different benefits offered by your seminars. Decide what is valuable and exciting about your seminar, then tell your audience how and why they need what you have to sell.

- *"Sell the sizzle, not the steak."* This old advertising axiom means: Sell the benefits of the seminar, not just the seminar itself. There's nothing wrong with talking about the features of your seminar, but unless you spell out how the customers directly benefit, your ad won't have maximum effectiveness. To excite your audience, you must describe your seminar in a captivating way. This does not mean using fancy words or constructions that might confuse the reader. Use plain, simple English. Be straightforward. Keep your ad copy at a level understandable by an 11- or 12-year-old. But highlight the benefits.

- *Evaluate other ads.* Collect all kinds of ads and study them. This is a practice among all good ad-makers. Use their ideas if they're worthwhile. It is certainly essential to put your own imagination to use, but learn to emulate the strengths of others who have succeeded with their advertising.

ELECTRONIC MEDIA

Television and Radio

As mentioned above, television advertising is generally too expensive to be cost-effective. However, as public relations media, both television and radio are great vehicles for promoting your seminar business.

Public-access television on a cable system can help you gain recognition and credibility. You can't go on public-access TV with a 30-minute commercial for your business, but you can present relevant weekly top-ics, such as "Stress Management for the 90s," "Asking for the Raise You Deserve," or "Loving Discipline for Parents of Toddlers."

Public-access channels offer local programming that interests cable subscribers. Stations in large cities may have 25 hours of quality programming per week, but stations in small towns are more likely to schedule local church services or basement shows.

What do you need to produce a show on a public-access channel? First, realize that you do *not* need television experience. Many cable sys-tems offer training or staff members who will work with you to produce your show. Additionally, many cable systems will offer studio space and equipment for free or at a low cost. Second, call your local cable station and ask about its guidelines. You may deal with either the cable com-pany or a nonprofit agency that organizes the public-access center. Most stations will have a contract that asks the number of shows you will pro-duce, how much studio time you will use, and when you would like your show to air.

Consider what type of show would work best with the type of in-formation offered in your seminars. Interview shows work well for top-ics that can draw on a large number of experts. Demonstration shows work best for topics such as office or closet organization. A live call-in show is effective for professional advisers such as management consul-tants. Public-access channels don't have a huge audience, but the expo-sure is valuable nonetheless.

Radio shows often have larger audiences. If possible, pitch a short-form show that becomes a small but regular part of an already es-tablished show. Key Seminars' Michael Podolinsky went one better. After Podolinsky did a talk show in Johannesburg, South Africa, the station manager called and hired him to tape "Success with Stress—A Motivational Moment with Michael Podolinsky," a regular two-minute spot that has mainly been aired in Africa and Asia for two years and is now going into syndication.

A Word on Infomercials

An infomercial is one of the most popular ways to sell your products once your business takes off. In general, there are two ways to market your product through an infomercial: (1) license or sell your product or idea to a company which then assumes all the marketing and production costs, or (2) go to a second type of firm, which takes none of the profits but charges you for all the production costs. Guthy-Renker Corp., in Palm Desert, California, and Kent & Spiegel Direct Inc., in Culver City, California, are examples of the former; Fairfield, Iowa-based Hawthorne

Communications Inc. is an example of the latter. San Francisco-based Impact Television Marketing blends these two types (it will work with an entrepreneur who has the money and the idea, or find financing if an entrepreneur has a good idea but lacks backing).

If you don't have a large sum of money to get started, don't panic. One solution is to get help. Hawthorne Communications, for example, works as a kind of "infomercial doctor." On a pay-per-service basis, you can go to them for an initial consultation, for help with the script, for fulfillment, or for production.

Other companies, like Guthy-Renker, will organize and finance the process, and will pay you a royalty from the proceeds. Depending on the arrangements you make, you can get an infomercial made with little or no money of your own.

If the products that complement your seminars don't warrant a full-length show, try the home shopping networks. QVC Network, in West Chester, Pennsylvania, and the Home Shopping Network, in St. Petersburg, Florida, are the best known. Many others are already operating, and still more are in the works.

The infomercial industry boasts revenues of roughly $2 billion; by some estimates, revenues should skyrocket in the coming years.

SPECIALTY ITEMS

Ad specialties are products that feature your company's name and/or logo. If you use them correctly, they can offer longer-lasting results than print or electronic ads. They work best for companies that are known for their service and expertise. You can inscribe your company's name and/or logo, or a theme from a popular seminar, on visors, T-shirts, sunglasses, matchbooks, calendars, pens, and any other item you can think of. The list of potential products is practically endless. You can sell the high-ticket items, and you can hand out the less expensive specialties to customers for free.

MEASURING ADVERTISING EFFECTIVENESS

As a business owner, you should never stop surveying and studying your customers. Check the effectiveness of your advertising programs regularly, using tests like the following:

1. Advertise a seminar with a special discount in one newspaper (or other medium) only, and track the number of respondents who call in about the discount offer.

2. Run the same ad in two different publications but put an identifying phrase on each ad. Ask those who call to enroll which phrase appears on their ad, and offer them a special price or discount. Keep track of how many calls come in from each ad.

3. Omit a regular advertising project for intermittent periods, and watch for any change in enrollment.

4. Be sure to track where each enrollment comes from. Ask every caller who does not have a brochure how he or she heard about your seminar.

These checks cannot provide precise measurements, but they can give you some idea of how your program is performing. Timing, topics, weather, season, economic conditions, and similar factors will affect any advertising program. If results are not significant, the program may still have served an institutional purpose by telling people your company is there. Some people may enroll in the future.

ADVERTISING PROFESSIONALS

Professional advertising agency personnel and media representatives may be able to help you plan your advertising efforts, though ad agencies earn a large portion of their profits in commissions from advertising media placed on behalf of their clients. Still, if you are not confident about your design, copywriting, conceptual, or other marketing skills, seek help. Remember, a thorough knowledge of advertising is essential to any businessperson.

PUBLICITY

A newspaper editor's main concern is to fill each edition with newsworthy items. When you introduce a unique topic; when you have a contest promotion; when you do something charitable; when something unusual happens to you, your business, or your employees—let the media know. The principal advantages of publicity are:

- A news story or magazine article takes more time to read than an ad. The more time a reader spends with your story, the more likely that reader will remember you.

- News and feature stories can appear in more periodicals than you could afford to reach through paid advertising.

- You will not receive any media coverage unless the media decide your story is worth covering. This kind of coverage gives

third-party credibility to your story, which you could not duplicate through paid advertisements.

You must make the right media contacts when you begin any publicity
campaign. Linda Pinson and Jerry Jinnett, in a *Business Start-Ups* magazine article,[1] suggest that you start by contacting the advertising directors for the various media in your area and asking for a copy of their
editorial schedules, which will give you a good idea of when the media
plan to cover particular subjects. Using this information, you can contact
radio and television programmers and newspaper and magazine editors.
Call the newspaper or broadcast station, ask for the appropriate person,
and be sure you have the correct spelling of his or her name and the correct business address. This is extremely important to most media people. Taking the time to contact the right people will pay off for you. You
might offer to write an article or take part in an interview focusing on
your area of expertise. You might also try to obtain coverage for your
business as part of a planned article or show.

Keep alert to anything that can give you publicity. The media may
not accept everything, but whatever they do accept will be free advertising for you. Be sure to reprint any stories that give you free publicity.
Use them as highly credible advertising in your handouts and mailers.

Reprints

Once a story on you or your business appears, reprints of the article
will make wonderful marketing tools. Potential customers, vendors,
and suppliers may be interested in reading the piece. Articles make
people think your company is important and unique because a publication chose to write about you.

Most magazines and newspapers offer reprinting services for a
fee—75¢ to $1 apiece for a four-color reprint. Once you have the reprints,
send them out with information kits or display them where your customers can see them.

Press Kits

You should have press kits prepared to send to local newspapers, television stations, radio stations, magazines, and similar outlets. Your press
kit should include a picture of you and/or your featured speaker(s). An
8 × 10-inch glossy black-and-white print should be fine. Include a press
release describing your background and your speakers' expertise, your
intended audience, and the need for the information presented in the

seminar. Send this press kit with the heading, "For Release on X Date." Be sure to emphasize any unique strengths of your seminar or your speaker. If your speaker is a celebrity in any way—a professional athlete, a former politician, a well-known speaker, or any other "newsmaker"— your program will be of special interest to the media.

There's no guarantee that you will receive publicity from any of the media to which you send press kits, but you can increase your chances if you send the kits early enough to meet various deadlines. Many magazines, for instance, are prepared months before they actually appear on the stands. If you know of a trade publication targeting your audience, call it to see how early you would need to send your press kit to meet the appropriate deadline. (If you're running a seminar in September, you would want the magazine to mention it in its August or September issues. To do so, however, the publication may need to receive your material as early as May or April.) Daily newspapers don't need as much advance notice; about two to three weeks should be enough. If nothing else, you may be contacted as an expert source in an upcoming article—free publicity at its finest.

CHOOSING A NAME

From an advertising standpoint, the best name for your business is one that describes your type of service, such as "Top-Flight Seminars." When new businesses strive for uniqueness by using nondescriptive names, many potential customers pass them by, not realizing the brochure they received is worth their perusal, offering just the information and insight they need.

If you use your full name in the title of the business, such as "Jonathan Harrington Seminars," or "Sue Younger Co.," you may improve your personal credit (if you pay your bills on time) as you build your company's credit, and you may find your products easier to market as your company grows. This process can also build prestige in the community. After a time, people will recognize your name.

On the other hand, it is generally easier to sell a business that has a nonfamily name, should you ever decide to sell. Consider building up your personal credit and then converting the business to a corporation, using only your last name.

CONSUMER PROTECTION

Advertising is regulated by agencies on the local, state, and federal levels. At the federal level, the Federal Trade Commission (FTC), the Food and Drug Administration (FDA), and the Federal Communications Commission (FCC) regulate the advertising practices of large corporations. On the smaller, local scale, advertising and business practices are handled by state departments of consumer affairs, local bureaus of consumer affairs, and the Better Business Bureaus.

Because advertising is subject to public and legal scrutiny and criticism, be careful about the claims you make for your seminars. They should conform to the regulations of federal, state, and local agencies, as well as to the standards of good taste.

9

OPERATIONS

Putting together a seminar is a complex, time-consuming project that requires a great deal of attention to detail as well as effective time management. Keep in mind that while you are making all the arrangements to run a particular seminar, you also have to run the day-to-day operations of your business.

To give you an idea of the tasks involved in producing a seminar, we'll look at a sample seminar, from beginning to end. We'll also cover the intricacies of day-to-day operations that we haven't discussed in previous chapters.

DESIGNING YOUR SEMINAR

Before you get started, decide how your actual presentations are going to run. Will you simply audition speakers and let them go forward with their own presentations, or do you want them to follow a set outline? The difference is an important one. "We do 6,700 seminars a year as a company, and it becomes pretty precise. The curriculum—what the speaker is talking about—is developed here, and our creative materials are developed here at CareerTrack," says Bill Hill, manager of seminar operations. "Equipment, by topic, becomes very standardized so that our planners can make proper arrangements, and every trainer pretty much uses the same thing."

If you can afford well-known speakers for your seminars and hope to draw in crowds based on name recognition, you won't want to tinker too much with each speaker's formula. The speakers are known because of what they do and how they do it. On the other hand, if you are selling your seminars based on the value of the topics being covered and your ability to market your "product," you will want to offer some consistency. "We want to stay true to the promise of our brochure," says Denise Dudley, co-founder of SkillPath Seminars. "Having a structure for your presentations becomes crucial when you work with hundreds of different speakers across the country. Should a large corporation decide to take advantage of your public seminars in 20 different cities one year, you will want all [the attendees] to receive the same information," says Dudley. "The only thing we don't control, and won't, is personal stories" she adds.

Structure offers at least three important elements to the seminars you sell:

1. It helps you answer questions from callers both before and after the seminars are held.
2. It allows you to better serve the lucrative corporate market. (Management will not want each employee group to hear different messages through the course of a specific training session.)
3. It allows your speakers to rehearse and perfect their presentations ahead of time, so that your attendees see a polished, professional performance.

It may help if you start out on a small local scale and experiment with different outlines and techniques for some time before settling on a set "script" for each seminar. You have to find speakers who can be themselves while addressing the points most important to your customers. Eve Cappello, PhD, a speaker, author, and consultant, says that she always takes notes on audience reactions to her presentations, to gauge what's going well, what's not going well, and why. These notes, along with postevent attendee evaluations, guide her as she works to perfect each new seminar.

SEMINAR TIMELINE

The following timeline lists the major steps involved in staging a seminar and the order in which you need to accomplish them.

Six months or more *before seminar.* Select your topic and speakers and start planning the dates. Remember to avoid any conflicts with holidays, major sporting events, or any other kind of event that is likely to take precedence over your seminar in the eyes of your target audience. If your show is aimed at salespeople, and a national sales industry convention is scheduled for a given week, you won't have many attendees if you schedule your seminar for the same week—unless you can "tack on" to that convention.

Check on any competitive activity in your selected city and your planned hotel or facility site. Competitive activity can be either a similar seminar event or something unrelated like the Super Bowl or Miss America pageant taking place in the same city. Contact speakers bureaus if you are seeking a big-name speaker, and finalize contracts with dates up front. Once the dates are finalized, you can start putting down deposits on your site and making other arrangements. (For more information on selecting sites and facilities, see Chapter 2.)

Five months before seminar. Price your seminar carefully. Don't underprice because you are nervous about turnout. Pricing is covered more thoroughly below (and in Chapter 7), but you need to consider pricing before many other steps. For example, you can only start printing your brochures, letters, ads, and flyers after you have set your price.

Decide whether to serve meals at your program. The length of your program and the time of day at which it takes place are important factors. Even if your seminar is an all-day affair, you don't have to serve lunch, but you do need to schedule a lunch break of about one and a half to two hours, and hold your seminar in a facility with or near a restaurant.

Do offer water, coffee, tea, and perhaps juice or lemonade at all seminars. Attendees remember clearly the "amenities" of the seminars they attend—comfortable chairs, the temperature of the room, and so on. If you just offer water, hotels will often include the setup price in your room rental. Coffee and other beverages can run you from $3 to $7 per person; in some cases, more. It may be cost-effective and worthwhile to offer continental breakfast through the hotel. Coffee, tea, and juice will be included *and* there will be muffins, croissants, and similar pickups.

Start preparing photographs. You may want camera-ready black-and-white or color photos of your speaker for your brochures or press kits. Contact the speaker or the bureau for photos. If you plan to send your press kits to any magazines, start now. (Newspapers don't need as much lead time; aim for one month ahead of your date.) If you plan to use temporary salespeople, now is the time to hire them.

Four months before seminar. Your brochure should be ready. This is when the promotion of your seminar really begins. Do all you can to encourage preregistration: offer a discounted price (mark up "at-the-door" tickets by 15 or 20 percent); assign seats in order of ticket purchase and say so on the brochure; offer even greater discounts for preregistered groups or students; give a $5 or $10 voucher for products to those who preregister; and so on. If you decide to use salespeople, have them begin calling on local businesses now.

Two months before seminar. Finalize your workbooks and place orders for signs, audio/visual equipment, and incidentals. If you plan to sell products at the seminar, order them from your supplier or from the speaker. Begin hiring or contacting site employees and firming up details on your seminar needs. Michael Podolinsky, a speaker and author, as well as founder of Key Seminars Speakers Bureau and TEAM Seminars, has a preprinted booklet that he sends out to site coordinators, explaining his specific needs and how he likes his room set up.

One month before seminar. By this time, you should have a good idea of how many attendees you will have. Place all the necessary printing orders (e.g., for workbooks, evaluation forms, agendas, and so on) now. By ordering in advance, you avoid paying express delivery charges, which you would incur by waiting until the last minute.

Finalize any necessary travel arrangements for yourself, an assistant, or your speaker. Many professional speakers are so busy that they may not know where they will be, on the day before your program, until two to four weeks before it takes place, so don't purchase tickets too early. Be sure to have a clear idea of the speaker's travel requirements. Does he or she demand first-class airfare, or will coach suffice? What type of hotel accommodations are desired?

Many seminar promoters use only local speakers for their seminars, to keep their costs down. But if you go for the big names, you will have to cover travel arrangements and costs.

The day before the seminar. If your speaker is from out of town, have him or her arrive a day early. This allows time to relax from the trip, which is particularly important if the trip began in a different time zone. Even if the speaker is local, have him or her check out the seminar site and become familiar with its layout. Where are the nearest restrooms? Pay phones? Copy machines? Be sure to call your site coordinator(s)—at the facility and for your seminar—to finalize all arrangements.

The day of the seminar. You or your seminar manager and your speaker should arrive at least one to two hours early to check the setup of the room and the equipment, and to ensure that any emergency can be handled well ahead of time. Make sure that all your "on-site" employees are in place. Set up tables for registration, handouts, products, and programs. Make sure your ushers and guards, if any, arrive on time and take their places.

REGISTRATION AND SEATING

Once your advertising goes out, you must be ready to answer questions and to accept calls for registration. Be sure your phone is answered professionally by someone who speaks well and knows about the seminar, the speaker, and your company. Have your computer database ready to accept the information taken over the phone. It is wise to accept payment via a credit card up front, rather than allowing for payment at the seminar. Have the operator accepting the information read it all back to the caller to be sure it is correct. Confirm dates, name of the seminar, location, and times. If you offer more than one seminar, be sure that you have registered the caller for the correct event, date, and city. Check all phone messages. If callers reach your business when no one is available to answer the phone, be sure their calls are returned within 48 hours.

You will probably receive up to half of your registrations by mail, if you offer that registration option. Again, be sure that you register the person for the correct event, date, and city. Send a confirmation letter, a ticket, and other necessary materials as soon as possible after you receive a registration. If payment is by check, deposit the check but wait a week or so to mail the confirmation package, just to ensure there are no problems with the check. If you have any trouble reading the personal information provided, call the registrant for clarification. (This is one reason why it is important to get a phone number on the mail-in registration forms.)

On the day of your seminar, set up a registration table at the entrance to the facility or room in which the seminar will take place. Place copies of the agenda for the seminar, the workbook, and any other handouts on this table. Registered attendees should come up and check in. Walk-ins can pay their fee and fill out a registration form at the table.

If you have open seating, ushers won't be necessary. If you have assigned seats or have reserved sections of seats, you will need ushers to guide people to the appropriate sections. You will also need some way of indicating on the ticket where an attendee should sit. You might use color-coded tickets, or you might arrange seating by the number on the ticket. (This latter method would require you to keep tight control of the tickets and the order in which they are sold.)

Don't forget to have a place for displaying any products for sale. You do not have to keep these products on the registration table, but they should be near the table and displayed in a very inviting fashion. You might offer a discount coupon for another seminar, or a drawing for a free product or seminar, at the table where your products are being displayed. Have someone at the table at all times to take payments and help answer questions.

Planning for Walk-Ins

If you decide to host big-name seminars with lots of newspaper and radio advertising, walk-ins may become a common part of your seminars. However, because most seminar promoters concentrate on direct mail and word-of-mouth referrals for new clients, it's possible to generate more than 90 percent of your attendance ahead of time, and thus be fully prepared for those attending.

Work with your facility site coordinator to prepare for walk-ins. Most hotels will allow for a 5 to 10 percent float on seating and pre-ordered food or beverages. If you expect many walk-ins, look for a seminar site or room that doesn't have fixed seating, so that you can adjust the number of seats in the room according to at-the-door ticket sales.

You also need to think about materials. It is wise to bring extra workbooks, programs, and so on, but you don't want to spend too much money on items that you might not actually need. Dudley says that when a SkillPath seminar brings in far more walk-ins than anticipated, her staff has a copy of one workbook ready to photocopy and makes arrangements with hotel staff up front to use a copy machine. "If anyone gets a photocopied workbook, we send them a real one the next day, [and give them] 10 percent off their next seminar. We really concentrate on keeping people happy," she says.

EVALUATIONS

According to a 1994 survey of corporate executives, association executives, and meeting planners, conducted by the National Speakers Association, the most common problems encountered when hosting a seminar were (1) the speaker did not tailor the presentation appropriately to the audience and (2) the speaker ran overtime.

Critiques like these are important; you can use them to improve your seminars and increase your attendance at future seminars. Every seminar should end with attendees filling out evaluation forms. This step is so important that you need to make it a part of the actual seminar. Encourage responses by holding a drawing or offering another incentive. Have your speakers make filling out the forms an easy part of the session. Be sure that your evaluation forms are simple to fill out. Your attendees should not find them burdensome. As Dudley notes, "Enrollees are very, very helpful. They want you to do well." Give them an evaluation form that gives you the information you need without becoming a burden. Three to four weeks after the seminar, you may want to send another, brief evaluation that simply says: "I would/would not attend another ABC Seminar" with a space for writing why or why not.

WEEKLY AND MONTHLY CONCERNS

There are a number of weekly and monthly tasks that you need to plan and carry out. Like any other business owner, you have to maintain your bookkeeping and record keeping to ensure your seminar business's cash flow in the short term and avoid confusion at the end of the fiscal year. If you can't find the hours during weekdays to update your financial records, devote a couple of hours to them at the end of the week. Allocate some additional time to performing payroll functions and looking over employee schedules. Entrepreneurs who carry out these weekly duties diligently improve their businesses' efficiency and reduce operating problems. (For a review of all the basic financial documents that a small business needs to prepare on a weekly, monthly, and yearly basis, refer to Chapter 7.)

You will also have a number of duties immediately following any seminar. Laura Lodato, owner of a Priority Management franchise in Tampa, Florida, says, "The day before a workshop, the day of a workshop and the day after a workshop are completely consumed for me." She spends mornings filling orders for her daily UPS noon pickup. She goes through evaluations and makes follow-up calls, writes letters, and handles other postseminar duties. Don't overlook the importance of handling administrative tasks in addition to putting on a good show. To prosper, you need to keep the entire operation running smoothly, encourage repeat business, and monitor your budget.

PRICING YOUR SERVICE

Coming up with a ticket price for your seminars will generally involve three variables:

1. Direct seminar costs.
2. Overhead.
3. Profit.

Direct Seminar Costs

Until you establish records to use as guides, you must estimate the costs associated with each seminar. Labor costs consist of the wages or daily rates you pay your on-site employees and/or contractors who manage your seminars, as well as your speakers' fees. If you will manage the seminars yourself, or serve as the speaker, you must include your personal involvement in the total labor charges.

You must also account for the direct, nonlabor costs associated with producing each seminar, including room rental, food and beverages, advertising, printing costs, and special equipment.

Overhead

Overhead comprises all the nonlabor, indirect expenses you incur to operate your business. If you have past operating expenses to guide you, figuring overhead is not difficult. Total all your expenses for one year, excluding direct seminar costs. Divide this number by your total cost of producing the year's seminars. The result is your overhead rate. For example, using the high-end sample business from Chapter 7, suppose your costs and expenses for a one-year period were as follows:

Overhead Expenses:	$154,744
Direct Seminar Costs:	$544,656
Overhead Rate:	$154,744 ÷ $544,656 = 28 percent

If you do not have past expenses to guide you, figuring your overhead rate can be tricky. For example, the hypothetical low-end business depicted in the income statement in Chapter 7 has an overhead rate of approximately 108 percent. The number of people you employ and the number of seminars you produce can vary greatly. Begin with an estimate that overhead will cost you from 25 to 75 percent of your direct seminar costs. You can later raise or lower that figure to suit the realities of your operation.

Using an overhead rate of 28 percent, as just computed, and continuing with our example on a per-seminar basis, we now have:

Direct Per-Seminar Costs:	$2,837
Overhead (28% of $2,837):	$ 794
Subtotal of Operating Expenses:	**$3,631**

Profit

Most operators in this business expect to net 15 to 40 percent of their gross revenues. You must include this net profit in your estimate by applying a percentage profit factor to your combined direct seminar costs and overhead costs. This profit factor will be larger than the actual percentage of gross revenue you'll end up with for your net profit. The markup table (Table 9–1) shows you how much you need to mark up your costs to reach a specific net profit. Find this in the "Net Profit" column. Applying the percentage in the "Markup" column will give you the desired net profit percentage in the "Net Profit" column.

For example, if you plan to net 20 percent before taxes out of your gross revenue, you will need to apply a profit factor of about 25 percent to your direct seminar costs, plus overhead, to achieve that target. Continuing our example, we have:

Subtotal of Operating Expenses:	$3,631
Net Profit (25% of $3,631):	$ 908
Total Income Needed per Seminar:	**$4,539**

Table 9–1   Mark-Up Table

Margin % of Selling Price	Markup % of Cost	Margin % of Selling Price	Markup % of Cost	Margin % of Selling Price	Markup % of Cost	Margin % of Selling Price	Markup % of Cost
4.8	5.01	18.0	22.0	32.0	47.1	50.0	100
5.0	5.3	18.5	22.7	33.3	50.0	52.4	110
6.0	6.4	19.0	23.5	34.0	51.5	54.5	120
7.0	7.5	20.0	25.0	35.0	53.9	56.5	130
8.0	8.7	21.0	26.6	35.5	55.0	58.3	140
9.0	10.0	22.0	28.2	36.0	56.3	60.0	150
10.0	11.1	22.5	29.0	37.0	58.8	61.5	160
10.7	12.0	23.0	29.9	37.5	60.0	63.0	170
11.0	12.4	23.1	30.0	38.0	61.3	64.2	180
11.1	12.5	24.0	31.6	39.0	64.0	65.5	190
12.0	13.6	25.0	33.3	39.5	65.5	66.7	200
12.5	14.3	26.0	35.0	40.0	66.7	69.2	225
13.0	15.0	27.0	37.0	41.0	70.0	71.4	250
14.0	16.3	27.3	37.5	42.0	72.4	73.3	275
15.0	17.7	28.0	39.0	42.8	75.0	75.0	300
16.0	19.1	28.5	40.0	44.4	80.0	76.4	325
16.7	20.0	29.0	40.9	46.1	85.0	77.8	350
17.0	20.5	30.0	42.9	47.5	90.0	78.9	375
17.5	21.2	31.0	45.0	48.7	95.0	80.0	400

Ticket Price

Once you have calculated all your expenses and added a sufficient profit factor to ensure that your seminar will provide you with the desired return, you must determine exactly what your ticket price will be. To do this, refer back to your market survey and estimate the number of attendees you can attract to your seminar through your marketing efforts.

In this example, we projected that you would draw a total of 51 attendees per seminar. Therefore, you would derive the ticket price for this particular seminar by dividing your total required income by the number of attendees. You then would have:

Total Required Income: $4,539
Ticket Price ($4,539 divided by 51): $ 89

PRICING GOALS

The goal in pricing a service is to mark up your labor and materials costs sufficiently to cover overhead expenses *and* generate an acceptable profit. First-time business owners often fail without realizing they priced their services too low.

It's fine to establish your prices based on the three elements we have outlined, but will your price float in the marketplace? There's one sure way to find out: Try it. If your competition is underpricing you, think carefully before lowering your price. Can you reduce your overhead? Are your cost estimates accurate? Don't forgo your budgeted profit just to sell more tickets. A business that does not earn an adequate profit is more vulnerable to total failure because it does not have the cushion that good profits provide for absorbing costly mistakes.

AVOIDING BANKRUPTCY

Developing a strong customer base, paying close attention to customers' needs, finding a small niche and sticking to what you know best, and coping with a changing economy are all proven ways to keep a business successful and out of bankruptcy.

To recognize crucial warning signs and head off disaster, analyze the following list:

1. Are you producing too many different kinds of seminars or carrying too much merchandise?

2. Are you blinded by "pride of parenthood," failing to cut back on money-losing operations?

3. Have you carefully analyzed seminar costs and the demand for your topics, monitored the marketplace, and adjusted quickly to changing conditions?

4. Are you employing sales reps or other employees who make little contribution to your bottom line?

5. Are your profits declining despite increased sales, or is your inventory increasing because of decreasing sales?

6. Have you prepared an accurate and realistic cash projection?

7. Are you maintaining unneeded space?

8. Have you diversified away from your main strengths or over-expanded during good times, only to find yourself cash-poor?

9. Are you taking stopgap measures like injecting additional cash to meet accounts payable, payroll, and other expenses, rather than facing the real problems and taking the necessary corrective steps?

Recognizing problems is a step in the right direction. Next, if you see a problem, you've got to take action to fix it and get your seminar business back on track. When deciding your course of action, make and update an accurate and realistic cash-flow projection that takes into account changing economic realities. Look at the entirety of your operations instead of taking a piecemeal approach to cost-cutting, and analyze both the short- and long-term effects of each cost-cutting activity.

SPONSORS

Once your business is established, you can consider attracting sponsors to pay for part of the cost of the seminar in return for an opportunity to exhibit their products and services at your program. If you establish a good track record for attracting members of a specific segment of the public—say, salespeople, or owners of small businesses—to your programs, you can seek out sponsors who want to present their services or products to that segment. Sponsors are particularly valuable if you are putting on an unusually large or expensive show, or if you are featuring a very well-known speaker who charges a hefty speaking fee.

In exchange for sponsorship, you would provide your sponsors a forum for reaching their desired audience. The sponsors may want to display promotional literature at a table during your program, or they may want to give a brief presentation to your audience. Whatever the arrangement, you and the sponsor should draw up a *contract* specifying the rights and obligations of both parties. Specify just what kind of forum the sponsor will have, and what you will ask for it. The sponsor is paying for the right to reach your audience, but you should make sure that the reaching is fairly unobtrusive.

Sponsors don't need to actually invest money in your program. You may be able to get free advertising space for your seminar in a local business magazine in exchange for letting the magazine display a banner at your program, crediting it as a sponsor in your brochure, and, if appropriate, giving tickets to its staffers.

Before you can expect to attract any sponsors, you must prove that you can draw those segments of the public that sponsors wish to reach. For this reason, you need to keep good records of your attendees. As we have discussed previously in this chapter, registration information and seminar evaluations are vital in helping you track your attendees.

Furthermore, if you plan to have more than one company sponsor a given seminar, make sure that you don't have more than one sponsor from a given field. If you had a seminar on business travel, for instance, a car rental company may be willing to sponsor your show. But if two or three different car rental companies sponsor the same show, then the uniqueness and appeal of each one will drop in the eyes of your attendees. If you choose to draw sponsors, consider guaranteeing exclusivity to them. In other words, if you have one car rental company sponsoring your show, you would guarantee that it's the only one there.

FAILURE FACTORS

Most small business surveys show that the primary reasons for business failure lie in the following areas:

1. Inefficient control of costs and quality of product.
2. Underpricing of goods sold.
3. Poor customer relations.
4. Poor relations with suppliers.
5. Inability of management to reach decisions and act on them.
6. Failure to keep pace with a management system.
7. Illness of key personnel.
8. Reluctance to seek professional assistance.
9. Failure to minimize taxation through tax planning.
10. Inadequate insurance.

For the seminar promoter, the two biggest "killers" are bound to be lack of market research and underestimating overhead costs. "Overhead is incredible," says Dudley. "And I think that's something that people don't think about in this business. It's very, very expensive to run one of these things. You have to think really hard before you do it, because you can literally go out of business overnight." You face a number of "hidden" costs, or costs that you can easily overlook. You must, for instance, pay for postage before you ever get a return from your attendees. Unlike a printer or a hotel, the U.S. Postal Service will not grant 60 or 90 days of credit, so you will have to pay for your direct mailings up front. You must watch changing prices for the materials you use. The cost of paper, for example, almost quadrupled in the early 1990s, forcing newspapers, magazines, and other paper-intensive businesses to find ways to cut costs. "I can't even remember what it cost us last year in increased paper costs," says Dudley.

This, of course, ties into the importance of market research. If you waste your brochures and postage on people who are unlikely to respond to your seminar offer, you can lose a bundle. On the other hand, if you carefully survey the marketplace, find your niche, change your topics as the market demands, and artfully entice your potential customers to your seminars, you can soon find yourself enjoying a hefty profit.

EDITOR'S NOTE

Although we have covered all the details necessary for you to set up and operate this business, business management experience and education will certainly increase your chances of success. If you don't have management education or experience, consider enrolling in a small business management course at one of your local community colleges. You may also wish to acquire *The Small Business Encyclopedia®*. For more information, call toll-free: (800) 421-2300.

10

THE START-UP PHASE

Many entrepreneurs fail to realize how much of themselves they will need to give to their businesses. Before you begin operations, be absolutely certain that you are ready to devote yourself entirely—emotionally and financially—to your new venture.

"I sold my car, my stocks, my boat . . . my little brother," jokes Michael Podolinsky, founder of Key Seminars Speakers Bureau and TEAM Seminars. "But if you really do what you enjoy, that's the neat thing about being an entrepreneur—you can put in the long hours. I've heard it said that entrepreneurs are people who work 80 hours a week for the privilege of not working 40 hours for someone else."

The start-up period is a trying time for any business. You need to invest considerable time and energy to run the business smoothly, and you may have to sacrifice your standard of living to find the extra money to keep things going. "I rented out every room in my house, slept in the basement, and worked as a security guard," says Podolinsky. "I'd work 60 hours a week as a security guard, get 2 hours of sleep, and then go put on my suit and go out and tell people how to be successful!" His dedication, however, paid off. Although he originally set out to start a seminar company with two partners, his partners quit after the first failed seminar. Podolinsky endured. "I was the only one who had quit my job to do this," he says. "I was the only one really excited about it."

Today, Key Seminars is one of the most successful bureaus in the country, representing such names as Zig Ziglar, Kenneth Blanchard, Og Mandino, Fran Tarkenton, and Mary Lou Retton. Podolinsky himself travels the world speaking to individuals and organizations on TEAM (Together Everyone Achieves More) building, leadership, motivation, customer satisfaction, time management, and dealing with change. He has a weekly radio show in Africa that is soon to be syndicated across North America, in Australia, and throughout Asia, and he is the author of *The Great Persuader, The Great Communicators II,* and *Marketing Masters.*

The key to early success, say experts, is to remember that this is a learning period and you should treat it as such. Learn from your early experiences so you will do things more efficiently and not repeat mistakes once the business has become established. "You've got to pay some dues. You've got to learn along the way. There are just some things that you can't learn out of a book," says Podolinsky, "like how to handle hostile questions and interruptions. Those are things you have to control. I give a lot of credit to my mentors. At the same time, until you've experienced it, you don't understand it." Like the passenger in an automobile, he says, you don't *really* pay much attention to the direction you're heading in until you have to do the driving.

When you first start out, you will need to work hard to get people interested in your abilities, topics, and seminars or speakers. Like movie stars, exceptional speakers go in and out of the limelight; even after achieving great success, they must continue to market themselves aggressively to stay busy in the long run. Speakers bureaus experience the same kind of ups and downs. The big names that command higher speaking fees bring in the largest profits, but you need to attract and serve as many speakers as possible to meet all the needs of your clients and to keep growing as a business. You must continually market your bureau as the best place to find quality speakers, good service, and support for personal growth. Seminar promotion companies are made on their reputations. People do not necessarily go to the SkillPath, Fred Pryor, and Dun & Bradstreet seminars because they know the trainers; they know the quality of the company. To achieve that kind of reputation takes hard work, exceptional customer service, quality speakers, and a dedication to investing in your business continually.

Therefore, before you begin your business, you need to have a substantial amount of capital with which to operate until you reach your break-even point. You can offset some of your start-up and operating expenses through various types of financing, as discussed in this chapter.

Table 10–1 gives an indication of how much money you will need to start out as a seminar promoter.

Table 10–1   Start-Up Costs

This table depicts the start-up costs for two hypothetical seminar promotion businesses. The low-end business has gross sales of $194,400 per year, and the high-end business grosses $954,624 per year. The owner of the low-end business operates out of his home, but holds seminars in rented meeting rooms in hotels. The owner also serves as the speaker. He produces highly specialized seminars that emphasize one-on-one follow-up sessions, which an employee conducts.

The owner of the high-end business also operates from home and holds seminars in various locations across the country. This business offers four different seminars, and puts on each one, once a week, for 50 weeks a year. This business employs a receptionist, an assistant, and a part-time marketing employee. This business also uses speakers to deliver the actual seminars, and independent contractors to serve as seminar staff.

Some of the start-up costs listed will be incurred before the businesses are established; others (such as payroll costs) will be incurred during the first month of operations. The Suggested Operating Capital will cover the first three months of operation.

Item	Low	High
Initial Inventory	5,386	49,998
Equipment	4,734	14,568
Licenses/Tax Deposits	150	850
Phone/Utilities Deposits	50	200
Employees	2,700	5,250
Marketing/Postage	500	6,180
Seminar Site Rental	200	4,160
Speakers' Fees/Seminar Workers	0	7,920
Seminar Equipment/Refreshments	280	2,240
Professional Services	1,200	3,200
Insurance	80	320
Miscellaneous	200	800
Total Costs	**$15,480**	**$95,686**
Suggested Operating Captial	**$ 9,936**	**$30,749**

THE BUSINESS PLAN

Most people manage their business ideas haphazardly. Assembling a business plan and writing down specifics gives you a chance to step away from your business and take a levelheaded approach to running it.

Every entrepreneur, in every line of business, stands to benefit from using a business plan. A recent AT&T Small Business Study reports that, of businesses with less than $20 million in sales during 1992, fewer than 42 percent used formal business plans to guide their daily operations.

Among businesses with sales of less than $500,000, which made up 68 percent of the total, only one-third had carried out even the most basic planning efforts. Those that did, however, were likely to be rewarded: More than half (59 percent) of the small businesses that exhibited growth, according to the study, said they had used formal business plans.

Very few owners, principals, or executives in charge of small businesses identify long-term planning as one of the strengths they bring to their companies. In fact, only 6 percent of these individuals say long-term planning is a strength. Experience shows they are wrong; long-term planning is paramount to success.

A finished business plan becomes an operating tool that will help you manage your business. A business plan is the chief instrument you will use to communicate your ideas to others—including businesspeople, bankers, and partners. If you seek financing for your business, the plan will also become the basis for your loan proposal.

A strong business plan conforms to generally accepted guidelines of form and content. Generally, a business plan has seven major components:

1. Executive summary.
2. Business description.
3. Market strategies.
4. Competitive analysis.
5. Design and development plans.
6. Operations and management plans.
7. Financial statements.

An optional component is a section for Small Business Administration (SBA) materials, which you should include only if the purpose of your business plan is to obtain financing from the SBA. Documents required by the SBA may also help you set up your business.

Additional Components

Three additional components are critical to the plan's success: (1) a cover, (2) a title page, and (3) a table of contents.

A business plan should have a cover but there is no need to bind the plan in leather; a neat cover large enough to hold your material will suffice. Buy a blue, black, or brown cover at a stationery store. A lender will think more highly of a conservatively presented business plan than of one that is needlessly elaborate. Subtle things like a cover choice reflect your business judgment and management ability.

On the title page, put the name of the business, the name(s) of the principals who own it, and the business's address and phone number. If you have a logo, use it to dress up your title page. Some plans list the names of any people who assisted the business owners in preparing the plans, but, unless some famous people are among your advisers or backers, listing your helpers can lessen the impact of the plan. A business plan should be compiled by the principals of the business.

The table of contents should follow the *executive summary* or *statement of purpose,* which is discussed below. When you or others look over your plan, you should be able to find certain information, such as financial data and market patterns, very quickly. Although the table of contents appears at the front of the plan, you will naturally prepare it last.

Executive Summary

The *executive summary* is also prepared after the other sections, but it should be placed before the table of contents. The summary should tell the reader of the plan what you want. Are you seeking a loan to finance expansion of your promotion company into several more states? Start-up capital to cover the expenses involved in marketing your seminars (e.g., to draw in big names)? Whatever the purpose of the business plan, state it clearly and concisely here. *This is very important.*

The statement should be short and businesslike—probably no more than half a page. It could be up to one page, depending on how complicated the use of funds is. Within that space, you'll need to provide a synopsis of the entire business plan. Key elements that you should include are:

1. *The business concept.* Describes the business, your seminars or your bureau, and the market you will serve. States exactly what you will sell, to whom, and why the business will hold a competitive advantage.
2. *Financial features.* Highlights the important financial points of the business, including sales, profits, cash flows, and return on investment.
3. *Financial requirements.* States how much capital you need to start the business and to expand it; how the capital will be used; and the equity, if any, that will be provided for funding. If the loan for initial capital will be based on security instead of equity within the company, you should specify the source of collateral.

4. *Current business position.* Furnishes relevant information about the company: its legal form of operation, when it was formed, the principal owners, and key personnel.

5. *Major achievements.* Details any developments that are essential to the success of the business, such as trademarks, rental agreements with expensive hotels or auditoriums, any crucial contracts that need to be in place (such as contracts with busy speakers), or results from any test marketing that you have conducted. If the statement of purpose is eight pages long, nobody's going to read it; it will be very clear that the business won't be a good investment because the principals don't really know what they want. By being concise, you enable the reader to discern your needs and capabilities instantly.

Business Description

Following the executive summary is the *business description*, which usually begins with a short examination of the industry's present state and future possibilities.

In the business description, first concentrate on its structure: wholesale, retail, food service, manufacturing, or service. State this right away, along with whether your operation is new or already established, and reiterate the legal form of the business. Detail whether the business is a sole proprietorship, a partnership, or a corporation; who its principals are; and what they will bring to the business.

Once again, mention to whom you will sell and the business's support systems. Support may come in the form of advertising, promotions, or customer service.

After you've described the structure of the business, itemize the actual seminars you intend to market. Your description should be complete enough to give the reader a clear idea of your intentions. Emphasize any unique features or variations from typical seminar concepts in the industry. If you're using your business plan to secure financing, explain why the added equity or debt money will make your business more profitable. Demonstrate how you will expand your business and create growth with the money you are seeking.

Show why your business is going to be profitable. A potential lender will want to know how successful you're going to be. Give a word sketch of the experience of the key people in your business. Report on what experts you've spoken to about your business, and their response to your idea. A lender may even ask you to clarify your choice of location or your reasons for marketing seminars. If you've done proper research and planning, you will be able to describe and defend your ideas in minute detail.

The business description can be a few paragraphs or a few pages long, depending on the complexity of your plan. If your plan is not too complicated, keep your business description short. Describe the industry in one paragraph, the product in another, and the business and its success factors in three or four additional paragraphs.

Market Strategies

Having described the business, you now need to define the market in the *market strategies* section. Begin your market analysis by defining the market in terms of size, structure, growth prospects, trends, and sales potential.

The aggregate sales of your competitors will provide you with a fairly accurate estimate of the total potential market. Once you have determined the overall size of the market, define your target market. Narrow the total market by concentrating on customer-characteristic segmentation factors that will identify potential customer groups.

Once you have detailed the target market, you must further define the total feasible market. You can do this in several ways, but most professional planners concentrate on product segmentation that may produce gaps within the market. Typical product segmentation factors include user characteristics, price sensitivity, and user benefits.

It is important to understand that the total feasible market is the portion of the market that you could capture, provided every condition within the environment were ideal and there were very little competition. In most industries, this is simply not the case. Other limiting factors will affect the share of the feasible market that a business can obtain. These factors are usually tied to the structure of the industry, the impact of competition, strategies for entry into the market and for continued growth, and the amount of capital the business is willing to invest to increase its market share.

A business plan must also estimate the company's future market share. There are two factors to consider when determining future sales potential:

1. Industry growth, which will increase the total number of users.
2. Conversion of users from the total feasible market.

Defining the market is just one step in your analysis. With the information you've gained through market research, you need to develop strategies that will allow you to fulfill your objectives.

How you price your seminars or speaking services will have a direct effect on the success of your business. In the business plan, thoroughly describe your pricing strategy and how it will affect the success of your company or your prospects within the defined market. Describe the going rates for the industry, and justify your chosen price for the services you will provide.

You will need to outline the cities or areas you are targeting and how you plan to expand into each of them. Analyze your competitors to determine which channels they use; then use the same channels or alternative ones that may provide you with a strategic advantage. Finally, describe the sales plan you intend to use to execute your expansion. You should base the sales strategy on several elements that will affect how your sales team will move you into your selected areas:

- *Pricing flexibility.* Determines the degree of flexibility the sales team will have when enforcing the pricing policy.
- *Sales presentation.* Establishes the strategies used to present sales information to potential customers.
- *Lead generation.* Dictates how sales leads will be developed. Direct mail sales leads, for instance, can be generated by using list brokers.
- *Compensation policy.* There has to be an incentive for the sales force to sell aggressively at all times.

After you have researched and analyzed the market, develop a sales projection, as described in Chapter 7. The sales projection for a business plan should chart the potential of the business at least 3 years into the future, although 5-year projections are becoming increasingly popular among lenders.

Competitive Analysis

The competitive analysis section probes the strengths and weaknesses of your competitors, outlining any strategies that will (1) provide you with a distinct advantage over current competitors and (2) develop barriers that will prevent future competition from entering your market.

First, identify your current and potential rivals. Look at the market from the customers' viewpoint and group all your competitors either by the degree to which they contend for the buyer's dollar, or according to their various competitive strategies for attacking the market. To cover all ground, do both exercises of grouping your competitors.

One way of identifying competitors through the customer-viewpoint method is by intensity of competition. You will usually encounter the following types of competitors:

1. *Primary.* Companies that compete directly and intensely with you for sales within the target market.
2. *Secondary.* Companies that compete for sales within the target market, but not as intensely as your primary competition.
3. *Indirect.* Companies that are not in the direct sphere of competition but are still threatening.

Grouping your rivals according to customers' viewpoint is only one way to analyze your competitors. Sorting them by strategy will make it easier to identify the methods they use. Classify your competitors by similar competitive strategies pursued over a period of time, by related characteristics, or by comparable assets and skills.

For the strategic-grouping method to work, there must be barriers between groups that exclude the entry of markedly different competitors and prevent those in one strategic group from moving into another. These barriers may be advertising budgets, dominance of a particular market region, the ability to sign exclusive contracts with speakers, and so on.

Probably one of the most essential parts of your competitor analysis is an examination of your rivals' weaknesses and strengths, usually based on the presence or absence of key assets and skills. Through your competitor analysis, you will also have to create a marketing strategy that will generate an asset or skill that gives you a distinct and enduring competitive advantage.

When you've established the key assets and skills and defined your distinct competitive advantage, communicate them in a way that will both attract and defend market share. Competitive strategies usually fall into five areas:

1. Product.
2. Distribution or, for this business, geographic reach.
3. Pricing.
4. Promotion.
5. Advertising.

Many of the factors leading to the formation of a strategy should have been highlighted in previous sections of your plan—specifically, in your marketing strategies.

Design and Development

The purposes of the design and development section are: to provide investors with a description of how you plan to expand your market, and to chart your company's development within the context of planning, marketing, and the company itself.

Generally, you'll cover three areas in the development plan section:

1. Seminar development/expansion.
2. Market development.
3. Organizational development.

Examine each of these elements from the funding of the plan to the point at which the business begins to generate a continuous income. Although these elements will differ in content, each will be based on the same structure and goals.

The first step in the development process is to set goals for the overall plan. Most of the product development goals will be apparent from your analysis of the market and your competition.

You can only achieve your goals if certain key assets and skills (as enumerated in previous sections) are present in your company. Reassure your reader that you have these assets.

With your goals set and your expertise in place, the development plan needs a set of procedures with which the development team can work. Procedures should address how resources will be allocated and who is in charge of accomplishing each goal. Develop a different set of procedures for seminar development/expansion, market development, and organizational development.

Your schedule for the procedural plan is one of the most important elements of the development plan. Scheduling includes all of the key work elements as well as the stages through which a seminar must pass before it is presented to the public. Tie the scheduling to the *development budget* so that you can track expenses. When forming your development budget, take into account all the expenses required to design each new seminar, and the costs of taking it from planning to presentation.

Costs that you should include in the development budget are:

- *Labor.* All labor costs associated with the development and delivery of the seminar.
- *Overhead.* All overhead expenses required to operate the business during the development phase.

- *General and Administrative (G&A) costs.* The salaries of executive and administrative personnel, along with any office support functions.
- *Miscellaneous costs.* All costs related to product development (i.e., workbooks, videotapes, audiotapes, and so on).
- *Capital equipment.*

Operations and Management Plan

The *operations and management plan* is designed to be a blueprint for ongoing operations, once the business becomes active.

The operations plan will highlight the logistics of the organization—the various responsibilities of the management team, the tasks assigned to each division within the company, and capital and expense requirements related to the operation of the business.

You must address two areas, when planning the operations of your company: (1) the organizational structure, and (2) the expense and capital requirements associated with its operation.

Outline the organizational structure of the company to provide a basis from which to project operating expenses. This is critical to the formation of sound financial statements, which will be heavily scrutinized by investors. The organizational structure has to be well-defined and realistic, given the parameters of the business.

After you have planned the organization's operations, you can calculate the expenses associated with the operation of the business—also known as overhead. Overhead expenses are all nonlabor expenses incurred in operating the business. You can divide expenses into *fixed*—those that you must pay (usually at the same rate) regardless of the volume of business—and *variable* (or semivariable)—those that change according to the volume of business. Within this section of the business plan, include an expense table detailing all your overhead costs.

You'll also need to develop a capital requirements table in which you (1) estimate the amount of money necessary to purchase equipment and (2) illustrate the amount of depreciation your company will incur, based on all equipment purchased with a lifetime of more than one year.

The last table you need to generate in the operations and management section projects the cost of goods. For your purposes, this table covers only your inventory products, such as audiotapes and videotapes. As in a retail business, the merchandise that is sold is included in the cost of goods, and merchandise that isn't sold is placed in inventory. You have to account for the cost of goods. It is an important measurement of the firm's profitability.

Financial Statements

Once the product, market, and operations have been defined, you are ready to address the real backbone of the business plan—your financial statements. The financial statements you must develop are: the *income statement*, the *cash-flow statement*, and the *balance sheet*. (See Chapter 7 for more information on financial statements.)

The income statement is a simple report on the proposed business's cash-generating ability. As a scorecard of the financial performance of your business, it combines the various financial models developed earlier, such as revenue, expenses, capital (in the form of depreciation), and cost of goods.

You should generate an income statement on a monthly basis during the first year, on a quarterly basis during the second year, and annually for each year thereafter. A short note analyzing its results should follow the income statement. The analysis should be very short, emphasizing key points within the income statement.

The cash-flow statement is one of the most critical information tools for your business. It shows how much cash you will need to meet obligations, when you will need it, and where it will come from, and projects a schedule of the money coming into the business and the expenses that you will need to pay. The result is the profit or loss at the end of the month or the year. In a cash-flow statement, both profits and losses are carried over to the next column to show the cumulative amount. If you show a loss on your cash-flow statement, it is a strong indication that you will need additional cash to meet expenses.

Like the income statement, you should prepare the cash-flow statement on a monthly basis during the first year, on a quarterly basis during the second year, and on an annual basis thereafter. As with the income statement, you will need to analyze the cash-flow statement in a short summary.

The last financial statement you'll need to develop is the balance sheet. It too uses information from all of the previous sections; however, unlike the previous statements, you will only generate the balance sheet on an annual basis for the business plan. It is, more or less, a summary of all the preceding financial information.

To obtain financing for a new business, you may have to generate two balance sheets: one that projects the condition of the proposed business over a set period of time, and one that summarizes your personal financial outlook. You can generate a personal balance sheet in the same manner as you would generate one for a business. Refer to the description of the balance sheet in Chapter 7.

You'll need to create an analysis statement for the balance sheet just as you did for the income and cash-flow statements. The analysis of the balance sheet should be short and should cover key points about the company.

This is just a brief overview of what you need in a business plan. For more information that will guide you through the preparation of a business plan, see Entrepreneur Magazine Group's detailed guide No. 1800, *Writing Effective Business Plans.* Entrepreneur Magazine Group also publishes software for DOS, Windows, and Macintosh that will help you write and compile your business plan.

SMALL BUSINESS DEVELOPMENT CENTERS (SBDC)

Created as a result of a cooperative effort involving the private sector, the educational community, and federal, state, and local governments, SBDCs offer current and prospective small business owners—for free or at a nominal cost—counseling, training, and technical assistance in all aspects of small business management.

There are 57 SBDCs, one or more in each of the 50 states, the District of Columbia, Puerto Rico, and the Virgin Islands, and they operate more than 700 service locations. Each SBDC has a "lead" organization that sponsors and manages a program and coordinates the services, which are offered through a network of subcenters and satellite locations at colleges, universities, vocational schools, chambers of commerce, and economic development corporations.

In addition to programs unique to their areas, all SBDCs provide training and technical assistance with business basics, such as finance, marketing, organization, human resources, and production.

Although the SBDC program is sponsored by the Small Business Administration (SBA), each center has leeway to develop services tailored to the local community and the needs of its individual clients.

FINANCING

You may find others to raise the necessary capital for you, or you can try to raise it through your own resources. A well-defined set of rules comes into play for whichever course you choose. If you seek all of your capital from one large investor, you will end up with a much smaller piece of your company. If you attempt to raise the money with the help of your own acquaintances, you can usually arrange a much better deal for yourself. If you're lucky, you can finance your business through your own personal lines of credit or savings accounts. If not, you will begin the search for financing.

If any single piece of advice is most appropriate for a new entrepreneur in need of money, it is to make a careful assessment of the proposed value of the business, the needed capital, the increments, and the period of time. Then, decide on the source—a Small Business Investment Company (SBIC), a single investor, a private placement of securities with friends and relatives, a private placement through a securities firm, or a public offering either through a securities firm or a self-issuer distribution.

For any of these approaches, you're going to need a business plan. Once you've chosen a course of action, follow it without deviation, and abandon it for another course only when your first choice has clearly proven unfeasible. Tenacity is everything. If your product has merit, you can usually find a formula that works.

Tap Yourself First

The best source of financing for anyone wishing to start a business is, as mentioned, his or her own money. It is immediately available capital, there is no interest to pay back, and the owner does not have to surrender any equity in the business. Getting any venture off the ground, however, can be a very costly proposition—one that may be beyond your immediate cash reserves. If this is the case, there are several avenues you can explore to obtain the necessary capital.

One of the most overlooked ways to obtain start-up capital is to use your credit cards. Most charge extremely high interest rates, but they do provide a way to get several thousand dollars quickly without dealing with paperwork, as long as you don't exceed your credit limit.

We know of one person who had three credit cards with a $3,000 credit line on each. He needed approximately $8,000 to start an auto detailing shop. He cashed in each of his credit cards for the full amount and started his shop. Within 6 months, he had built up a very good business and approached his bank for a loan of $10,000. He received the loan for a 3-year term at 12 percent. With the $10,000, he paid off his credit card balances, which were incurring a 20 percent annual interest rate. After another 6 months, he paid off the bank loan of $10,000.

Friends and Relatives

After using your own money, borrowing from your friends and relatives is the next best choice. Any money raised this way, however, should be treated as any other loan. Have your lawyer draw up loan papers for each friend or relative who contributes money to your venture.

Disclose your plans and intentions, and explain to friends and relatives what the risks are. Having friends and relatives who loan you money sign loan papers serves two purposes: (1) it protects their loans, and (2) it prevents them from gaining equity in your business, unless you default on the loans.

Borrowing from Banks

Banks are probably the most visible source of ready financing, and you should already have contact with a few through your personal and business accounts. Although banks are logical places to go for capital, they are notoriously conservative.

Most banks will require some sort of collateral as security for a loan. Banks will also want to know the purpose of the loan, so be prepared to show them your business plan. Your personal background will have a direct bearing on how a bank treats your loan applications.

Depending on the size of the loan you request, there are several bank loan and collateral possibilities. If you have a savings account at a bank, you can use this money as collateral for a short-term loan.

It may also be possible to use your life insurance policy as collateral, if it has any cash value. Loans can usually be made for up to 95 percent of the policy's cash value. By borrowing against your life insurance policy, you don't actually have to repay the loan; you need only pay the interest charges along with your premium. However, if you don't repay the amount at some time, your policy will decrease in value by that amount.

Signature (personal) loans are a possibility if your credit is good. You can usually take out a loan of this type for several thousand dollars—or even more, if you have a good relationship with the bank. Personal loans usually have short terms and very high interest rates.

Another type of short-term loan is a commercial loan, which is usually issued for a 6-month period and can be paid in installments during that time or in one lump sum. Stocks and bonds, your life insurance policy, or your personal guarantee can be used as collateral. If the loan is exceptionally large compared to your assets, the bank may require you to post a cash reserve equal to 20 percent of the loan amount.

You can also use, as collateral, any real estate you own. Loans of this nature can be secured for up to 75 percent of the real estate's value and can be set up for terms of up to 20 years, if necessary.

If you own a home, you may want to consider a home equity loan. However, there are two valid and opposing points of view about using home equity as a money source. On the positive side, if you have equity in your home, you can take it out, invest it in a business, and make it work for you. On the other hand, if you have equity in your home but you don't own it free and clear, and something happens that prevents you from making payments, you can lose your home *and* your equity. The decision is up to you.

Other loan possibilities include equipment and accounts receivable financing. These types of loans use the value of your equipment or accounts receivable as security for a loan. If you use your equipment or accounts receivable as collateral, you can usually secure a loan for 80 percent of their value.

The SBA

Although it is difficult to get a loan through the Small Business Administration, it is not impossible. By law, the SBA may not make or guarantee a loan if a business can obtain funds on reasonable terms from some other source. Therefore, a borrower must first seek private financing before applying to the SBA. The SBA considers itself to be a lender of last resort.

To qualify for an SBA loan, your loan application must be for the financing of an independently owned and operated business. Loans cannot be made to speculative businesses, newspapers, or businesses engaged in gambling, nor can they be made to pay off a creditor who is adequately secured and in a position to sustain loss; to provide funds for distribution to the principals of the applicant; or to replenish funds previously used for such purposes.

Be prepared to prove to the SBA that your proposed company has the ability to compete successfully in its field. Whether you're seeking a loan for a new concept or an established one, don't underestimate the importance of the category into which the SBA groups it. The success or failure of your application may rest on this classification. Decide which field your business can best compete in, state this on your application, and be prepared to back it up.

To help you prepare for this question, you should know how the SBA formulates its guidelines. A key publication it relies on is the *Standard Industrial Classification (SIC) Manual*, published by the Bureau of the Budget, in Washington, DC. The SBA also uses published information concerning the nature of similar companies, as well as your description of the proposed business. The SBA will not intentionally work against you, but it is up to you to steer the agency in the direction that is best for you.

The maximum amount you may borrow under an SBA-guaranteed loan is $833,333. Interest on the loan will be set according to a statutory formula based on the cost of money to the government.

Although loans are available for as few as 1 or 2 years and as many as 25 years (in the case of construction and real estate loans), the vast majority of loans run for 5 to 8 years, with 10 years being the limit (except for working-capital loans, which are limited to 7 years).

You can use certain assets as collateral for an SBA loan:

1. Land and/or buildings.
2. Machinery and/or equipment.
3. Real estate and/or chattel mortgages.
4. Warehouse receipts for marketable merchandise.
5. Personal endorsement of a guarantor (someone who is able and willing to pay off the loan if you fail).

The LowDoc Loan Program

The Small Business Administration has adopted a program that makes applying for a loan somewhat easier. Called the LowDoc Loan Program, it combines a simplified application process with a more rapid response from SBA loan officers of up to 2 weeks, slashing much red tape out of the loan process.

The LowDoc program was created in response to complaints that the SBA's loan application process for smaller loans was needlessly cumbersome for both borrowers and lenders that participate in the SBA's 7(a) General Business Loan Guarantee Program. The process tended to discourage borrowers from applying for, and lenders from making, loans of less than $100,000.

LowDoc streamlines the loan application process for guaranteed loans of less than $100,000. The approval process relies heavily on the lender's experience and judgment of the borrower's credit history and character. The primary considerations are the borrower's willingness and ability to repay debts, as shown by his or her personal and business credit history, and by past or projected cash flow. No predetermined percentage of equity is required, and lack of full collateral is not necessarily a determining factor.

The application form for loans of less than $50,000 is just one page long. Applications for loans of $50,000 to $100,000 include that form and the applicant's income tax returns for the previous three years, plus personal financial statements from all other guarantors and co-owners of the business. Commercial lenders are likely to require additional paperwork to satisfy their own requirements. Other documents required by legislation, regulation, and executive order are dealt with at the loan closing.

Any small business eligible under the regular 7(a) loan program can apply under LowDoc if its average annual sales for the previous 3 years are $5 million or less and it employs 100 or fewer individuals, including the owner, partners, or principals.

Finance Companies

Finance companies will take greater risks than banks, but they also charge higher interest rates. Generally, finance companies will be more interested in your collateral, your past track record, and the potential of your new business than in the strength of your credit.

Using Suppliers as Loan Sources

Although you won't be able to finance your complete start-up through suppliers, you may be able to offset the cost of merchandise during your start-up period by obtaining a lengthy payment period, or trade credit. When you first start your business, suppliers will usually not extend trade credit. One of the things you can do to get credit is to have a properly prepared financial plan and negotiate with the owner of the business or the chief financial officer.

If you're successful, you may defer payment for supplies from the time of delivery to 30, 60, or even 90 days, interest-free. Although this is not actually a loan, you still have the money you would otherwise spend on those supplies during the crucial start-up period.

Selling Equity

Sometimes, raising start-up capital requires giving up a portion of a business to private investors. Money you receive this way is called equity capital. With equity financing, you divide your business ownership among investors who contribute capital but may or may not participate in the operation of the business. There aren't any loans associated with equity capital, and you have no legal obligation to pay back the amount invested. All the investor gets is a percentage of the business—and the losses or profits associated with it.

Equity capital may, at first glance, seem like the best way to raise start-up capital, but it has many drawbacks. First, you give up a portion of your business and, with it, some control. That means you have to share your profits with your new partners, and, depending on how you set up the company—as a partnership, a limited partnership, or a corporation—you could become responsible for the actions of your partner(s). If partners go into debt, you and your company may join them.

Second, with some types of equity financing, you might relinquish control of your company. Have your lawyer draw up documents for equity investors to sign that state the amount and value of the equity being offered. The individual with the idea will usually retain 50 percent of the equity in the company, and the other 50 percent will be sold to investors. While the 50–50 rule is fairly common, everything is negotiable in a deal such as this.

Venture Capital

Obtaining start-up money from venture capitalists is another popular, albeit riskier, financing route. Although venture capital funds invest $2 to $3 billion annually in more than 2,000 new and existing businesses, they do so in only about 1 percent of the proposals they see each year.[1] Venture capitalists, whether institutional funds or individuals (often referred to as "angels"), usually like to invest in relatively new businesses that are risky but have a successful track record and the potential for relatively high profit and growth.

There are over 500 venture capital funds throughout the United States. The funds are controlled by professional fund managers who oversee about $35 billion. Venture capitalists are a diverse group of investors with different investment interests, skills, and objectives. They differ with regard to the industries they will finance and the stages of development of the companies they will fund. Some prefer to provide "seed" money for start-ups; others only do later rounds of financing or leveraged buyouts. Some may specialize in a particular geographic area or may choose to finance businesses within certain industries. They also have differing parameters on the minimum amount of money they will invest. Some may invest in $50,000 to $100,000 minimums; others will not invest less than $200,000 to $500,000.

Venture capitalists expect two things from the companies they finance: (1) high returns and (2) a method of exit. Because venture capitalists make money from only a small percentage of the companies they back, they must go into each deal with the possibility of a return of 5 to 10 times their investment in 3 to 5 years if the company is successful. This may mean that they will own anywhere from 20 to 70 percent or more of your company. Each situation is different, and the amount of equity the venture capitalist will hold depends on the stage of the company's development at the time of the investment, the risk perceived, the amount of capital required, and the background of the entrepreneur.

The key to attracting venture capital is the potential growth of the company. If your company does not have the potential to be a $30 to $50 million company in 5 to 7 years, you are going to have a difficult time obtaining money from most venture capitalists. They do not invest in small businesses. They invest in large businesses that are just getting started. There are some firms that may finance your new seminar promotion venture even though your growth prospects are not that high, but those firms are more difficult to find.

However, if you're willing to give a venture capitalist a piece of the action, and if you're prepared to accept the venture capitalist as a partner in your business, you might be a candidate for venture financing. The best way to begin your search for funds is to obtain a comprehensive list of venture capital companies. Contact The National Venture Capital Association (NVCA), 1655 N. Fort Myer Dr., Suite 700, Arlington, VA 22209; (703) 351-5269.

Appendix A

SEMINAR PROMOTION RESOURCES

(Although the editors at Entrepreneur Media, Inc. have made every effort to verify the following information to ensure its accuracy at the time of publication, businesses and other organizations do move or cease to conduct business. Due to these circumstances, Entrepreneur Media, Inc. cannot be held responsible for the reliability of the sources listed. If you are unable to contact any of the following organizations, first try calling directory assistance in the area code listed. You can do this by dialing 1-[area code]-555-1212 and asking for the organization listed.)

Associations

National Speakers Association, 1500 S. Priest Dr., Tempe, AZ 85281; (602) 968-2552

Meeting Professionals International, 4455 LBJ Freeway, Suite 1200, Dallas, TX 75244; (214) 702-3000

Franchise

Priority Management Systems Inc., 500 108th Ave. NE, Suite 1740, Bellevue, WA 98004; (800) 221-9031

Promotional Consulting Service

Eve Cappello, PhD, ACT International, 518 S. El Molino Ave., #303, Pasadena, CA 91101; (818) 432-1981

Speakers Bureaus and Seminar Producers

Key Seminars Speakers Bureau and TEAM™ Seminars, 18885 Valley View Rd., Eden Prairie, MN 55346; (612) 949-8833
Speakers Unlimited, Box 27225, Columbus, OH 43227; (614) 864-3703 (Michael Frank, who owns this bureau, also offers consulting services to seminar producers.)

Seminar Producers Offering Mailing Lists

CareerTrack, 3085 Center Green Dr., Boulder, CO 80301; (303) 447-2323
SkillPath, 6900 Squibb Rd., Suite 300, Mission, KS 66202; (913) 362-3900

Related Books by Entrepreneur Magazine Group

To order any of the following business guides 24 hours a day, 7 days a week, call (800) 421-2300 or fax your order to (714) 851-9088.

Home-based Business Resource, #1804
Managing Personnel, #1801
Small Business Encyclopedia, #3500 (3-volume set)
Smart Selling, #1803
Writing Effective Business Plans, #1800

SOURCES OF SUPPLY

The following are representative but certainly not the only suppliers of services such as the duplication, packaging, printing, and production of audio, video, and other materials used by seminar promoters at their seminars and as additional sources of revenue. New companies are coming into the market all the time, and you should watch for the announcements of their development in trade magazines. To source equipment locally, look in your Business-to-Business Yellow Pages.

Audio/Video Packaging or Duplication

American Packaging, 90 Dayton Ave., Passaic, NJ 07055; (201) 471-1111
Audio Video Color Corp., 7045 Radford Ave., North Hollywood, CA 91605; (818) 982-6800
Cassette Duplicators, Inc., 2211 W. Printers Row, South Lake City, UT 84119; (800) 829-0077 or (801) 977-0077
Duplication Factory, Inc., 4275 Norex Dr., Chaska, MN 55318; (800) 279-2009
Global Cassettes, 14804 N. Cave Creek Rd., Phoenix, AZ 85032; (602) 483-0398
Multi-Media Publishing & Packaging, Inc., 9430 Topanga Canyon Blvd., Suite 200, Chatsworth, CA 91311; (818) 341-7484 (full service company)
Vaughn Duplication Services Inc., 2009 McKenzie Dr., Suite 110, Carrollton, TX 75006; (214) 620-7978
Video Central, 13455 Ventura Blvd., Suite 203, Sherman Oaks, CA 91423; (818) 789-9801

Photocopiers/Facsimile Machines

Canon U.S.A., Inc., One Canon Plaza, Lake Success, NY 11042; (516) 488-6700
Sharp Electronics Corp., Sharp Plaza, Mahwah, NJ 07430; (800) 237-4277

Cellular Phones

JRC International: (800) 231-5100
Matsushita Consumer Electronics Co., One Panasonic Way, Secaucus, NJ 07094; (201) 348-9090
Motorola, 600 N. U.S. Hwy. 45, Libertyville, IL 60048; (800) 331-6456
Oki, 437 Old Peachtree Rd., Suwanee, GA 30174; (800) 554-3112

Computers

Apple Computer, Inc., 1 Infinite Loop, Cupertino, CA 95014; (408) GO
   APPLE (462-7753)
Compaq Computer Corp., 20555 State Hwy. 249, Houston, TX 77070-
   2698; (713) 370-0670 or (800) 345-1518
Hewlett-Packard Co., 3000 Hanover St., Palo Alto, CA 94304-1181; (415)
   857-1501
IBM, Old Orchard Rd., Armonk, NY 10504; (914) 765-1900

Software

Borland Software, P.O. Box 660001, Scotts Valley, CA 95067-0001; (408)
   461-9000
Data Storm Technologies, Inc. (PROCOMM PLUS), P.O. Box 1471,
   Columbia, MO 65205; (573) 443-3282
Intuit (Quicken), P.O. Box 7850, Mountain View, CA 94039-7850;
   (415) 624-8742
Lotus Development Corp., 55 Cambridge Pkwy., Cambridge, MA
   02142; (617) 577-8500
Microsoft (Windows, Word, Excel, FoxPro, FoxBASE+ and Money), One
   Microsoft Way, Redmond, WA 98052-6399; (800) 426-9400 or (206)
   882-8080
Symantec Corp. (Norton AntiVirus and Utilities, Q&A), 10201 Torre
   Ave., Cupertino, CA 95014-2132; (408) 253-9600 or (800) 336-0291

Appendix B

ADDITIONAL BUSINESS RESOURCES

GENERAL SMALL BUSINESS RESOURCES

Associations

American Management Association, 135 W. 50th St., New York, NY
    10020; (212) 586-8100
Center for Entrepreneurial Management, Inc., 180 Varick St., 17th Fl.,
    New York, NY 10014; (212) 633-0060
National Association for the Self-Employed, P.O. Box 612067, Dallas,
    TX 75261-2067; (800) 232-6273
National Management Association, 2210 Arbor Blvd., Dayton, OH
    45439; (513) 294-0421
Small Business Network, 10451 Mill Run Circle, Suite 400, Owings
    Mills, MD 21117; (410) 581-1373
Small Business Service Bureau, 554 Main St., P.O. Box 15014, Worces-
    ter, MA 01615-0014; (508) 756-3513

Publications

Barron's National Business & Financial Weekly, 200 Liberty St., New York, NY 10281; (212) 416-2700

The Business Owner, 383 S. Broadway, Hicksville, NY 11801; (516) 681-2111

Business Review, P.O. Box 777, Cypress, TX 77429; (713) 373-3535

Business Week, 1221 Avenue of the Americas, 39th Fl., New York, NY 10020; (212) 512-3896

Entrepreneur Magazine, 2392 Morse Ave., P.O. Box 19787, Irvine, CA 92714-6234; (800) 421-2300

Entrepreneurial Manager's Newsletter, 180 Varick St., 17th Fl., New York, NY 10014; (212) 633-0060

Journal of Small Business Management, West Virginia University, College of Business Economics, Bureau of Business Research, P.O. Box 6025, Morgantown, WV 26506-6025; (304) 293-5837

Nation's Business, 1615 H St. NW, Washington, DC 20062-2000; (202) 463-5650

The Pricing Advisor, 3277 Roswell Rd., #620, Atlanta, GA 30305; (404) 252-5708

The Wall Street Journal Customer Service: (800) 568-7625

Books

The Entrepreneur and Small Business Problem Solver: An Encyclopedic Reference and Guide, William Cohen; John Wiley & Sons, Inc., 605 3rd Ave., New York, NY 10158

Minding Your Own Small Business, Nancy Holt, Joe Shuchat, and Mary Lewis Regal; CDC Education and Human Development, Inc., U.S. Printing Office, Dept. 33, Washington, DC 20402

HOME-BASED BUSINESS RESOURCES

Home Business Institute, Inc., P.O. Box 301, White Plains, NY 10605-0301; (914) 946-6600

National Association for the Cottage Industry, P.O. Box 14850, Chicago, IL 60614; (312) 472-8116

National Association of Home-Based Businesses, 10451 Mill Run Circle, Owings Mills, MD 21117; (410) 363-3698

Publication

Self-Employment Survival Letter, P.O. Box 2137, Naperville, IL 60567; (708) 717-4188

Start-Up Assistance—Associations

America's Community Bankers, 900 19th St. NW, Suite 400, Washington, DC 20006; (202) 857-3100

American Bankers Association, 1120 Connecticut Ave. NW, Washington, DC 20036; (202) 663-5000

American League of Financial Institutions, 900 19th St. NW, Suite 400, Washington, DC 20006; (202) 628-5624

Association of Small Business Development Centers, 1050 17th St. NW, Suite 810, Washington, DC 20036; (202) 887-5599

Bancard Services Trust Company, 22311 Ventura Blvd., Suite 125, Woodland Hills, CA 91364-1522; (818) 999-3333

Independent Bankers Association of America, One Thomas Circle NW, Suite 950, Washington, DC 20005; (202) 659-8111

National Association of Small Business Investment Companies (NASBIC), 1199 N. Fairfax St., Suite 200, Alexandria, VA 22314; (703) 683-1601

National Commercial Finance Association, 225 W. 34th St., Suite 1815, New York, NY 10122; (212) 594-3490

National Venture Capital Association (NVCA), 1655 N. Fort Myer Dr., Suite 700, Arlington, VA 22209; (703) 351-5269

SBA Online—Telephone Assistance and General Information: (202) 205-6400; Direct-Dial Access: (202) 401-9600; 800-Number Access: (800) 697-4636; 900 Service Access: (900) 463-4636

SBA Small Business Answer Desk; (800) 827-5722

SCORE National Office, 409 3rd St. SW, 4th Fl., Washington, DC 20024; (202) 205-6762

Books

A Banker's Guide to Small Business Loans, American Bankers Association, 1120 Connecticut Ave. NW, Washington, DC 20036

Banking and Small Business, Derek Hansen; Council of State Planning Agencies, Hall of the States, 400 N. Capitol St., Washington, DC 20001

Business Loans: A Guide to Money Sources and How to Approach Them Successfully, Rick Hayes; CBI Publishing Co., Inc., 135 W. 50th St., New York, NY 10020

Encyclopedia of Banking and Finance, F. L. Garcia; Bankers Publishing Co., 210 South St., Boston, MA 02111

Financing the Smaller Business, Thomas Martin; Center for Video Education, Inc., 103 S. Bedford Rd., Mount Kisco, NY 10549

Financing Your Business, Price Waterhouse, 1251 Ave. of the Americas, New York, NY 10020

Handbook of Business Finance and Capital Sources, Dileep Rao; Inter-Finance Corp., 511 11th Ave. S., Minneapolis, MN 55415

How and Where to Raise Venture Capital to Finance a Business, Ted Nicholas; Enterprise Publishing Co., 725 Market St., Wilmington, DE 19801

How to Ask for a Business Loan, Benton Gup; R. F. Dame, Inc., 1905 Huguenot Rd., Richmond, VA 23235

How to Obtain Financing and Make "Your Best Deal" with Any Bank, Finance or Lending Company!, I. M. Fytenbak; Cambrian Financial Corp., 2775 Park Ave., Santa Clara, CA 95050

How to Raise Venture Capital, Stanley Pratt; Charles Scribner's Sons, 597 5th Ave., New York, NY 10017

Maximizing Profits in Small- and Medium-Sized Businesses, Jerome Braverman; Van Nostrand Reinhold Co., Inc., 135 W. 50th St., New York, NY 10020

Raising Cash: A Guide to Financing and Controlling Your Business, Sol Postyn and Jo Postyn; Lifetime Learning Publications, 10 Davis Dr., Belmont, CA 94002

Small Business and Venture Capital, Rudolph Weissman; Arno Press, 382 Main St., P.O. Box 958, Salem, NH 03079

Small Business Financing, American Bankers Association, 1120 Connecticut Ave. NW, Washington, DC 20036

Small Business Financing: Federal Assistance & Contracts, Anthony Chase; McGraw-Hill Book Co., 1221 Avenue of the Americas, New York, NY 10020

Sourceguide for Borrowing Capital, Leonard Smollen, Mark Rollinson, and Stanley Rubel; Capital Publishing Co., 10 S. LaSalle St., Chicago, IL 60603

The Small Business Guide to Borrowing Money, Richard Rubin and Philip Goldbert; McGraw-Hill Book Co., 1221 Avenue of the Americas, New York, NY 10020

Trade Financing, Charles Gmur; Business Press International, Ltd., 205 E. 42nd St., New York, NY 10017

Understanding Money Sources, SBA, 1441 L St. NW, Washington, DC 10416

Up Front Financing: The Entrepreneur's Guide, David Silver; John Wiley & Sons, Inc., 605 3rd Ave., New York, NY 10158

Venture Capital: The Complete Guide for Investors, David Silver; John Wiley & Sons, Inc., 605 3rd Ave., New York, NY 10158

Who's Who in Venture Capital, David Silver; John Wiley & Sons, Inc., 605
3rd Ave., New York, NY 10158

Magazines

American Banker, One State St. Plaza, 26th Fl., New York, NY 10004;
(212) 803-8200
Bankers Digest, 7515 Greenville Ave., Suite 901, Dallas, TX 75231; (214)
373-4544
Business Credit, 8815 Centre Park Dr., Suite 200, Columbia, MD 21045-
2158; (410) 740-5560
Corporate Cashflow, 6151 Powers Ferry Rd. NW, Atlanta, GA 30339; (404)
955-2500
Corporate Finance, 1328 Broadway, New York, NY 10001; (212) 594-5030
Corporate Financing Week, 488 Madison Ave., New York, NY 10022; (212)
303-3300
Credit, 919 18th St. NW, 3rd Fl., Washington, DC 20006; (202) 296-5544
Going Public: The IPO Reporter, 2 World Trade Center, 18th Fl., New
York, NY 10048; (212) 227-1200
The Independent Banker, 518 Lincoln Rd., P.O. Box 267, Sauk Centre, MN
56378; (612) 352-6546
Journal of Cash Management, 7315 Wisconsin Ave., Suite 1250 West,
Bethesda, MD 20814; (301) 907-2862
The Secured Lender, 225 W. 34th St., Suite 1815, New York, NY 10122;
(212) 594-3490

MARKET RESEARCH SERVICES

Dun & Bradstreet Small Business Services, 3 Sylvan Way, Parsippany,
NJ 07054; (800) 544-3867; fax: (800) 525-5980
FIND/SVP, 625 Avenue of the Americas, New York, NY 10011;
(212) 645-4500
Gale Research, Inc., 835 Penobscot Bldg., Detroit, MI 48226; (313)
961-2242
Giga Information Group, One Longwater Circle, Norwell, MA 02061;
(617) 982-9500

ONLINE SERVICES

America Online Inc., 8619 Westwood Center Dr., Vienna, VA 22182;
(703) 448-8700 or (800) 827-6364

CompuServe, 5000 Arlington Centre Blvd., Columbus, OH 43220; (800) 848-8990

Delphi, General Videotex Corp., 1030 Massachusetts Ave., Cambridge, MA 02138; (800) 544-4005

Dow Jones News/Retrieval Service, P.O. Box 300, Princeton, NJ 08543-0300; (609) 452-1511

GEnie, P.O. Box 6403, Rockville, MD 20849-6403; (800) 638-9636

Knight-Ridder Information Services, Inc., 2440 El Camino Real, Mountain View, CA 94040; (800) 334-2564

NewsNet, 945 Haverford Rd., Bryn Mawr, PA 19010; (215) 527-8030 or (800) 345-1301

Ovid Technologies, 333 7th Ave., New York, NY 10001; (800) 955-0906

Prodigy Services Company, 445 Hamilton Ave., White Plains, NY 10601; (800) 776-0845 [1-800-PRODIGY]

VU/TEXT Information Services, Inc., 1 Commerce Square, 2005 Market St., Suite 1010, Philadelphia, PA 19103; (215) 587-4400

Publication

The Whole Internet User's Guide and Catalog, O'Reilly & Associates, 103-A Morris St., Sebastopol, CA 95472; (800) 998-9938

ADVERTISING AND MARKETING

Associations

American Advertising Federation, 1101 Vermont Ave. NW, Suite 500, Washington, DC 20005; (202) 898-0090

American Marketing Association, 250 S. Wacker Dr., Suite 200, Chicago, IL 60606; (312) 648-0536

Association of National Advertisers, 155 E. 44th St., New York, NY 10017-4270

Cable Television Advertising Bureau, 757 3rd Ave., 5th Fl., New York, NY 10017; (212) 751-7770

Invention Marketing Institute, 345 W. Cypress St., Glendale, CA 91204; (818) 246-6540

Marketing Research Association, 2189 Silas Deane Highway, Suite 5, Rocky Hill, CT 06067; (203) 257-4008

Outdoor Advertising Association of America, 12 E. 49th St., 22nd Fl., New York, NY 10017; (212) 688-3667

Point-of-Purchase Advertising Institute, 66 N. Van Brunt St., Englewood, NJ 07631; (201) 894-8899

Radio Advertising Bureau, 304 Park Ave. S., 7th Fl., New York, NY 10010; (212) 254-4800

Books

Advertising—How to Write the Kind that Works, David Nalickson; Charles Scribner's Sons, 597 5th Ave., New York, NY 10017

Advertising and Communication Management, Michael Ray; Prentice-Hall, Inc., Route 9W, Englewood Cliffs, NJ 07632

Advertising and Public Relations for a Small Business, Diane Bellavance; DBA Books, 77 Gordon St., Boston, MA 02135

Advertising and Sales Promotion; Cost Effective Techniques for Your Small Business, William Brannen; Prentice-Hall, Route 9W, Englewood Cliffs, NJ 07632

Advertising Doesn't Cost . . . and Other Lies, L. S. Enterprises, 120 Enterprise Ave., Secaucus, NJ 07094

Advertising Media Models: A Practical Guide, Roland Rust; Lexington Books, 125 Spring St., Lexington, MA 02173

Advertising Small Business, Andrea Dailey; Bank of America, Dept. 3120, P.O. Box 37000, San Francisco, CA 94137

Big Paybacks from Small-Budget Advertising, Webster Kuswa; Dartnell Corp., 4660 Ravenswood Ave., Chicago, IL 60640

Essentials of Advertising Strategy, Don Schultz; Crain Books, 740 Rush St., Chicago, IL 60611

Handbook of Small Business Advertising, Michael Anthony; Addison-Wesley Publishing Co., Reading, MA 01867

How to Advertise: A Handbook for Small Business, Sandra Linville Dean; Enterprise Publishing, Inc., 725 Market St., Wilmington, DE 19801

How to Advertise and Promote Your Small Business, Connie Siegel; John Wiley & Sons, Inc., 605 3rd Ave., New York, NY 10158

How to Maximize Your Advertising Investment, Philip Johnson; CBI Publishing, 135 W. 50th St., New York, NY 10020

How to Promote Your Own Business, Gary Blake; New American Library, 1633 Broadway, New York, NY 10019

Marketing Management, Kenneth Davis; John Wiley & Sons, Inc., 605 3rd Ave., New York, NY 10158

Profitable Advertising Techniques for Small Business, Harvey Cook; Entrepreneur Press, 3422 Astoria Circle, Fairfield, CA 94533

Profitable Methods for Small Business Advertising, Ernest Gray; John Wiley & Sons, Inc., 605 3rd Ave., New York, NY 10158

Step-by-Step Advertising, Cynthia Smith; Sterling Publishing Co., Inc., 2 Park Ave., New York, NY 10016

Strategic Advertising Campaigns, Don Schultz, Dennis Martin, and William Brown; Crain Books, 740 Rush St., Chicago, IL 60611

Strategy in Advertising: Matching Media and Messages to Markets and Motivation, Leo Bogart; Crain Books, 740 Rush St., Chicago, IL 60611

Streetfighting: Low-Cost Advertising/Promotion Strategies for Your Small Business, Jeff Slutsky and Woody Woodruff; Prentice-Hall, Route 9W, Englewood Cliffs, NJ 07632

The 27 Most Common Mistakes in Advertising, Alec Benn; AMACOM, 135 W. 50th St., New York, NY 10020

The Secrets of Practical Marketing for Small Business, Herman Holtz; Prentice-Hall, Inc., Route 9W, Englewood Cliffs, NJ 07632

Magazines

Adcrafter, 1249 Washington Blvd., Detroit, MI 48226-1852; (313) 962-7225

Advertising Age, 220 E. 42nd St., New York, NY 10017; (212) 210-0100

Advertising Communications Times, 121 Chestnut St., Philadelphia, PA 19106; (215) 629-1666

Adweek, 1515 Broadway, New York, NY 10036-8986; (212) 536-5336

American Advertising, 1101 Vermont Ave. NW, Suite 500, Washington, DC 20005; (202) 898-0089

American Demographics, P.O. Box 68, Ithaca, NY 14851; (607) 273-6343

Business Marketing, 740 N. Rush St., Chicago, IL 60611; (312) 649-5200

Inside Media, Cowles Business Media, 911 Hope St., Bldg. 6, P.O. Box 4949, Stamford, CT 06907-0949; (203) 358-9900

Journal of Marketing Research, 250 S. Wacker Dr., #200, Chicago, IL 60606

Quirk's Marketing Research Review, 8030 Cedar Ave. S., Suite 229, Bloomington, MN 55425; (612) 854-5101

Tradeshow Week, 12233 W. Olympic Blvd., Suite 236, Los Angeles, CA 90064; (310) 826-5696

RECORD KEEPING AND TAXES

Associations

American Accounting Association, 5717 Bessie Dr., Sarasota, FL 34233; (813) 921-7747

Independent Accountants International, 9200 S. Dadeland Blvd., Suite 510, Miami, FL 33156; (305) 661-0580

International Credit Association, 243 N. Lindbergh Blvd., P.O. Box 419057, St. Louis, MO 63141-1757; (314) 991-3030

Publications

Taxes: The Tax Magazine, 4025 W. Peterson Ave., Chicago, IL 60646; (312) 583-8500

The Tax Adviser, Harborside Financial Center, #201 Plaza 3, Jersey City, NJ 07311-3881; (201) 938-3447

Appendix C

GOVERNMENT LISTINGS

GOVERNMENT AGENCIES

Copyright Clearance Center, 222 Rosewood Dr., Danvers, MA 01923; (508) 750-8400

The Copyright Office, Library of Congress, Washington, DC 20540; (202) 707-3000

Export-Import Bank of the United States, 811 Vermont Ave. NW, Washington, DC 20571; (202) 565-3946

Internal Revenue Service, 1111 Constitution Ave. NW, Washington, DC 20224; (202) 622-5000

U.S. Small Business Administration, P.O. Box 34500, Washington, DC 20043-4500; (800) 827-5722

U.S. Dept. of Agriculture, 14th St. & Independence Ave. SW, Washington, DC 20013; (202) 720-7420

U.S. Dept. of Commerce, Herbert C. Hoover Bldg., 14th St. & Constitution Ave. NW, Washington, DC 20230; (202) 482-2000

U.S. Dept. of Energy, 1000 Independence Ave. SW, Washington, DC 20585; (202) 586-5000

U.S. Dept. of the Interior, 1849 C St. NW, Washington, DC 20240; (202) 208-3100

U.S. Dept. of Labor, 200 Constitution Ave. NW, Room S-1004, Washington, DC 20210; (202) 219-6666

U.S. Dept. of Treasury, Main Treasury Bldg., 1500 Pennsylvania Ave. NW, Washington, DC 20220; (202) 622-2000

U.S. Government Printing Office, Washington, DC 20402; (202) 512-1800

U.S. Patent and Trademark Office, Washington, DC 20231; (800) 786-9199

U.S. Securities and Exchange Commission, 450 5th St. NW, Washington, DC 20549; (202) 942-8088

STATE COMMERCE AND ECONOMIC DEVELOPMENT DEPARTMENTS

Alabama Development Office, 401 Adams Ave., Montgomery, AL 36130; (334) 242-0400

Alaska State Dept. of Commerce and Economic Development, State Office Bldg., P.O. Box 110800, Juneau, AK 99811-0800; (907) 465-2500

Arizona State Dept. of Commerce, Small Business Advocate, 3800 N. Central Ave., Phoenix, AZ 85012; (602) 280-1480

Arkansas Industrial Development Commission, Minority & Small Business, One State Capitol Mall, Little Rock, AR 72201; (501) 682-1060

California State Dept. of Commerce, 801 K St., Suite 1600, Sacramento, CA 95814; (916) 322-1394

Colorado Office of Economic Development, 1625 Broadway, Suite 1710, Denver, CO 80202; (303) 892-3840

Connecticut Economic Resource Center, 805 Brook St., Bldg. 4, Rocky Hill, CT 06067; (860) 571-7136

Delaware State Chamber of Commerce, 1201 N. Orange St., Suite 200, Wilmington, DE 19801; (302) 655-7221

District of Columbia, Office of Economic Development, 717 14th St. NW, 12th Fl., Washington DC 20005; (202) 727-6600

Florida Dept. of Commerce, 536 Collins Bldg., 107 W. Gaines St., Tallahassee, FL 32399-2000; (904) 488-3104

Georgia Dept. of Community Affairs, 100 Peachtree St., Suite 1200, Atlanta, GA 30303; (404) 656-2900

Hawaii: Business Action Center, 1130 N. Nimitz Hwy., Suite A-254, Honolulu, HI 96817; (808) 585-2600

Idaho State Dept. of Commerce, P.O. Box 83720, Boise, ID 83720; (208) 334-2470

Illinois Dept. of Commerce and Community Affairs, 100 W. Randolph St., Chicago, IL 60601; (312) 814-7179

Indiana State Dept. of Commerce, One N. Capitol, Suite 700, Indianapolis, IN 46204-2288; (317) 232-8782

Iowa Dept. of Economic Development, 200 E. Grand Ave., Des Moines, IA 50309; (515) 281-3251

Kansas Dept. of Commerce and Housing, Business Development Dept., 700 SW Harrison St., Suite 1300, Topeka, KS 66603; (913) 296-3483

Kentucky Dept. of Economic Development, Business Information Clearinghouse, Capitol Plaza Tower, 22nd Fl., Frankfort, KY 40601; (800) 626-2250

Louisiana Dept. of Economic Development, P.O. Box 94185, Baton Rouge, LA 70804-9185; (504) 342-5388

Maine: Business Answers, Dept. of Economic and Community Development, 33 Stone St., 59 Statehouse Station, Augusta, ME 04333; (207) 287-2656

Maryland Dept. of Business and Economic Development, Division of Regional Development, 217 E. Redwood St., Baltimore, MD 21202; (410) 767-0095

Massachusetts Office of Business Development, 1 Ashburton Pl., Boston, MA 02108; (617) 727-3221

Michigan Jobs Commission, Ombudsman, 201 N. Washington Sq., Victor Office Center, 4th Fl., Lansing, MI 48933; (517) 335-1847

Minnesota Small Business Assistance Office, 500 Metro Sq., 121 Seventh Pl. E., St. Paul, MN 55101; (612) 282-2103

Mississippi Dept. of Economic and Community Development, Division of Existing Industry and Business, P.O. Box 849, Jackson, MS 39205; (601) 359-3593

Missouri: Community and Economic Development, Business Information Program, P.O. Box 118, Jefferson City, MO 65102; (573) 751-4982

Montana: Dept. of Commerce, 1424 9th Ave., Helena, MT 59620; (406) 444-4780

Nebraska: Dept. of Economic Development, P.O. Box 94666, Lincoln, NE 69509; (402) 471-3782

Nevada State Dept. of Business and Industry, Office of the Director, Center for Business Advocacy Services, 2501 E. Sahara Ave., Suite 202, Las Vegas, NV 89104; (702) 486-4335

New Hampshire State Dept. of Resources and Economic Development, P.O. Box 330, Concord, NH 03302-1856; (603) 271-2591

New Jersey: State of New Jersey Dept. of Commerce and Economic Development, Division of Small Businesses, Women and Minority Businesses, CN 835, Trenton, NJ 08625-0835; (609) 292-3860

New Mexico Economic Development Dept., P.O. Box 20003, Santa Fe, NM 87504; (505) 827-0300

New York: Division for Small Business, Empire State Development, One Commerce Plaza, Albany, NY 12245; (518) 473-0499

North Carolina: Small Business and Technology Development Center, 333 Fayetteville St. Mall, Suite 1150, Raleigh, NC 27601-1742; (919) 715-7292

North Dakota: Center for Innovation and Business Development, P.O. Box 8372, Grand Forks, ND 58202; (701) 777-3132

Ohio One-Stop Business Permit Center, 77 S. High St., 28th Fl., Columbus, OH 43216; (614) 644-8748

Oklahoma: Dept. of Commerce, P.O. Box 29680, Oklahoma City, OK 71326-0980; (405) 843-9770

Oregon Dept. of Economic Development, 775 Summer St. NE, Salem, OR 97310; (503) 986-0123

Pennsylvania Business Resource Center, The Forum Building, Room 404, Harrisburg, PA 17120; (717) 783-5700

Rhode Island Economic Development Corp., 7 Jackson Walkway, Providence, RI 02903; (401) 277-2601

South Carolina: Enterprise Development Dept., South Carolina State Development Board, P.O. Box 927, Columbia, SC 29202; (803) 737-0400

South Dakota: Governor's Office of Economic Development, 711 E. Wells Ave., Pierre, SD 57501; (605) 773-5032

Tennessee: Office of Small Business, Dept. of Economic and Community Development, 320 6th Ave. N., 7th Fl., Nashville, TN 37243-0405; (615) 741-2626

Texas Dept. of Commerce, Small Business Division, P.O. Box 12728, Austin, TX 78711; (512) 936-0100

Utah Dept. of Community and Economic Development, 3600 Constitution Blvd., West Valley City, UT 84119; (801) 963-3286

Vermont: Development and Community Affairs, 109 State St., Montpelier, VT 05609-0501; (802) 828-3221

Virginia: Dept. of Economic Development, Office of Small Business and Financial Services, 901 E. Byrd St., Suite 1800, Richmond, VA 23319. Call (804) 371-8253 for information on the Virginia Small Business Development Center in your area.

Washington: Business Assistance Division, Community Trade and Economic Development, 906 Columbia St. SW, P.O. Box 48300, Olympia, WA 98504-8300; (360) 753-4900

West Virginia Small Business Development Center, 950 Kanawha Blvd., Charleston, WV 25301; (304) 558-2960

Wisconsin: Dept. of Development, 123 W. Washington Ave., Madison, WI 53703; (608) 266-9467

Wyoming Dept. of Economic and Community Development, 6101 Yellowstone Rd., Cheyenne, WY 82002; (307) 777-7284

STATE SMALL BUSINESS DEVELOPMENT OFFICES

Note: The following offices are the lead Small Business Development Centers for each state. Most states have other regional centers as well.

Alabama Small Business Development Consortium, 1717 11th Ave. S., Suite 419, Birmingham, AL 35294; (205) 934-7260

Alaska: UAA SBDC, 430 W. 7th Ave., Suite 110, Anchorage, AK 99501; (907) 274-7232

Arizona Small Business Development Center, 1414 W. Broadway, Suite 165, Tempe, AZ 85282; (602) 966-7786

Arkansas Small Business Development Center, University of Arkansas at Little Rock, 100 South Main, Suite 401, Little Rock, AR 72201; (501) 324-9043

California Small Business Development Center, Office of Small Business, 801 K St., Suite 1700, Sacramento, CA 95814; (916) 324-5068

Colorado Small Business Development Center, 1625 Broadway, Suite 1710, Denver, CO 80202; (303) 892-3809

Connecticut: University of Connecticut, Connecticut Small Business Development Center, 2 Bourne Pl., U-94, Storrs, CT 06269-5094; (203) 486-4135

Delaware Small Business Development Center, 005 Purnell Hall, Newark, DE 19716; (302) 831-2747

District of Columbia: Howard University, School of Business, Small Business Development Center, Room 125, Washington, DC 20059; (202) 806-1550

Florida Small Business Development Center, University of West Florida, 11000 University Pkwy., Pensacola, FL 32514; (904) 474-2908

Georgia Small Business Development Center, University of Georgia, 1180 E. Broad St., Athens, GA 30602-5412; (706) 542-7436

Hawaii: University of Hawaii at Hilo, Small Business Development Center, 200 West Kawili St., Hilo, HI 96720-4091; (808) 933-3515

Idaho Small Business Development Center, Boise State University, 1910 University Dr., Boise, ID 83725; (208) 385-1640

Illinois Small Business Development Center, 620 E. Adams St., Springfield, IL 62701; (217) 524-5858

Indiana Small Business Development Center, One N. Capitol, Suite 425, Indianapolis, IN 46204; (317) 264-6871

Iowa Small Business Development Center, 137 Lynn St., Ames, IA 50014; (515) 292-6351

Kansas: Please call the Small Business Administration at (316) 269-6273.

Kentucky Center for Business Development, Carol Martin Gatton Business and Economics Building, Room 225, University of Kentucky, Lexington, KY 40506-0034; (606) 257-7668

Louisiana Small Business Development Center, College of Business Administration, Admin. 2-57, Northeast Louisiana University, Monroe, LA 71209-6435; (318) 342-5506

Maine: University of Southern Maine, Maine Small Business Development Center, 96 Falmouth St., P.O. Box 9300, Portland, ME 04104-9300; (207) 780-4420

Maryland Small Business Development Center, 217 E. Redwood St., Baltimore, MD 21202; (410) 767-6552

Massachusetts: University of Massachusetts, Massachusetts Small Business Development Center, P.O. Box 34935, Amherst, MA 01003-4935; (413) 545-6301

Michigan Small Business Development Center, 2727 2nd Ave., Detroit, MI 48201; (313) 964-1798

Minnesota Small Business Development Center, Dept. of Trade and Economic Development, 500 Metro Sq., 121 7th Pl. E., St. Paul, MN 55101-2146; (612) 297-5770

Mississippi Small Business Development Center, University of Mississippi, Old Chemistry Building, Suite 216, University, MS 38677; (601) 232-5650

Missouri Small Business Development Center, 300 University Pl., Columbia, MO 65211; (314) 882-0344

Montana: Small Business Development Center, Dept. of Commerce, 1424 9th Ave., Helena, MT 59620; (406) 444-4780

Nebraska Business Development Center, University of Nebraska—Omaha, 60th and Dodge St., College of Business Administration, Room 407, Omaha, NE 68182; (402) 554-2521

Nevada Small Business Development Center, University of Nevada—Reno, College of Business/032, Reno, NV 89577-0100; (702) 784-17171

New Hampshire Small Business Development Center, 108 McConnell Hall, 15 College Rd., Durham, NH 03824; (603) 862-2200

New Jersey Small Business Development Center, Ackerson Hall, 180 University Ave., Newark, NJ 07102; (201) 648-1110

New Mexico Small Business Development Center, P.O. Box 4187, Santa Fe, NM 87502-4187; (505) 438-1237

New York Small Business Development Center, State University of New York, State University Plaza, S-523, Albany, NY 12246; (518) 443-5398

North Carolina Small Business and Technology Development Center, 3333 Fayetteville St. Mall, Suite 1150, Raleigh, NC 27601; (919) 715-7272

North Dakota Small Business Development Center, P.O. Box 7308, University of N. Dakota, Grand Forks, ND 58202; (701) 777-3700

Ohio Dept. of Development, P.O. Box 1001, Columbus, OH 43216-1001; (614) 466-2480

Oklahoma Small Business Development Center, Station A, P.O. Box 2584, Durant, OK 74701; (405) 924-0277

Oregon Small Business Development Center Network, 44 W. Broadway, Suite 501, Eugene, OR 97401; (503) 726-2250

Pennsylvania Small Business Development Center, 3733 Spruce St., Room 423, Vance Hall, Philadelphia, PA 19104; (215) 898-1219

Rhode Island Small Business Development Center, Bryant College, 1150 Douglas Pike, Smithfield, RI 02917; (401) 232-6111

South Carolina Small Business Development Center, College of Business Administration, Room 652, University of South Carolina, Columbia, SC 29208; (803) 777-5118

South Dakota Small Business Development Center, University of South Dakota, School of Business, 414 E. Clark St., Vermillion, SD 57069; (605) 677-5498

Tennessee Small Business Development Center, University of Memphis, South Campus, Bldg. 1, Memphis, TN 38152; (901) 678-2500

Texas Small Business Development Center, 1402 Corinth St., Corinth, TX 75215; (214) 565-5837

Utah Small Business Development Center, 8811 S. 700 E., Salt Lake City, UT 84070; (801) 255-5878

Vermont Small Business Development Center, 60 Main St., Suite 103, Burlington, VT 05401; (802) 658-9228

Virginia Small Business Development Center, P.O. Box 798, Richmond, VA 23206-0798; (804) 371-8258

Washington: Community Trade and Economic Development, 906 Columbia St. SW, P.O. Box 48300, Olympia, WA 98504-8300; (360) 753-2200

West Virginia Small Business Development Center, 950 Kanawha Blvd., Charleston, WV 25301; (304) 558-2960

Wisconsin Small Business Development Center, 432 Lake St., Madison, WI 53706; (608) 262-3878

Wyoming Small Business Development Center, 111 W. 2nd St., Suite 502, Casper, WY 82601; (307) 234-6683

SBA DISTRICT OFFICES

The Small Business Administration has several types of field offices. Of these, the district offices offer the fullest range of services to small businesses.

ALABAMA: 2121 8th Ave. N., Suite 200, Birmingham, AL 35203-2398; (205) 731-1344

ALASKA: 222 W. 8th Ave., Room A36, Anchorage, AK 99513-7559; (907) 271-4022

ARIZONA: 2828 N. Central Ave., Suite 800, Phoenix, AZ 85004-1093; (602) 640-2316

ARKANSAS: 2120 Riverfront Dr., Suite 100, Little Rock, AR 72202; (501) 324-5871

CALIFORNIA: 2719 N. Air Fresno Dr., Suite 107, Fresno, CA 93727-1547; (209) 487-5189

    330 N. Brand Blvd., Suite 1200, Glendale, CA 91203-2304; (818) 552-3210

    550 West C St., Suite 550, San Diego, CA 92188-3540; (619) 557-7250

    211 Main St., 4th Fl., San Francisco, CA 94105-1988; (615) 744-6820

    660 J St., Suite 215, Sacramento, CA 95814-2413; (916) 498-6410

    200 W. Santa Ana Blvd., Suite 700, Santa Ana, CA 92701; (714) 550-7420

COLORADO: 721 19th St., Suite 426, Denver, CO 80202-2599; (303) 844-3984

CONNECTICUT: 330 Main St., 2nd Fl., Hartford, CT 06106; (203) 240-4700

DELAWARE: (branch office) 824 N. Market St., Suite 610, Wilmington, DE 19801-3011; (302) 573-6294

DISTRICT OF COLUMBIA: 1110 Vermont Ave. NW, Suite 900, Washington, DC 20005; (202) 606-4000

FLORIDA: 1320 S. Dixie Hwy., Suite 501, Coral Gables, FL 33146-2911; (305) 536-5521

    7825 Baymeadows Way, Suite 100-B, Jacksonville, FL 32256-7504; (904) 443-1900

GEORGIA: 1720 Peachtree Rd. NW, 6th Fl., Atlanta, GA 30309; (404) 347-4749

HAWAII: 300 Ala Moana Blvd., Room 2314, Honolulu, HI 96850-4981; (808) 541-2990

IDAHO: 1020 Main St., Suite 290, Boise, ID 83702-5745; (208) 334-1696

ILLINOIS: 500 W. Madison St., Suite 1250, Chicago, IL 60661-2511; (312) 353-4528

    511 W. Capitol Ave., Suite 302, Springfield, IL 62704; (217) 492-4416

INDIANA: 429 N. Pennsylvania St., Suite 100, Indianapolis, IN 46204-1873; (317) 226-7272

IOWA: 216 6th Ave. SE, Suite 200, Cedar Rapids, IA 52401-1806; (319) 362-6405

    210 Walnut St., Room 749, Des Moines, IA 50309-2186; (515) 284-4422

KANSAS: 100 E. English St., Suite 510, Wichita, KS 67202; (316) 269-6616
KENTUCKY: 600 Dr. Martin Luther King Jr. Pl., Room 188, Louisville, KY 40202; (502) 582-5971
LOUISIANA: 365 Canal St., Suite 2250, New Orleans, LA 70130; (504) 589-6685
MAINE: 40 Western Ave., Room 512, Augusta, ME 04330; (207) 622-8378
MARYLAND: 10 S. Howard St., Suite 6220, Baltimore, MD 21201-2525; (410) 962-4392
MASSACHUSETTS: 10 Causeway St., Room 265, Boston, MA 02222-1093; (617) 565-5590
MICHIGAN: 477 Michigan Ave., Room 515, Detroit, MI 48226; (313) 226-6075
MINNESOTA: 100 N. 6th St., Suite 610, Minneapolis, MN 55403-1563; (612) 370-2324
MISSISSIPPI: 101 W. Capital St., Suite 400, Jackson, MS 39201; (601) 965-4378
MISSOURI: 323 West 8th St., Suite 501, Kansas City, MO 64105; (816) 374-6708
815 Olive St., Room 242, St. Louis, MO 63101; (314) 539-6600
MONTANA: 301 South Park Ave., Room 334, Helena, MT 59626; (406) 441-1081
NEBRASKA: 11145 Mill Valley Rd., Omaha, NE 68154; (402) 221-4691
NEVADA: 301 E. Stewart Ave., Room 301, Las Vegas, NV 89101; (702) 388-6611
NEW HAMPSHIRE: 143 N. Main St., Suite 202, Concord, NH 03301; (603) 225-1400
NEW JERSEY: 2 Gateway Center, 4th Fl., Newark, NJ 07102; (201) 645-2434
NEW MEXICO: 625 Silver SW, Suite 320, Albuquerque, NM 87102; (505) 766-1870
NEW YORK: 111 West Huron St., Room 1311, Buffalo, NY 14202; (716) 551-4301
26 Federal Plaza, Suite 31-00, New York, NY 10278; (212) 264-2454
100 South Clinton St., Suite 1071, Syracuse, NY 13260; (315) 448-0423
NORTH CAROLINA: 200 N. College St., Suite A-2015, Charlotte, NC 28202-2137; (704) 344-6563
NORTH DAKOTA: 657 2nd Ave. N., Room 219, Fargo, ND 58108-3086; (701) 239-5131
OHIO: 1111 Superior Ave., Suite 630, Cleveland, OH 44114-2507; (216) 522-4180
2 Nationwide Plaza, Suite 1400, Columbus, OH 43215-2592; (614) 469-6860

OKLAHOMA: 210 Park Ave., Suite 1300, Oklahoma City, OK 73102; (405) 231-5521

OREGON: 222 SW Columbia St., Suite 500, Portland, OR 97201-6695; (503) 326-2682

PENNSYLVANIA: 475 Allendale Rd., Suite 201, King of Prussia, PA 19406; (610) 962-3800

960 Penn Ave., 5th Fl., Pittsburgh, PA 15222, (412) 644-2780

PUERTO RICO: 252 Ponce De Leon Ave., Suite 201, Hato Rey, PR 00918; (809) 766-5572

RHODE ISLAND: 380 Westminster Mall, 5th Fl., Providence, RI 02903; (401) 528-4561

SOUTH CAROLINA: 1835 Assembly St., Room 358, Columbia, SC 29201; (803) 765-5377

SOUTH DAKOTA: 110 South Phillips Ave., Suite 200, Sioux Falls, SD 57102-1109; (605) 330-4231

TENNESSEE: 50 Vantage Way, Suite 201, Nashville, TN 37228-1500; (615) 736-5881

TEXAS: 4300 Amon Carter Blvd., Suite 114, Ft. Worth, TX 76155; (817) 885-6500

10737 Gateway West, Suite 320, El Paso, TX 79935; (915) 540-5676

9301 Southwest Freeway., Suite 550, Houston, TX 77074-1591; (713) 773-6500

222 E. Van Buren St., Room 500, Harlingen, TX 78550-6855; (210) 427-8625

1611 10th St., Suite 200, Lubbock, TX 79401-2693; (806) 743-7462

727 E. Durango Blvd., Room A-527, San Antonio, TX 78206-1204; (210) 229-5900

UTAH: 125 S. State St., Room 2237, Salt Lake City, UT 84138-1195; (801) 524-5804

VERMONT: 87 State St., Room 205, Montpelier, VT 05602; (802) 828-4422

VIRGINIA: 1504 Santa Rosa Rd., Suite 200, Richmond, VA 23229; (804) 771-2400

WASHINGTON: 1200 6th Ave., Suite 1700, Seattle, WA 98101-1128; (206) 553-7310

WEST VIRGINIA: 168 W. Main St., 5th Fl., Clarksburg, WV 26301; (304) 623-5631

WISCONSIN: 212 E. Washington Ave., Room 213, Madison, WI 53703; (608) 264-5261

WYOMING: 100 East B St., Room 4001, Casper, WY 82602-2839; (307) 261-6500

Appendix D

BUSINESS BANKS

Knowledge is power and, in 1996, for the second consecutive year, the Small Business Administration (SBA) Office of Advocacy gave entrepreneurs a powerful tool to help them obtain loans from commercial banks.

In its *Micro Business Lending in the United States*, 1995 edition, the Office of Advocacy found that, since the 1994 study was released, commercial bank credit to microfirms (defined as companies seeking loans of $100,000 or less) had increased by $2.7 billion.

Jere W. Glover, Chief Counsel for Advocacy at the SBA, attributes the increase to the study and the SBA's LowDoc loan program.

"LowDoc got banks in the habit of making smaller loans and convinced them to change the procedure to make it faster," says Glover. "Also, the fact that there is published information about the amount of loans they are making and where they rank in their state is a competitive incentive for banks to be in this market."

Banks have also become much more serious about courting small businesses, contends Glover, who says he has been visited by a number of banking executives touting their new small business programs. "Each looked me straight in the eye and said, 'Jere, this year it's real.'"

For banks, the need to truly become small business friendly is powerful, Glover says, because an entrepreneur whose institution doesn't make small business loans might just move to a more welcoming bank.

The SBA's report, which for the first time provides the number and amount of small business loans, relies on the call report data filed quarterly by financial institutions.

Glover acknowledges that the study has its limitations; for example, call reports don't provide separate information on SBA-guaranteed lending. This means financial institutions that are active SBA lenders but sell the guaranteed portion of their loans in the secondary market are likely to be underrepresented in the rankings because the call reports contain only information on the unguaranteed portion of their SBA loans.

Some banks may also be making microloans through credit cards, second mortgages, or other forms of consumer credit, which again would preclude their small business activities from appearing in the reports.

Nor do call reports reflect demand conditions. Consequently, a bank with fewer branches in a geographic area, or a bank in a location where few people seek microloans, will appear not to be small business friendly.

Even with these limitations, however, Glover believes the study can be a valuable tool for an entrepreneur seeking capital. In addition to helping pinpoint friendly banks, he says, the report might help turn around unfriendly ones. "You could go in and talk to a banker and say, 'Look, you only made 100 small business loans. You ought to be making more, and I'm here to help you. Here's my application.'" And that's a powerful tool for an entrepreneur, concludes Glover.

—*Cynthia E. Griffin*

The SBA defines microbusiness-friendly banks as those whose microloans (loans of under $100,000) comprise at least 25 percent of their total assets. Following is a list of the top banks in each state. Please note that not all states have lenders that meet this criterion.

Alabama

CB&T Bank of Russell City, P.O. Box 2400, Phenix City, AL 36838-2400; (334) 297-7000

First Bank of Dothan, 1479 W. Main St., Dothan, AL 36301; (334) 794-8090

First National Bank of Union Springs, P.O. Box 570, Union Springs, AL 36089; (334) 738-2060

Independent Bank of Oxford, 402 Main St., Oxford, AL 36203; (205) 835-1776

Peoples Exchange Bank of Monroe County, 1112 Main St., Beatrice, AL 36425; (334) 789-2490

Southland Bank, 3299 Ross Clark Cir., Dothan, AL 36303; (334) 671-4000

Arizona

Bank of Casa Grande Valley, 1300 E. Florence Blvd., Casa Grande, AZ 85222 (520) 836-4666

Arkansas

Bank of Eureka Springs, P.O. Box 309, Eureka Springs, AR 72632; (501) 253-8241

Bank of Little Rock, 305 E. Broadway, North Little Rock, AR 72116; (501) 228-9818

Calhoun County Bank, P.O. Box 8, Hampton, AR 71744; (501) 798-2207

First Bank of Arkansas, 500 N. Falls, Wynne, AR 72396; (501) 238-2265

First Bank of Arkansas, 825 Hwy. 463, Trumann, AR 72472;(501) 483-6433

Stephens Security Bank, 108 Ruby St., Stephens, AR 71764; (501) 786-5416

California

Centennial Thrift & Loan Association, 18837 Brookhurst, #100, Fountain Valley, CA 92708; (714) 964-9111

Inland Community Bank, N.A., 851 W. Foothill Blvd., Rialto, CA 92376; (909) 874-4444

Monument National Bank, 1450 N. Norma Ave., Ridgecrest, CA 93555; (619) 446-3576

North State National Bank, P.O. Box 3235, Chico, CA 95927; (916) 893-0415

Redding Bank of Commerce, 1177 Placer St., Redding, CA 96001; (916) 241-2265

Six Rivers National Bank, 402F Frank St., Eureka, CA 95501; (707) 443-8400

Taft National Bank, 523 Cascade Pl., Taft, CA 93268; (805) 763-5151

Colorado

Bank at Broadmoor, 4 Elm Ave., Colorado Springs, CO 80906; (719) 633-2695

Bank of Durango, 15 Bodo Dr., P.O. Drawer G, Durango, CO 81302; (970) 259-5500

Bank of Grand Junction, 2415 F Rd., Grand Junction, CO 81505; (970) 241-9000

Bank of the Southwest, N.A., 523 San Juan St., Pagosa Springs, CO 81147; (970) 264-4111

Cheyenne Mountain Bank, 1580 E. Cheyenne Mtn. Blvd., Colorado Springs, CO 80906; (719) 579-9150

Citizens Bank of Pagosa Springs, P.O. Box 1508, Pagosa Springs, CO 81147; (970) 264-2235

Clear Creek National Bank, P.O. Box 337, Georgetown, CO 80444-0337; (303) 569-2393

Eagle Bank of Broomfield, 1990 W. 10th Ave., Broomfield, CO 80020; (303) 460-9991

Farmers Bank, 100 Elm Ave., Eaton, CO 80615; (970) 454-3434

First State Bank of Colorado Springs, 1776 S. Nevada Ave., Colorado Springs, CO 80906; (719) 475-1776

First State Bank of Hotchkiss, P.O. Box 38, Hotchkiss, CO 81419; (970) 872-3111

First State Bank, P.O. Box 3309, Idaho Springs, CO 80452; (303) 567-2696

Fort Morgan State Bank, 520 Sherman St., Fort Morgan, CO 80701; (970) 867-3319

Gunnison Bank & Trust Co., 232 W. Tomichi Ave., Gunnison, CO 81230; (970) 641-0320

Lafayette State Bank, 811 S. Public Rd., Lafayette, CO 80026; (303) 666-0777

Mountain National Bank, 361 W. Hwy. 24, Woodland Park, CO 80863; (719) 687-3012

Olathe State Bank, 302 Main St., Olathe, CO 81425; (970) 323-5565

Florida

American Bank & Trust Co., 101 W. Garden St., Pensacola, FL 32501; (904) 432-2481

Apalachicola State Bank, P.O. Box 370, Apalachicola, FL 32329; (904) 653-8805

C & L Bank of Blountstown, P.O. Box 534, Blountstown, FL 32424; (904) 674-5900

Dadeland Bank, 7545 N. Kendal, Miami, FL 33156; (305) 667-8401

First American Bank of Indian River County, 4000 20th St., Vero Beach, FL 32960; (407) 567-0552

First National Bank of Southwest Florida, 2724 Del Prado Blvd., Cape Coral, FL 33904; (941) 772-2220

First National Bank of Wauchula, 406 N. 6th Ave., Wauchula, FL 33873; (941) 773-4136

Putnam State Bank, 350 State Rd., 19 N., Palatka, FL 32177; (904) 328-5600

Seminole National Bank, P.O. Box 2057, Sanford, FL 32772; (407) 330-5190

South Hillsborough Community Bank, P.O. Box 3430, Apollo Beach, FL 33572; (813) 645-0886

Wewahitchka State Bank, 125 N. Main St., Wewahitchka, FL 32465; (904) 639-2222

Georgia

Adel Banking Co., P.O. Box 191, Adel, GA 31620; (912) 896-7402

Bank Atlanta, 1221 Clairmont Rd., Decatur, GA 30030; (404) 320-3300

Bank of Dudley, P.O. Box 7, Dudley, GA 31022; (912) 676-3196

Bank of Milan, P.O. Box 38, Milan, GA 31060; (912) 362-4483

Bank of Thomas County, 2484 E. Pinetree Blvd., Thomasville, GA 31799; (912) 226-5755

Bank of Toccoa, P.O. Box 430, Toccoa, GA 30577; (706) 886-9421

Bryan Bank & Trust, P.O. Box 1299, Richmond Hill, GA 31324; (912) 756-4444

Coastal Bank, P.O. Box 529, Hinesville, GA 31310; (912) 368-2265

Cordele Banking Co., 1620 16th Ave. E., Cordele, GA 31015; (912) 273-2416

Farmers & Merchants Bank, 301 W. 4th St., Adel, GA 31620; (912) 896-4585

First Bank & Trust, P.O. Box 545, Carnesville, GA 30521; (706) 384-4545

First National Bank of Alma, P.O. Box 2028, Alma, GA 31510; (912) 632-7262

First National Bank of Barnesville, 315 Thomaston St., Barnesville, GA 30204; (770) 358-1100

First National Bank of Effingham, 501 S. Laurel, Springfield, GA 31329; (912) 754-6111

McIntosh State Bank, 210 S. Oak St., Jackson, GA 30233; (770) 775-8300

Patterson Bank, 6365 Hwy. 84, Patterson, GA 31557; (912) 647-5332

White County Bank, 153 E. Kytle St., Cleveland, GA 30528; (706) 865-3151

Idaho

Panhandle State Bank, P.O. Box 967, Sandpoint, ID 83864; (208) 263-0505

Twin River National Bank, 1507 G St., Lewiston, ID 83501; (208) 743-2565

Illinois

Ashland State Bank, 9443 S. Ashland Ave., Chicago, IL 60620; (312) 445-9300

Bank of Bourbonnais, 1 Heritage Plaza, Bourbonnais, IL 60914; (815) 933-0570

Bank of Edwardsville, 330 W. Vandalia, Edwardsville, IL 62025; (618) 656-0057

Banterra Bank of Gallatin County, P.O. Box 680, El Dorado, IL 62979; (618) 272-3151

Du Quoin State Bank, 15 E. Main, P.O. Box 468, Du Quoin, IL 62832; (618) 542-2111

First National Bank of Antioch, 485 Lake St., Antioch, IL 60002; (708) 395-3111

First National Bank of Danville, 1 Town Center, Danville, IL 61832; (217) 442-0362

First National Bank of Wheaton, 1151 E. Butterfield Rd., Wheaton, IL 60187; (708) 260-2200

Mercantile Trust & Savings Bank, 440 Maine St., Quincy, IL 62301; (217) 223-7300

Northwest Bank of Rockford, 125 Phelps Ave., Rockford, IL 61108; (815) 987-4550

Peoples National Bank, 108 S. Washington St., McLeansboro, IL 62859; (618) 643-4303

State Bank of Geneva, P.O. Box 108, Geneva, IL 60134; (708) 232-3200

West Pointe Bank & Trust Co., 5701 W. Main St., Belleville, IL 62223; (618) 234-5700

Indiana

Farmers State Bank, P.O. Box 455, Mentone, IN 46539; (219) 353-7521

Jackson County Bank, 125 S. Chestnut, Seymour, IN 47274; (812) 522-3607

Kansas

Admire Bank & Trust Co., 1104 E. 12th Ave., P.O. Box 1047, Emporia, KS 66801; (316) 343-1940

Coffeyville State Bank, 313 W. 9th St., P.O. Box 219, Coffeyville, KS 67337; (316) 251-1313

First National Bank of Wamego, P.O. Box 226, Wamego, KS 66547; (913) 456-2221

First National Bank, 2160 W. Hwy. 50, Emporia, KS 66801; (316) 343-1010

Peoples Bank & Trust Co., P.O. Box 1226, McPherson, KS 67460; (316) 241-2100

Kentucky

Bank of Ohio County, 11658 State Rte. 69 N., P.O. Box 127, Dundee, KY 42338; (502) 276-3631

Citizens Deposit Bank & Trust, 400 2nd St., Vanceburg, KY 41179; (606) 796-3001

Community First Bank, P.O. Box 198, Mount Olivet, KY 41064; (606) 724-5403

Farmers State Bank, P.O. Box 68, Main St., Booneville, KY 41314; (606) 593-5151

First & Farmers Bank of Somerset Inc., 100 Public Sq., Somerset, KY 42501; (606) 679-7451

First Southern National Bank of Fayette County, 3060 Harrodsburg Rd., Lexington, KY 40503; (606) 223-3743

First Southern National Bank of Jessamine County, 980 N. Main St., P.O. Box 430, Nicholasville, KY 40356; (606) 885-1222

First Southern National Bank of Lincoln County, Main St., P.O. Box 27, Hustonville, KY 40437; (606) 346-4921

First Southern National Bank of Wayne County, 216 N. Main St., P.O. Box 489, Monticello, KY 42633; (606) 348-8421

Franklin Bank & Trust Co., 317 N. Main St., Franklin, KY 42134; (502) 586-7121

Leitchfield Deposit Bank & Trust Co., 76 Public Sq., P.O. Box 188, Leitchfield, KY 42755-0188; (502) 259-5611

Peoples Bank & Trust Co., 524 Main St., Hazard, KY 41701; (606) 436-2161

Louisiana

Acadia State Bank, 2237 S. Acadian Thruway, #100, Baton Rouge, LA 70808; (504) 924-0984

Acadian Bank, 1001 Canal Blvd., Thibodaux, LA 70301; (504) 446-8161

Bank of Jackson, P.O. Box 248, Jackson, LA 70748; (504) 634-7741

First Bank of Natchitoches, 315 Royal, Natchitoches, LA 71457; (318) 352-9089

Gulf Coast Bank, 221 S. State St., Abbeville, LA 70510; (318) 893-5010

Metro Bank, 3417 Williams Blvd., Kenner, LA 70065; (504) 443-5626

Peoples State Bank, 880 San Antonio Ave., Many, LA 71449; (318) 256-2071

Progressive National Bank of Desoto Parish, P.O. Box 233, Mansfield, LA 71052; (318) 872-3661

Sabine State Bank & Trust Co., P.O. Box 670, Many, LA 71449; (318) 256-7000

Southeast National Bank, P.O. Box 2488, Hammond, LA 70404; (504) 542-9700

Maine

United Bank, 145 Exchange St., Bangor, ME 04401; (207) 942-5263

Katahdin Trust Co., Main St., P.O. Box I, Patten, ME 04765; (207) 528-2211

Maryland

Commercial & Farmers Bank, 8593 Baltimore National Pike, Ellicott City, MD 21043; (410) 465-0900

Home Bank, 8305 Langmaid Rd., P.O. Box 10, Newark, MD 21841; (410) 632-2151

Maryland Permanent Bank & Trust Co., 9612 Reisterstown Rd., Owings Mills, MD 21117; (410) 356-4411

Massachusetts

Enterprise Bank & Trust Co., 222 Merrimack St., Lowell, MA 01852; (508) 459-9000

Michigan

1st Bank, 502 W. Houghton, West Branch, MI 48661; (517) 345-7900

First Community Bank, 200 E. Main, Harbor Springs, MI 49740; (616) 526-2114

First National Bank in Ontonagon, 601 River St., Ontonagon, MI 49953; (906) 884-4114

Grant State Bank, 10 W. Main, P.O. Box 38, Grant, MI 49327-0038; (616) 834-5685

MFC First National Bank, 1205 Ludington St., Escanaba, MI 49829; (906) 786-5010

MFC First National Bank, 962 First St., Menominee, MI 49858; (906) 863-5523

MFC First National Bank, P.O. Box 191, Iron River, MI 49935; (906) 265-5144

Peoples State Bank of Munising, 100 E. Superior, P.O. Box 158, Munising, MI 49862; (906) 387-2006

Minnesota

Chisago State Bank, 1135 Lake Blvd., P.O. Box G, Chisago City, MN 55013; (612) 257-6561

CreditAmerica Saving Co., 2019 S. 6th St., Brainerd, MN 56401; (218) 829-1484

First National Bank and Trust, 101 N.W. 2nd St., P.O. Box 190, Pipestone, MN 56164; (507) 825-3344

Grand Marais State Bank, P.O. Box 100, Grand Marais, MN 55604; (218) 387-2441

Highland Bank, 701 Central Ave. E., Saint Michael, MN 55376; (612) 497-2131

Itasca State Bank, P.O. Box 160, Grand Rapids, MN 55744; (218) 327-1121

Lakes State Bank, P.O. Box 366, Pequot Lakes, MN 56472; (218) 568-4473

Mountain Iron First State Bank, P.O. Box 415, Mountain Iron, MN 55768; (218) 735-8201

Princeton Bank, 202 S. LaGrande Ave., Princeton, MN 55371; (612) 389-2020

Roseville Community Bank, N.A., 1501 W. County Rd., Suite C, Roseville, MN 55113; (612) 631-1040

Saint Stephen State Bank, 2 Central Ave. S., Saint Stephen, MN 56375; (612) 251-0902

State Bank of Delano, P.O. Box 530, Delano, MN 55328; (612) 972-2935

Town & Country Bank of Almelund, P.O. Box 88, Almelund, MN 55002; (612) 583-2035

United Community Bank, 155 2nd St. S.W., P.O. Box 249, Perham, MN 56573; (218) 346-5700

Mississippi

Community Bank, P.O. Box 28, Indianola, MS 38751; (601) 887-4513

First Bank, P.O. Box 808, McComb, MS 39648; (601) 684-2231

Pike County National Bank, 350 Rawls Dr., McComb, MS 39648; (601) 684-7575

Union Planters Bank of Mississippi, P.O. Box 947, Grenada, MS 38902; (601) 227-3361

Missouri

Allegiant Bank, 2550 Schuetz Rd., Maryland Heights, MO 63043; (314) 534-3000

Bank of Warrensburg, P.O. Box 477, Warrensburg, MO 64093; (816) 429-2101

Carter County State Bank, P.O. Box 129, Van Buren, MO 63965; (314) 323-4246

Centennial Bank, 9850 St. Charles Rock Rd., St. Ann, MO 63074; (314) 423-6800

Central Bank of Kansas City, 2301 Independence Blvd., Kansas City, MO 64124; (816) 483-1210

Citizens National Bank of Springfield, 1465 E. Sunshine, Springfield, MO 65804; (417) 887-4200

Commerce-Warren County Bank, 104 N. Hwy 47, Warrenton, MO 63383; (314) 456-3441

Community Bank of Raymore, P.O. Box 200, Raymore, MO 64083; (816) 322-2100

Community Bank of the Ozarks, P.O. Box 43, Sunrise Beach, MO 65079; (314) 374-5245

First Bank of Kansas City, 3901 Main St., Kansas City, MO 64111; (816) 561-8866

First Commercial Bank, P.O. Box 195, Gideon, MO 63848; (314) 448-3514

First Midwest Bank, P.O. Box 160, Poplar Bluff, MO 63902; (573) 785-8461

First Missouri State Bank, P.O. Box 430, Poplar Bluff, MO 63902; (573) 785-6800

First State Bank of Joplin, P.O. Box 1373, Joplin, MO 64802; (417) 623-8860

Lawson Bank, 401 N. Pennsylvania, Lawson, MO 64062; (816) 296-3242

Mercantile Bank of Poplar Bluff, P.O. Box 700, Poplar Bluff, MO 63902; (314) 785-4671

Northland National Bank, 99 N.E. 72nd St., Gladstone, MO 64118; (816) 436-3500

Peoples Bank & Trust Co. of Lincoln County, P.O. Box G, Troy, MO 63379; (314) 528-7001

Peoples Bank, P.O. Box H, Cuba, MO 65453; (573) 885-2511

Rockwood Bank, P.O. Box 710, Eureka, MO 63025; (314) 938-9222

United Bank of Union, P.O. Box 500, Union, MO 63084; (314) 583-2555

Montana

BankWest, N.A., P.O. Box 7070, Kalispell, MT 59904; (406) 758-2256
Bitterroot Valley Bank, LoLo Shopping Center, P.O. Box 9, LoLo, MT 59847; (406) 273-2400
Citizens State Bank, P.O. Box 393, Hamilton, MT 59840; (406) 363-3551
First Bank of Lincoln, P.O. Box 9, Lincoln, MT 59639; (406) 362-4248
First Bank of Montana, 2801 Brooks, P.O. Box 4787, Thompson Falls, MT 59806; (406) 523-2300
First Boulder Valley Bank, P.O. Box 207, Boulder, MT 59632; (406) 225-3351
First Citizens Bank, N.A., P.O. Box 1728, Columbia Falls, MT 59912; (406) 892-2122
First Security Bank of West Yellowstone, P.O. Box 550, West Yellowstone, MT 59758; (406) 646-7646
Mountain Bank, Third & Spokane, Whitefish, MT 59937; (406) 862-2551
Mountain West Bank of Helena, 1225 Cedar St., Helena, MT 59604; (406) 449-2265
Rocky Mountain Bank, 2615 King Ave. W., Billings, MT 59102; (406) 656-3140
State Bank and Trust Co., P.O. Box 1257, Dillon, MT 59725; (406) 683-2393
United States National Bank of Red Lodge, P.O. Box 910, Red Lodge, MT 59068; (406) 446-1422
Valley Bank Glasgow, 110 6th St. S., Glasgow, MT 59230; (406) 228-4364
Valley Bank of Helena, 3030 N. Montana Ave., Helena, MT 59601; (406) 443-7443
Valley Bank of Ronan, P.O. Box 129, Ronan, MT 59864; (406) 676-2000

Nebraska

American National Bank of Fremont, 99 W. 6th St., Fremont, NE 68025; (402) 727-8600
City State Bank, P.O. Box 370, Sutton, NE 68979; (402) 773-5521
First National Bank, 100 W. Fletcher Ave., Lincoln, NE 68521; (402) 435-7233
Dakota County State Bank, 2024 Dakota Ave., South Sioux City, NE 68776; (402) 494-4215

New Mexico

First National Bank, P.O. Box 1107, Tucumcari, NM 88401; (505) 461-3602

Bank Of The Southwest, 226 N. Main, Roswell, NM 88201; (505) 625-1122

Centinel Bank of Taos, P.O. Box 828, Taos, NM 87571; (505) 758-6700

Valley Bank Of Commerce, 217 W. 2nd, Roswell, NM 88201; (505) 623-2265

Valley National Bank, 333 Riverside Dr., Espanola, NM 87532; (505) 753-2136

New York

Continental Bank, 118 7th St., Garden City, NY 11530; (516) 741-2400

Habib American Bank, 99 Madison Ave., New York, NY 10016; (212) 532-4444

Solvay Bank, 1537 Milton Ave., Solvay, NY 13209; (315) 468-1661

North Carolina

Bank of Currituck, P.O. Box 6, Moyock, NC 27958; (919) 435-6331

Old North State Bank, P.O. Box 995, King, NC 27021; (910) 983-0682

Triangle Bank, 4300 Glenwood Ave., Raleigh, NC 27612; (919) 881-0455

United National Bank, 320 Green St., Fayetteville, NC 28301; (910) 483-1131

Yadkin Valley Bank & Trust Co., 110 W. Market St., Elkin, NC 28621; (910) 526-6300

North Dakota

First Southwest Bank of Bismarck, P.O. Box 777, Bismarck, ND 58502; (701) 223-6050

First Western Bank & Trust, 900 S. Broadway, Minot, ND 58701; (701) 852-3711

Kirkwood Bank & Trust Co., 919 S. 7th St., Bismarck, ND 58506; (701) 258-6550

Page State Bank, P.O. Box 5, Page, ND 58064; (701) 668-2261

Union State Bank of Fargo, P.O. Box 9399, Fargo, ND 58106-9399; (701) 282-4598

Ohio

Citizens National Bank of Norwalk, 12 E. Main St., Norwalk, OH 44857; (419) 668-3736

First Bank of Marietta, 320 Front St., Marietta, OH 45750; (614) 373-4904

New Richmond National Bank, 110 Front St., New Richmond, OH 45157; (513) 553-3101

Peoples Banking Co., 1330 N. Main St., Findlay, OH 45840; (419) 423-4741

Oklahoma

American State Bank, P.O. Box 280, Broken Bow, OK 74728; (405) 584-9135

Bank of Cushing & Trust Company, 224 E. Broadway, Cushing, OK 74023; (918) 225-2010

Bank of Inola, 11 W. Commercial, Inola, OK 74036; (918) 543-2421

Bank of Western Oklahoma, 201 E. Broadway, Elk City, OK 73644; (405) 225-3434

Citizens Bank of Tulsa, 2500 W. Edison, Tulsa, OK 74127; (918) 582-2600

Community State Bank, 103 S. Main, P.O. Box 220, Cashion, OK 73016; (405) 433-2675

First Bank of Hennessey, 101 N. Main, P.O. Box 724, Hennessey, OK 73742; (405) 853-2530

First National Bank of Roland, P.O. Box 308, Roland, OK 74954; (918) 427-7474

Peoples National Bank, P.O. Box 599, Kingfisher, OK 73750; (405) 375-5911

Union National Bank of Chandler, 1001 Manville, Drawer 278, Chandler, OK 74834; (405) 258-1795

Oregon

Bank of Astoria, 1122 Duane St., Astoria, OR 97103; (503) 325-2228

Bank of Wallowa County, P.O. Box X, Joseph, OR 97846; (503) 432-9050

Columbia River Banking Company, 316 E. Third St., The Dalles, OR 97058; (541) 298-6647

Valley Commercial Bank, P.O. Box 766, Forest Grove, OR 91716; (503) 359-4495

Pennsylvania

First Columbia Bank & Trust Co., 11 W. Main St., Bloomsburg, PA 17815; (717) 784-1660

South Carolina

Anderson Brothers Bank, P.O. Box 310, Mullins, SC 29574; (803) 464-6271

Bank of Walterboro, 1002 N. Jefferies Blvd., Walterboro, SC 29488; (803) 549-2265

Bank of York, P.O. Box 339, York, SC 29745; (803) 684-2265

Enterprise Bank of South Carolina, 206 E. Broadway, Erhardt, SC 29081; (803) 267-3191

M.S. Bailey & Son, Bankers, 211 N. Broad St., Clinton, SC 29325; (803) 833-1910

Saluda County Bank, 200 N. Main St., P.O. Box 247, Saluda, SC 29138; (803) 445-8156

Sandhills Bank, P.O. Box 127, Bethune, SC 29009; (803) 334-6241

South Dakota

American State Bank of Rapid City, P.O. Box 2530, Rapid City, SD 57709; (605) 348-3322

Tennessee

American City Bank, 340 W. Lincoln St., Tullahoma, TN 37388; (615) 455-0026

Community Bank & Trust Co., P.O. Box 866, Lawrenceburg, TN 38464; (615) 762-5518

First State Bank, 301 Main St., Jacksboro, TN 37757; (423) 562-7443

Lincoln County Bank, P.O. Box 677, Fayetteville, TN 37334; (615) 433-7041

Traders National Bank, 120 N. Jackson St., Tullahoma, TN 37388; (615) 455-3426

Texas

Bloomburg State Bank, P.O. Box 155, Bloomburg, TX 75556; (903) 728-5211

Charter Bank - Northwest, 10502 Leopard St., Corpus Christi, TX 78410; (512) 241-7681

Citizen State Bank, P.O. Box 4007, Corpus Christi, TX 78469; (512) 887-3000

East Texas National Bank, P.O. Box 8109, Marshall, TX 75671; (903) 935-1331

First Bank of Conroe, N.A., 1426 Loop 336, Conroe, TX 77304; (409) 760-1888

First Commercial Capital, 1336 E. Court, Seguin, TX 78155; (210) 379-8390

First International Bank, P.O. Box 629, Bedford, TX 76095; (817) 354-8400

First National Bank, P.O. Box 37, Newton, TX 75966; (409) 379-8587

First State Bank, 201 S. Old Betsy Rd., Keene, TX 76059; (817) 645-7060

First Waco National Bank, 1700 N. Valley Mills Dr., Waco, TX 76710; (817) 776-0160

Founders National Bank, Skillman, 9696 Skillman, #150, Dallas, TX 75243; (214) 340-7400

Guaranty Bank, P.O. Box 1158, Mount Pleasant, TX 75456-1158; (903) 572-9881

Heritage Bank, 557 Ovilla Rd., Red Oak, TX 75154; (214) 617-0222

Home State Bank, P.O. Box 219, Rochester, TX 79544; (817) 743-3511

Inter National Bank, 1700 S. Tenth St., McAllen, TX 78505; (210) 630-1700

Justin State Bank, 412 S. Hwy. 156, Justin, TX 76247; (817) 648-2753

Lone Star National Bank, P.O. Box 1127, Pharr, TX 78577; (210) 781-4321

Midland American Bank, 401 W. Texas, Midland, TX 79701; (915) 687-3013

National Bank of Andrews, 1501 N. Main, Andrews, TX 79714; (915) 523-2800

North Texas Bank & Trust Co., P.O. Box 1299, Gainesville, TX 76240; (817) 665-8282

Security State Bank & Trust, P.O. Box 471, Fredericksburg, TX 78624; (210) 997-7575

Sundown State Bank, 5th & Slaughter, Sundown, TX 79372; (806) 229-2111

Surety Bank, 600 S. First, Lufkin, TX 75901; (409) 632-5541

Texas Bank, 102 N. Main, Weatherford, TX 76086; (817) 594-8721

Texas Bank, 4101 John Ben Sheppard Pkwy., Odessa, TX 79762; (915) 368-0931

Texas Bank, P.O. Box 1990, Henderson, TX 75653; (903) 657-1466

United Bank & Trust, P.O. Box 3157, Abilene, TX 79604; (915) 676-3800

Van Horn State Bank, 100 E. Broadway St., Van Horn, TX 79855; (915) 283-2283

Western National Bank, 8200A Nashville, Lubbock, TX 79423; (806) 794-8300

Woodhaven National Bank, 6750 Bridge St., Fort Worth, TX 76112; (817) 496-6700

Utah

Advanta Financial Corp., 11850 S. Election Dr., Salt Lake City, UT 84020; (801) 264-2920
Cache Valley Bank, 101 N. Main, Logan, UT 84321; (801) 753-3020
Bonneville Bank, 1675 N. 200 W., Provo, UT 84604; (801) 374-9500
First Commerce Bank, 5 E. 1400 North, Logan, UT 84341; (801) 752-7102

Vermont

Union Bank, 20 Main St./P.O. Box 667, Morrisville, VT 05661; (802) 888-6600

Virginia

Benchmark Community Bank, 100 S. Broad St., Kenbridge, VA 23944; (804) 676-8444
First Bank & Trust Co., 236 W. Main St., Lebanon, VA 24266; (540) 889-4622
Highlands Union Bank, P.O. Box 1128, Abingdon, VA 24212; (540) 628-9181
Marathon Bank, P.O. Box 998, Stephens City, VA 22655; (540) 636-9241
Virginia Community Bank, 408 E. Main St., Louisa, VA 23093; (540) 967-2111

Washington

Bank of Fife, 1507 54th Ave. E., Fife, WA 98424; (206) 922-7870
Bank of Pullman, 300 E. Main, Pullman, WA 99163; (509) 332-1561
Bank of the West, P.O. Box 1597, Walla Walla, WA 99362; (509) 527-3800
Farmers State Bank, P.O. Box 489, Winthrop, WA 98862; (509) 996-2243
First American State Bank, 1100 Harrison Ave., Centralia, WA 98531; (360) 736-0722
First National Bank of Port Orchard, 1488 Olney Ave. S.E., Port Orchard, WA 98366; (360) 895-2265
National Bank of Tukwila, 505 Industry Dr., Tukwila, WA 98138; (206) 575-1445
Pend Oreille Bank of Washington, P.O. Box 1530, Newport, WA 99156; (509) 447-5641
Towne Bank, P.O. Box 645, Woodinville, WA 98072; (206) 486-2265

West Virginia

Traders Bank, 303 Main St., Spencer, WV 25276; (304) 927-3340

Wisconsin

Bank of Fort Atkinson, 200 Sherman Ave. W., Fort Atkinson, WI 53538; (414) 563-2461

Bank of Mauston, 503 State Rd. 82, Mauston, WI 53948; (608) 847-6200

Bank of Milton, P.O. Box 217, Milton, WI 53563; (608) 868-7672

Bradley Bank, 227-W. Wisconsin Ave., Tomahawk, WI 54487; (715) 453-2112

Cambridge State Bank, 221 W. Main St., Cambridge, WI 53523; (608) 423-3226

Citizens Bank, N.A., 129 E. Division St., Shawano, WI 54166; (715) 526-6131

Community Bank and Trust Co., 1214 Tower Ave., Superior, WI 54880; (715) 392-8241

Community Bank of Grafton, 2090 Wisconsin Ave., Grafton, WI 53024; (414) 375-9150

Community First State Bank, 118 Elm St., Spooner, WI 54801; (715) 635-2161

DeForest-Morrisonville Bank, 321 N. Main St., DeForest, WI 53532; (608) 846-3711

F & M Bank-New London, 401 N. Water St., New London, WI 54961; (414) 982-4410

F & M Bank Kaukauna, 4th Street Plaza/P.O. Box 920, Kaukauna, WI 54130; (414) 766-8160

F & M Bank Portage City, 31 Park Ridge/P.O. Box 808, Stevens Point, WI 54481; (715) 341-6691

F & M Bank Winnebego County, P.O. Box 501, Omro, WI 54963-0501; (414) 685-2771

F & M Bank, P.O. Box 890, Pulaski, WI 54162; (414) 822-3225

Fidelity National Bank, 215 S. 8th St., Medford, WI 54451; (715) 748-5333

First National Bank Fox Valley, 161 Main St., Menasha, WI 54952; (414) 729-6900

First National Bank of Hartford, 116 W. Sumner St., Hartford, WI 53027; (414) 673-5800

First National Bank of New Richmond, 109 E. 2nd St., New Richmond, WI 54017; (715) 246-6901

First National Bank of Park Falls, 110 N. 2nd Ave., Park Falls, WI 54552; (715) 762-2411

First National Bank of Park Falls, P.O. Box 250, Park Falls, WI 54552; (715) 762-2411

First National Bank of Platteville, 170 W. Main St., Platteville, WI 53818; (608) 348-7777

First National Bank, P.O. Box 269, Waupaca, WI 54981; (715) 258-5511

Green Lake State Bank, 515 Hill St., Green Lake, WI 54941; (414) 294-3369

Headwaters State Bank, P.O. Box 149, Land O'Lakes, WI 54540; (715) 547-3383

Heritage Bank of Hayward, Hwy. 63 N., Hayward, WI 54843; (715) 634-2611

Ixonia State Bank, W. 1195 Marietta Ave., Ixonia, WI 53036; (414) 567-2881

Lincoln County Bank, 401 W. Main St., Merrill, WI 54452; (715) 536-8301

M & I Bank, 100 Main St. E., Ashland, WI 54806; (715) 682-3422

M & I Merchants Bank, 7 N. Brown St., Rhinelander, WI 54501; (715) 369-3000

Park Bank, 1200 Main St., Holmen, WI 54636; (608) 526-2265

Security State Bank, P.O. Box 157, Iron River, WI 54847; (715) 372-4242

State Bank of Chilton, 26 E. Main St., Chilton, WI 53014; (414) 849-9371

State Bank of Stockbridge, 401 W. Lake St./P.O. Box 38, Stockbridge, WI 53088; (414) 439-1414

Stephenson National Bank & Trust, 1820 Hall Ave., Marinette, WI 54143; (715) 732-1650

The Necedah Bank, 212 Main St., Necedah, WI 54646; (608) 565-2296

The RiverBank, 204 3rd Ave., Osceola, WI 54020; (715) 294-2183

Wyoming

Equality State Bank, P.O. Box 1710, Cheyenne, WY 82003; (307) 635-1101

First Interstate Bank of Commerce, 4 S. Main St., Sheridan, WY 82801; (307) 674-7411

Frontier Bank of Laramie County, 1501 S. Greeley Hwy., Cheyenne, WY 82007; (307) 637-7244

Riverton State Bank, 616 N. Federal, Riverton, WY 82501; (307) 856-2265

Western Bank Cheyenne, P.O. Box 127, Cheyenne, WY 82001; (307) 637-7333

GLOSSARY

accounts receivable: A record used to account for the total number of sales made through the extension of credit.

accrual basis: An accounting method used for record-keeping purposes in which all income and expenses are charged to the period to which they apply, whether money has actually changed hands or not.

acid-test ratio: An analysis method used to measure the liquidity of a business by dividing total liquid assets by current liabilities.

asset earning power: A common profitability measure used to determine the profitability of a business by taking its total earnings before taxes and dividing them by total assets.

Audit Bureau of Circulation (ABC): A third-party organization that verifies the circulation of print media through periodical audits.

balance sheet: A financial statement used to report a business's total assets, liabilities, and equity.

book-out policy: A policy whereby hotels "hold" meeting rooms for groups that also book blocks of guest rooms. Generally speaking, only hotels in major metropolitan areas employ book-out policies.

break-even analysis: An analysis method used to determine the number of jobs or products that a business needs to sell to pay its expenses and start making a profit.

business identity: A kind of *executive suite* arrangement without the offices, a "business identity" service provides mail collection and personalized phone answering services, along with copy centers and meeting rooms that can be scheduled when "tenants" need to meet with clients. Such a service can be useful for home-based entrepreneurs desiring a more professional image.

business plan: A plan used to chart a new or ongoing business's strategies, sales projections, and key personnel in order to obtain financing and provide a strategic foundation for growth.

Business Publications Audit (BPA): Like the Audit Bureau of Circulation, the BPA is a third-party organization that verifies the circulation of print media through periodical audits.

255

capitalization: Every company has capital—in the form of money, common stock, long-term debt, or some combination of all three. It is possible to have too much capital (in which case the firm is over-capitalized) or too little capital (in which case the firm is under-capitalized).

cash basis: An accounting method used for record keeping in which income is logged when received and expenses are charged when they occur.

Certified Speaking Professional (CSP): A designation bestowed by the National Speakers Association to certain individuals who have, among other qualifications, been speaking professionally for a minimum of 5 years and served a minimum of 100 different clients.

chattel mortgage contract: A credit contract used for the purchase of equipment in which the purchaser receives title of the equipment upon delivery but the creditor holds a mortgage claim against it.

collateral: Assets used as security for a loan.

commercial loan: A loan made to a business by a commercial bank.

conditional sales contract: A credit contract used for the purchase of equipment. The purchaser doesn't receive title of the equipment until the amount specified in the contract has been paid in full.

copyright: A form of protection used to safeguard original literary works, performing arts, sound recordings, and visual arts.

corporation: A legal form of operation that declares the business to be a separate legal entity guided by a group of officers known as the board of directors.

cost-of-living lease: A lease under which yearly increases are tied to the cost-of-living index.

cost per thousand (CPM): A measurement used in buying media. CPM refers to the cost it takes to reach a thousand people using a given medium.

current ratio: The ratio of total current assets to total current liabilities.

demographic characteristics: The attributes such as income, age, and occupation that best describe your target market.

depreciation: The lessening in value of fixed assets that provides the foundation for a tax deduction, based on either the declining-balance or straight-line method.

disability insurance: A payroll tax required in some states that is deducted from employee paychecks to ensure income during periods in which the employee is unable to work due to an injury or illness.

disclosure document program: A form of protection that safeguards an idea while it is in its developmental stage.

dollar control system: A system used in inventory management that reveals the cost and gross profit margin of individual inventory items.

Dun & Bradstreet: An agency that furnishes clients with market statistics and financial standings and credit ratings of businesses.

equipment loan: A loan used for the purchase of capital equipment.

equity capital: A form of financing in which private investors buy equity in a business.

exploratory research: Research used to gather market information. Targeted consumers are asked very general questions that are intended to elicit lengthy answers.

Fair Labor Standards Act: A federal law that enforces minimum standards by which employers must abide when hiring.

Federal Insurance Contributions Act (FICA): A law that requires employers to match the amount of Social Security tax deducted from an employee's paycheck.

fictitious name: A business name other than that of the owner(s) or partner(s).

first in, first out (FIFO): An accounting system used to value inventory for tax purposes. Under FIFO, inventory is valued at its most recent cost.

fixed expenses: Expenses that must be paid each month and do not fluctuate with the sales volume.

flat lease: A lease under which the cost is fixed for a specific period of time.

frequency: The number of times you hope to reach your target audience through your advertising campaign.

401(k) Plan: A retirement plan that allows employees to deduct money from their paychecks and place it in a tax-sheltered account.

The Hotel Index: A popular travel and planning resource that lists the available hotels in every city in the United States. (See also *Official Airlines Guide.*)

income statement: Also called a profit and loss statement, an income statement charts the sales and operating costs of a business over a specific period of time, usually a month.

inventory loan: A loan that is extended based on the value of a business's inventory.

inventory turnover: An analysis method used to determine the amount of capital invested in inventory and the total number of times per year that the investment will revolve.

investment tax credit: A federal tax credit that allows businesses to reduce their tax liability if they purchase new equipment for business use.

investment turnover: A profitability measure used to evaluate the number of times per year that total investment or assets revolve.

Keogh: A pension plan that lets business owners contribute a specific portion of their profits toward a tax-sheltered account. There are several Keoghs to choose from, including profit-sharing and defined-contribution plans.

leasehold improvements: The repairs and improvements a lessee makes to rented property. These improvements become the property of the lessor at the end of the lease.

liability: The legal responsibility for an act, especially as it pertains to insurance risks. Although there are numerous comprehensive and special coverages for almost every possible liability, three forms of liability coverage are usually underwritten by insurers. *General liability* covers any kind of bodily injury to nonemployees, except injury caused by automobiles and professional malpractice. *Product liability* covers injury to customers arising directly from goods they purchased from a business. *Public liability* covers injury to members of the public when they are on an owner's premises.

last in, first out (LIFO): An accounting system used to value inventory. Under LIFO, inventory is valued according to the remaining stock in inventory.

market survey: A research method used to define the market parameters of a business.

markup: The amount added to the cost of goods or cost of service to produce the desired profit.

measure of liquidity: An analysis method used to measure the amount of liquid assets available to meet accounts payable.

media plan: A plan that details the usage of media in an advertising campaign, including costs, running dates, markets, reach, frequency, rationales, and strategies.

net leases: There are three kinds of net leases: (1) the net lease, (2) the double-net lease, and (3) the triple-net lease. Under a net lease, the lessee pays a base rent plus an additional charge for taxes. A double-net lease adds an additional charge for insurance. Under a triple-net lease, the lessee pays yet another additional charge for common area expenses.

net profit on sales: A profitability measure in which net income before taxes is divided by gross sales.

Occupational Safety and Health Act (OSHA): A federal law that requires employers to provide employees with a workplace that is free of hazardous conditions.

Official Airlines Guide: A popular travel and planning resource that lists the available hotels in every city in the United States. (See also *The Hotel Index.*)

open to buy: The dollar amount budgeted by a business for inventory purchases for a specific time period.

overhead: All nonlabor expenses needed to operate a business.

partnership: A legal form of business operated by two or more individuals who act as co-owners. The federal government recognizes several types of partnerships. The two most common are general and limited partnerships.

patent: A form of protection that provides a person or legal entity with exclusive rights to exclude others from making, using, or selling a concept or invention for the duration of the patent. Three types of patents are available: design, plant, and utility.

percentage lease: Under this type of lease, the landlord charges a base rent plus an additional percentage of any profits the business tenant produces.

personal loans: A loan made to a person.

profit: There are generally two kinds of profit: gross profit and net profit. Gross profit is the difference between gross sales and cost of sales. Net profit is the difference between gross profit and all costs associated with operating a business.

reach: The total number of people in a target market contacted through an advertising campaign.

return on investment (ROI): A profitability measure that evaluates the performance of a business by dividing net profit by total assets.

return on owner's equity: A profitability measure used to gauge the earning power of the owner's total equity in the business by dividing the average equity investment of the owner by the net profit.

signature loans: See *personal loans.*

sole proprietorship: A legal form of operation in which one person owns and operates the business.

speakers' agreement: A legal document outlining all parties' obligations in regard to a planned engagement.

specific research: Research used to perform a market survey in which targeted consumers are asked very specific and in-depth questions that are intended to solve problems found through exploratory research.

Standard Rate and Data Service (SRDS): A company that produces a group of directories for each different type of advertising medium. Rates, circulation, contacts, markets serviced, etc., are listed.

step lease: A type of lease outlining annual rent increases based on the landlord's estimates of increases in his or her expenses.

Subchapter S: A portion of the Internal Revenue Code that allows small corporations to be taxed as partnerships. The corporations distribute income directly to their shareholders, who then report the income on their personal income tax forms.

variable expenses: Business costs that fluctuate from one payment period to another, according to sales volume.

venture capital: Start-up or expansion capital that a business obtains from private investors in exchange for equity positions within the business.

Worker's Compensation: State and federal insurance funds that reimburse employees for injuries they suffer on the job.

working capital: Net current assets available for a company to carry on with its work.

NOTES

Chapter 1 Defining Your Market

1. Nancy K. Austin, "The New Motivators." *Working Women*, July 1993: 24ff.
2. *Ibid.*
3. Richard Reeves, "Let's Get Motivated." *TIME*, May 2, 1994: 66–68.
4. *Ibid.*
5. Austin, "The New Motivators."
6. L. Gubernick and P. Mao, "The Happiness Hucksters." *Forbes*, October 9, 1995: 82–88.
7. William A. Cohen, *The Entrepreneur & Small Business Problem Solver*, 2nd ed. (New York: John Wiley & Sons, Inc., 1990), 192.
8. Dan Steinhoff and John F. Burgess, *Small Business Management Fundamentals*, 4th ed. (New York: McGraw-Hill, 1986), 65.
9. Stevie Cameron, "Evasive Action." *Maclean's*, October 9, 1995: 60.

Chapter 3 Equipment and Inventory

1. Ron Mansfield, "Ten Golden Rules," *New Business Opportunities* (September 1992): 12–15.

Chapter 4 Personnel

1. Richard J. Maturi, "Pension Headaches," *Entrepreneur* (August 1993): 134–137.

Chapter 5 Legal Requirements

1. Richard D. Bank, "Law Review," *Business Start-Ups* (November 1993): 94–96.

Chapter 7   Financial Management

1. U.S. Small Business Administration, *A Handbook of Small Business Finance* (Washington: Author, 1981) 19.

Chapter 8   Advertising and Promotion

1. Linda Pinson and Jerry Jinnett, "Spread the Word," *Business Start-Ups* (September 1994): 12.

Chapter 10   The Start-Up Phase

1. John Freear, Jeffrey E. Sohl, and William E. Wetzel, Jr., "The Private Investor Market for Venture Capital," *The Financier: ACMT* (May 1994): 7.

INDEX

http://www.entrepreneurmag.com

If its related to small business, you'll find it at the Small Business Square.

Front Page

Catch daily news and feature articles of significance to small business owners.

Soho Mall

Shop for small business products online in a secured environment.

Convention Center

Attend chat-room seminars with small business experts.

Forum & Roundtable

Network with other small business owners and aspiring entrepreneurs through our online message boards.

Resource Center

Access a wealth of small business information from resources like the Franchise 500 and Business Opportunity 500 Online Listings, the Small Business Encyclopedia, and FormNET™.

Watercooler

Chill out in our online fun zone where you can participate in contests, product giveaways, or download games and business software. And check out our weekly cartoon "In Business."